Introduction to
The Sociologies of Everyday Life

Introduction to
The Sociologies of
Everyday Life

JACK D. DOUGLAS
University of California, San Diego

and

PATRICIA A. ADLER
University of California, San Diego

PETER ADLER
University of California, San Diego

ANDREA FONTANA
University of Nevada, Las Vegas

C. ROBERT FREEMAN
University of California, San Diego

JOSEPH A. KOTARBA
University of Houston

Allyn and Bacon, Inc.
Boston   London   Sydney   Toronto

Library of Congress Cataloging in Publication Data

Douglas, Jack D
  Introduction to the sociologies of everyday life.

  Bibliography: p.
  1. Sociology—Addresses, essays, lectures.
2. Social psychology—Addresses, essays, lectures.
I. Title.
HM51.D66   301   79–16308
ISBN 0–205–06813–8

PRINTED IN THE UNITED STATES OF AMERICA

Contents

Phenomenological-Existential Sociology • Existential
Sociology • Other Sociologies and Existential Sociology

Preface

The sociologists of everyday life have for many years been rebuilding the foundation for understanding all human life and thus rebuilding the foundations of all theory and method in the social sciences. While some of the roots of the sociologies of everyday life are quite old, their specific forms are being continually created and re-created. Their emergent status has made some of their basic ideas seem highly problematic for sociologists and often murky for beginning students. The premises set forth by the sociologies of everyday life have elicited a great deal of confusion and a considerable amount of controversy. For example, many major works in the sociologies of everyday life are reviewed initially in terms that make these works almost unrecognizable to the authors themselves. The authors are accused of meaning things they never meant to imply and are sometimes charged with concluding the opposite of what they did conclude.

The failure to understand the basic ideas of the different sociologies of everyday life also leads to theory labelling games. Some people refer to all sociologies of everyday life as "labelling theory." Others consider them "phenomenology" or "ethnomethodology." Imprecise use of theoretical labels sometimes turns simple confusion into an intellectual swamp that defeats any attempt at rational analysis. These misunderstandings and confusions tempt some people who do not understand the works to conclude that "It's all a matter of academic jargon" or "They're all cultists trying to create a new object of worship." None of this sort of criticism contributes to serious consideration of the fundamental issues involved.

The great importance of communicating the creative ideas of the sociologies of everyday life as simply and clearly as possible led me several years ago to conclude that a systematic exposition of the fundamental ideas of all the sociologies of everyday life was very much needed. I quickly found that most of my co-workers and colleagues agreed. Some of us set to work and, after several years of writing, critical analysis, and rewriting—here we are at last!

We have tried above all to cut through the vast complexity of details to get at the basic ideas and then to present them as clearly and systematically as possible. This has been a difficult enterprise because the emergent ideas that make up the theoretical perspectives in this book are often concerned with the "ultimate realities" of life. Moreover, a crucial aspect of some of the perspectives, especially that of existentialism, is that they present ideas that are *open-ended*, ideas that point to basic but inherently problematic experiences of all human beings. For example, Heidegger's idea of "being-in-the-world" (*Dasein*) simply cannot be given any definitive meaning without destroying its basic purpose. In cases such as this absolute clarity is absurd and impossible, so we have not attempted to clarify by imposing an ad hoc definition. The idea of being incapable of rendering an exact definition may seem strange to anyone who does not understand the sociologies of everyday life. We hope that after reading this book, however, such readers will realize that the inherently emergent and undefinable property of the sociologies of everyday life—their openness to the inherently situated and problematic nature of all life—is one of their greatest strengths.

In addition to basic problems of systematizing and clarifying the ideas of these sociologies, there are the many lesser ones that plague all emerging, creative activities. The most creative thinkers in any human endeavor are often more prophetic than systematic. Their creativity springs more from the vastly rich pre-conscious realms of their minds and only slowly are clearly defined symbols found to communicate their emergent ideas to other people. Andrea Fontana in Chapter 3, for example, finds Erving Goffman's work fundamentally enigmatic, not clearly defined and systematized. In these cases, the true clarifier tries to show how and why enigmas exist within the sociologies of everyday life, rather than imposing pseudo-clarity or a pseudo-system. The true clarifier tries to help communicate the truths the author has grasped by helping to put them into currently used words, but he must do so cautiously to avoid distorting the inspirations. We hope to clarify, not to distort, so we are cautious, not sweeping in our interpretations. And, inevitably, there are times when we can only present alternative interpretations, and times when we can only tiptoe around some mystery, admitting that we do not know.

We have concentrated our efforts on what seem to clearly be the five major bodies of theoretical ideas we call the sociologies of everyday life: symbolic interactionism, dramaturgical analysis, labelling theory, phenomenology and ethnomethodology, and existential sociology. As far as we know, these contain all of the fundamental ideas of the sociologies of everyday life thus far created. We have first presented and analyzed each of the theoretical perspectives in its own terms. In fact, we selected authors to write each chapter who were basically sympathetic to the perspective being presented, but who were not in any way blind partisans. We also chose only authors who had spent some years studying a given perspective, but who also had wide exposure to the other perspectives. In each chapter, the particular theory is presented, empirical examples are described, and the major criticisms advanced thus far are answered from the standpoint of the theory under discussion. We have also tried to show how the different perspectives are related to each other, both how they are similar and how they are different. A brief history of the emergence of the sociologies of everyday life is included in the Appendix.

Our goal has been to present a clear, systematic, and unbiased picture of the major theories at this time. It has certainly not been our intention to replace the original works to make it appear there are no problems of interpretation, or to give any impression that this is the whole thing. This book is a *guide* to a complex, emergent, and problematic reality. It introduces the subject in a way that will invite direct and more detailed exploration of the original works.

All of the authors of this text are deeply involved in exploring the sociologies of everyday life. This might tempt some readers to conclude that we are biased against classical sociology. I should mention, therefore, that all of us started out as classical sociologists, as did almost all the sociologists of everyday life. We are not committed to the sociologies of everyday life because we were first trained and rewarded to be so. We are not saying that classical sociology is completely irrelevant. We do present brief overviews of classical sociology (especially in Chapter 1) to show why and how sociologists of everyday life are rebuilding the foundations of all our understanding of human life. But that is not a major goal. Some of us have done that at great length before and do not feel it necessary here.

Conflicts and partisanship exist not only between classical theorists and sociologists of everyday life, but also among the proponents of the five major sociologies of everyday life. We have tried to avoid the tendency of sociologists and other academics today to march under the banners of "schools of thought." All of us believe, as our analyses in this book will show, that there are both major agreements and disagreements among these five perspectives. These disagreements are largely, but not entirely, the result of using different realms of our vastly complex society as the empirical source of the perspectives. Labelling theory, for example, was built largely on information about delinquency, drug rules and violations, and Western social responses to mental illness. It is not surprising that labelling theory greatly increases our understanding of labelling and similar phenomena, nor that it shows weaknesses when extended to very different social phenomena. We believe these five special theories roughly share a common theoretical perspective, which we call the sociology of everyday life; this perspective, however, is not a partisan school. (The label "interactionism" is often used to refer generically to all of these sociologies. This is especially common in the field of deviance. However, that label sounds too similar to the label for George Herbert Mead's special theory of symbolic interactionism.) Each sociology is also more or less useful as a special theory in understanding various realms of our vastly variegated society. We have tried to show their strengths and weaknesses, their uses and misuses, with as much balance as possible.

But let us not end this preface on a negative note. This book is inspired by a great affirmation, an affirmation of the value of understanding the human species in nature. We would disagree with the ancient philosophical assertion that the unexamined life is not worth living. Life, not mind, is the ultimate reality, the foundation of all caring, of all value. But the ancient quest for understanding human life in nature adds immensely to human life, in and of itself. We believe that such understanding will eventually have practical values. But, unlike the structural sociologies with their commitments to "rational state policies" and merchandising and political questionnaire polls, the basic goals of the sociologists of everyday life are concerned with building the foundation for understanding human life in nature. The values of all practical goals, as well as the possibilities of using knowledge about the human being to achieve them, must ultimately depend upon that foundation of human understanding. Indeed, we believe the radically new technologies and sweeping political passions of our age make it urgent that we build this foundation for understanding. We hope this work will be a significant contribution to that effort.

J. D.
La Jolla, California

Acknowledgments

This work owes more than most of our works to our many colleagues. We have worked on it for several years, during which we have communicated on an everyday basis with many other sociologists of everyday life. Each of the chapters has been through various drafts, and each draft has benefitted from criticisms made of earlier ones. And of course we have benefitted from responses from around the world to earlier works in which we expressed preliminary versions of most of the ideas presented here.

We have profited most from our long and deep involvement in what is now a rather large community of sociologists of everyday life at the University of California at San Diego. There are now sociologists of everyday life scattered around the world, and in the United States most major departments of sociology now have at least one sociologist studying human beings in their natural situations. But there are only a few sociology departments in the entire world in which there is such a community large enough to constitute a "critical mass" that generates creative research and theory. The University of California at San Diego has had such a critical mass for over ten years. We have also benefitted from some criticisms from a few brave structuralists able to survive in that critical mass. They have forced us to continually sharpen, modify and broaden our ideas.

Introduction to
The Sociologies of Everyday Life

1

Introduction to the Sociologies of Everyday Life

Jack D. Douglas

The sociology of everyday life is a sociological orientation concerned with the experiencing, observing, understanding, describing, analyzing, and communicating about people interacting in concrete situations. There are three important points in this definition.

First, the sociologist of everyday life studies social interactions by observing and experiencing them in natural situations, that is, in situations that occur independently of scientific manipulation. These are situations common to everyday life. The focus leads to the name, the sociology of everyday life. Other names referring to this sociological orientation are "micro-sociology," "interactionism," and "naturalistic sociology." Natural situations are the opposite of experimentally controlled situations. This does not mean that the sociologists of everyday life never use experimental controls to study human beings. On the contrary, the social scientist of everyday life sometimes makes use of a previously established understanding of everyday life to manipulate variables in a study. These studies are called "natural experiments." (See the discussion of natural experiments in Douglas, 1976.) All such scientific controls, however, are derived from earlier experience and observation of natural situations. We must first learn what human beings feel,

1

perceive, think, and do in natural situations before we can determine how to conduct observations with controls that will not distort or bias the realities we observe.

Second, the sociology of everyday life begins with the experience and observation of people *interacting in concrete, face-to-face situations. Concrete situations* * are those in which the members of society actually are engaged in face-to-face interaction with other members of society— feeling, perceiving, thinking, and doing things. Sociologists of everyday life begin by experiencing and observing what is happening naturally, rather than by hypothesizing about what *might* happen or by questioning the members of society about what they think happens or did happen or will happen. Introspection and questioning are sometimes used by the sociologists of everyday life after they know from experience and observation what in fact does happen naturally. The sociologists of everyday life do not record what people say on an abstract level (such as their responses to an opinion poll or questionnaire survey), because abstract responses are often quite different from what people really feel, perceive, think and do in concrete situations.

Third, all analysis of everyday life, of concrete interactions in concrete situations, begins with an analysis of the *members' meanings.* Members' meanings are often called "common-sense meanings" or "everyday-life meanings" by sociologists of this school. "Meaning" is used to refer to the feelings, perceptions, emotions, moods, thoughts, ideas, beliefs, values, and morals of the members of society. In short, "meaning" refers to the internal experience of the members that is most relevant to a particular social interaction. Sociologists of everyday life do not begin by imposing their own meanings on their observations. They do not say "I think premarital intercourse is immoral because. . . ." They are concerned with finding what the members perceive, think, and feel. For example, do those being studied feel premarital intercourse is immoral? Sociologists of everyday life, then, first try to understand and analyze social situations *from the standpoint of the members.* Later analyses generally go beyond members' meanings, but they try to retain those meanings in as undistorted a way as possible. (This is what sociologists of everyday life often call "being true to the natural phenomena.")

In this book we shall see why the sociologists of everyday life have concluded that these three points are so crucial in developing a science of society. We shall also see that various theorists of this orientation give slightly different meanings to some of these points (one reason why there are different names for some of the key ideas). But they agree on the crucial points and generally on a good deal more. It is this set of basic agreements that sets sociologists of everyday life apart from the

---

* Other terms frequently used to refer to concrete situations and interactions are "face-to-face situations," "immediate situations," "mundane interaction," "practical interaction," and "micro-interaction."

classical theorists of society, called macro-structural theorists or structural-positivist theorists. The sociologists of everyday life have developed five more specific theories that diverge in some important ways, but each of these five special theories is built on a shared theoretical foundation. This is a new foundation for sociology and related disciplines that has grown out of a thorough re-examination of human life in its natural context. The basic ideas of the sociology of everyday life presented in the following sections must be grasped clearly in order to understand the complex details of the more specific theories examined in this book.

The Partial Situatedness of Life

All life is partially interdependent with the concrete situations or environments in which it exists. This truth is well recognized in everyday life and is expressed by numerous common-sense expressions, such as "It depends on the situation," "It all depends," "That depends on the circumstances," and so on. The great complexity of modern life has made it more difficult to see the obvious. Biologists have been able to show that in simpler forms of life very clear patterns of interdependency exist between a form of life and the immediate situation it faces. These patterns of interdependency often develop into extremely complex hierarchies of stimuli and responses. Although human beings are directly interdependent with their environments through stimulus-response hierarchies only in the simplest forms of reflex actions, it is helpful to see such interdependence at work in their most striking form. One of the classic examples of this interdependency is between environmental stimuli, male reactions, and female reactions of the stickleback fish during mating season:

> The three-spined stickleback is brought into reproductive motivation by the gradual increase in day length in spring and begins migration inland into shallow fresh-water habitats. This factor, together with the rise in water temperature and the visual stimulation of heavily vegetated sites, is a releasing mechanism for the establishment of a suitable territory by the males. A territory is necessary for the male to acquire its characteristic red belly. Only then does it begin to react to particular stimuli which previously had no effect. The male will build a nest with suitable material, fight against rival males (where the releasing stimulus is the red belly of the male intruding into his territory), and court passing females, which present their silvery, swollen, egg-filled bellies to the male in a characteristic manner. Thus, the stimuli emanating from a territory will activate the fighting, building, and mating drives, which must then be elicited by special releasers. Fighting itself consists of a number of behavior patterns (chasing, threatening, tail-beating, biting), each dependent upon still further, highly specific stimuli emanating from the intruder's behavior. The be-

havioral sequences of male and female form an alternating chain of reactions, each action of one partner releasing the following appropriate reaction of the other partner until the female spawns and the male fertilizes the eggs. The act of fertilization initiates brood care in the male; he now fans fresh water onto the eggs and continues to drive off rivals but does not exhibit further courtship until the young hatch. It is thus clear that there are chains of behavioral tendencies connected at higher and lower levels of integration and that these different levels are organized into a hierarchical system. The advantage of a hierarchy, as opposed to a stereotyped series of single fixed actions, lies in its adaptability to unpredictable sequences of events (Eibl-Eibesfeldt and Wickler, 1968, p. 191).

The immediate reason for the partial situatedness of life is simple enough, though the ultimate processes underlying it are complex. (For the complex biological arguments, see Wilson, 1975, and Dawkins, 1976.)

Each individual of every species since the beginning of life, perhaps a billion years ago, has a probability of determining future life; this probability rests on how that individual acts toward its environmental situation. Certain actions, called "unadaptive," lead to a lower probability that a particular individual will propagate future life; other actions, called "adaptive," lead to a higher probability that it will propagate future life. In simple terms, we could say that the individual proposes (or acts), and the natural situation disposes (determines whose genes will be passed on and whose will not). By this probabalistic natural selection process the natural situations and the actions that have proved the most adaptive in the past are transmitted by the genetic material (DNA) of each individual. This process has an overwhelming implication for all studies of life: one cannot completely understand any species without knowing the situation within which the members of the species exist. And, at a lower level of generalization, one cannot completely understand any human action without knowing the ways in which the situation affects that action. *Being-in-the-situation* is the fundamental idea of all modern behavioral biology and of all sociologies of everyday life. This idea has been producing a Copernican revolution in the biological and social sciences in recent years.

It is a biological truism that the human species is the most adaptive form of life. Humans are able to adapt successfully to more kinds of environmental situations than any other animal. They are more *transsituational* than any other animals—more able to abstract themselves from the many concrete situations of their lives. Human adaptability has been possible because humans have replaced part of their dependence on the physical environment with a dependence on culture. Microbial forms of life are commonly born fully developed. Human beings are born totally dependent on adults, must have very extensive adult care for many years before they can even maintain their own lives, and are thus necessarily dependent on social interaction. As Adam Smith insisted in 1759 in *The Theory of Moral Sentiments,* humans can "subsist only in society."

The basic fact of the *physical and social situatedness of human life* has an important implication for all attempts to study human beings scientifically. The most general implication is emphasized at the beginning of this chapter in the definition of the sociology of everyday life: human beings, like all animals, must be observed scientifically in their natural situations. Only by first learning what human beings feel, perceive, think, and do in their natural situations by natural (non-experimental) methods of observation, will we ever know reliably what human patterns of existence are. The more specific implication of the general truth is that, since all observations of human life will be made in social situations, scientific observers must participate in natural social situations and observe what takes place naturally.

The basic importance of observing human animals in their natural situations perhaps can be best grasped by looking at the history of biological studies of other animals, especially of other primates. Many areas of specialization within biology are important to this argument, but the most important are ethology, primatology, mammology, social biology, and vertebrate biology. Some social scientists mistakenly lump all of these specialties under the name "sociobiology," but this is very misleading. "Sociobiology" is a very specific theory most commonly associated with the work of Wilson (1975).

Although a few studies of animals in their natural situations were made in the nineteenth century, these were almost totally overlooked until they were rediscovered in recent years, primarily because their unique importance was not understood. Until approximately the 1920s almost all studies of animal behavior were done in the captive or controlled situation of the laboratory or the zoo. This was done partly because it was the easiest thing to do. As all later students of animals, especially of the extremely perceptive and "nervous" primates, in natural situations were to discover, it is extremely difficult to get near enough to animals in nature to observe what they are doing. (It took Van-Lawick-Goodall [1971] four years to get close enough to chimpanzees to observe them in detail without binoculars.) Captives, however, could not run away; indeed, they were so used to human observers that they did not try. On the basis of such controlled studies, it was concluded that primates are very aggressive, very sexual, and very inflexible (or "neurotically compulsive") compared to human beings.

By the 1920s, various studies were being carried out in natural settings, often by naturalists, but increasingly by biologists. As with anthropological studies, these were normally done for only brief periods, usually three or four months. (Details of such studies can be found in sources such as Dolhinow, 1972.) Even such brief periods of observation made it increasingly apparent that animals in natural situations are very different from animals in controlled situations. This led to a gradual increase in the periods of observation of animals in natural situations. The longer and more detailed these studies, the more complex and variable their behavior was realized to be, the more it was seen to be affected by the situations within which animals were observed—and the more the other primates appeared to behave like human beings in many basic respects. By the late 1970s, studies such as that of Van-Lawick-Goodall had been under way for as long as fifteen years and had expanded from one person to large teams of observers.

Dolhinow has summarized some of the more obvious differences found between primates studied in captive situations and those observed in natural situations:

> Some attempt should be made to assess the extent and kinds of behavior deprivation and alternations of behavior patterns that occur when animals are reared in captivity. Under these necessarily artificial and highly controlled conditions the animal is usually subjected to surroundings and handling that may have exceedingly long-lasting effects on its behavior and physical well-being. No documentation is available on the exact degree and kinds of behavioral changes that occur under differing captive conditions. It is not possible at this time to say precisely what percentage of behaviors or responses vary in clearly defined ways in captivity. Some species are affected much more than others; some simply do not survive or reproduce in captivity. Many laboratory traumas and stresses are obvious, as for example those associated with crowding, catching, transporting, and medication. The experienced field-workers has little or no difficulty in identifying laboratory-reared animals, especially if they have been caged in pairs or singly during most of the formative months. Stereotyped motor patterns and other forms of neurotic behavior are well documented among laboratory animals and may appear, along with normal species-typical patterns, in the behavior repertoires of captive animals. . . .
>
> Artificial colonies are limited in their usefulness for investigating some problems. Social groups in captivity, although they may be composed of approximately the same age-sex structure as a free-ranging group, seldom if ever replicate the generational and sibling ties that form part of social experience for a wild monkey or ape. Space is a severe problem in most captivity situations, including space for a group, a home range, as well as the more immediately important social space for each member of the group. Many and possibly most dominance fights are avoided in the wild by animals moving out of sight of each other, either by running away once a chase starts or by moving away cautiously in the early stages of tension build-up. Often in the wild, animals hostile to one another tend to avoid each other by staying in different parts of the troop, and nature is full of trees, shrubs, or tall grasses behind which an animal may move to escape being seen.
>
> How much energy, anger, or tension directed by a captive animal into an attack on a cagemate that cannot escape in flight might be

dissipated by running 100 yards? This is one of several important questions that deserve attention before there can be an assessment of the extent to which a laboratory colony can provide adequate surroundings for the expression and development of specific kinds of behavior. Species differ in their requirements, as for example with respect to space and open-area, ground-living forms probably need much more space than does a group of arboreal monkeys that inhabits dense forest treetops. Designing colony space in ways that maximize psychological distances and provide hiding places or complex surfaces may go a long way toward increasing the square feet of space usable by the animals (Dolhinow, 1972: 17–18).

All of this may sound simple enough and almost obvious today. But it was anything but obvious to most social scientists before the 1960s. Sociology and psychology in the nineteenth and early twentieth centuries was primarily built on methods that imposed controlled situations of observation on the human beings studied and that arrived at theories that include no direct consideration of the partial situatedness of concrete actions. In order to understand the importance, problems, and nature of the sociologies of everyday life, we must first understand how these earlier theories came about and what their basic ideas were.

Probably the most important mistake the early social scientists made as a result of their imitating the natural scientists was their adoption of the experimental method and the hypothetical model with which to formulate their theories. (For detailed treatments of this see, for example, Douglas, 1967 and 1971.) We now know from our own experience, as well as from experience in the numerous fields of behavioral biology, that the experimental method and the hypothetical model were the wrong approaches for a new science of human beings. The reasons are simple. The experimental method assumes, first, that one can make controlled observations of phenomena without the method itself changing the phenomena observed. And, second, the experimental method assumes that all of the important natural phenomena can be precisely reproduced under the controlled conditions of an experiment, so the scientist can see in the controlled situation all of the phenomena of fundamental importance. Both assumptions are quite untrue when applied to higher forms of life, especially to social animals—and especially untrue when applied to human beings. All higher forms of life, especially the higher social animals, are highly reactive to social observations; above all to any observation by strangers. Most animals will not allow people to get near enough to them to observe their natural behavior in any detail. Indeed, most early observations of animal life were of flight behavior only, which is important but hardly representative of the whole repertoire of animal behavior. Human beings also are extremely sensitive about being observed by other people. The distinction between private areas (not observable by strangers) and public areas (observable by strangers) varies in intensity from one group or individual to another, but it is always there and always important. In our society the distinction is basic. As Sartre noted, the difference between being unobservable (completely private), and the *possibility* of being observed by any human being, is a vast difference for human beings. We all know how carefully people "put their best foot forward" when they are observed. Goffman (*see* Chapter 3) has shown in detail the elaborate social armor most Americans present in public.

The failure to see the interdependency of life with its concrete situations led to the assumption that the observational reactivity of human beings is insignificant. Once scholars assumed that rigorous experimental methods should be used to study human beings, then they began to observe people in labs, to use "objective" tests or questionnaires to study their intelligence or their love lives, and even to study their physiological responses with computers. Of course, many scientists using experimental methods for observing people recognized that people change according to the situation they are in. Not all social scientists used the methods of the Skinnerians or others who studied human beings by putting pigeons or rats into mazes and boxes. Those who studied human beings in labs often tried to hide the experimenter's presence by using one-way mirrors. Over time, subjects studied in this way probably became less reactive to the observations of scientists, as long as the "subjects" were engaging in public forms of behavior. But that does not mean that their "subjects" were not affected by the methods of observation, nor does it mean that they were ever able to study anything but the most unconflictful forms of public behavior. In a sense, social scientists using the natural scientist's controlled approach were still studying the sticklebacks in a fishbowl, not recognizing that sticklebacks in a fishbowl are deprived of all those natural variations in light, warmth, territoriality, mates, competitors, and predators. People being studied in labs or by questionnaires resemble people in their natural, everyday situations even less than the stickleback in a fishbowl resembles its relative in a natural environment.

The failure of sociologists to see the fundamental interdependency of human beings and their situations also derived from the abstractionist fallacy of the structural sociologies. If one assumes the situation does not affect what people feel, think, or do, then one does not bother to observe concrete situations and instead looks for the causes of human behavior only in non-situational factors. The sociologies of the nineteenth and early twentieth centuries found those non-situational factors in the abstract shared values of social groups. The structuralists (also called structural-functionalists because they were concerned with the functions social structures supposedly served) produced a great deal of literature arguing that the abstract and publicly expressed values of a society determine the basic patterns of actions in the society.

One well-known work of the structuralists was Seymour Martin Lipset's *First New Nation* (1973). The basic argument of this book is that the major patterns of American society over the past two centuries have been determined by the conflict between a commitment to equality and a commitment to achievement, both of which are abstract values. The evidence for such a position is obvious enough. When asked in public-opinion questionnaires whether they believe in the values of equality and achievement almost all Americans will say yes. They will also express agreement on a large number of other abstract values such as love and honesty. It seems likely that even more agreement would be found on abstract values like "individual freedom," which, after all was the "slogan" of Americans in the nineteenth century and remains so for many millions. Almost all the members of all the industrial societies of the Western world express roughly the same abstract values in response to public opinion polls. This led Talcott Parsons (1951) and others to argue that Western societies can be described in terms of their position on general value dimensions. Parsons' structural analysis was far more abstract than Lipset's and thus even more removed from concrete situations.

Anyone assuming that the concrete actions of Americans are determined by abstractly shared values would expect to find almost universally similar human behavior. Such an analyst might expect to find everyone doing the same things. For example, the structuralist might expect all Americans to act in such a way as to produce total equality and total freedom. There are, however, intense social conflicts over specific or concrete interpretations of the values of equality or freedom. For example, today government officials and many judges insist that equality of education can be achieved through "busing," but approximately 80 percent of the people disagree, some violently. Again, libertarians insist that "individual freedom" means that individuals should be able to make their own decisions on economic matters, public nudity, drugs, or prostitution. What one person defines in a concrete situation as "equality," another sees as "government tyranny"; what one defines concretely as "freedom," another defines as "licentiousness" or "social disorder."

The pervasiveness of such conflicts led Lipset and other structuralists to argue that the abstractly shared values conflict with each other. They argued that abstract value conflicts produce conflicts over meanings and actions. But what determines which particular values will come into conflict in any given situation? What determines who will invoke what values in what order, to what degree? Above all, what determines which value will win out or which interpretation of what values will win out? Suppose, for example, that American history is determined by a conflict between an abstract value of equality and an abstract value of achievement. What determines why some people will line up on the side of "universal equality," while the other 80 percent line up on the side of "achievement"? Even more to the point, what determines which side will win in such a conflict? How, for example, would one predict that a society committed above all to freedom and due process of law would be one in which the minority of 20 percent would win out over the majority of 80 percent?

Thus, the recognition of a vast gap between the social theory of the structuralists and the everyday world around us led more and more sociologists to question the meanings imputed by the structuralists to the members of society. Were these meanings the ones the members of society were using in their everyday lives to determine what they did? Durkheim and other structural sociologists, for example, had given an abstract definition to suicide, that of a "death resulting from the act of an individual against himself which he knew would have the consequence of producing death." Durkheim argued against using a definition that involved any idea of intention, because he thought intention was too problematic or uncertain for a social scientist to be able to determine reliably. Durkheim also assumed that his abstract definition of suicide was the same as the concrete meanings of suicide imputed in concrete cases by coroners, medical examiners, and others who had gathered the official statistics on suicide that Durkheim used in his study. It was easy to show that the truth was the exact opposite. "Intention to kill oneself" is the most common idea involved in the everyday use of the word suicide; the officials who constructed the statistics used by Durkheim were using the term in that way. (The officials rarely even knew what the legal definition might be, but it also generally involved some idea of intention. See Douglas, 1967, 1971). If it was so simple to find that, why did not a brilliant man like Durkheim find it? The reason was simple: he did not look at human beings in everyday life. He *assumed* that concrete situations do not affect the meanings and actions of human beings. Durkheim assumed that the concrete meanings and actions are determined by the abstract meanings. In the long run, however, concrete situations are of fundamental importance and determine abstract meanings.

The Partially Problematic Nature of Life

Everyone knows that life is partially problematic, that is, unpredictable. We cannot always predict whether we shall go to work in the morning or whether we shall eat dinner at home at the usual time. More importantly, we all know, or recognize as soon as we think about it, that we cannot predict *exactly* what will happen in any given concrete situation. If we could predict with complete accuracy the exact details of what will happen in concrete situations, then we would say that life worked like "clock work," because clocks work as automatically as anything. Yet we know that clocks do break down and do run fast or slow. "Clock work" is about as unproblematic as anything ever gets in natural situations, yet clock work remains partially problematic. Needless to say, we all know that the important things and situations in our lives, such as love and marriage, are far more problematic than that. The question "What is love?" has perplexed human beings of all ages, and the question "Am I in love?" perplexes most people most of the time. The situatedness of life and its problematic nature are actually two different ways of looking at the same thing. If natural situations and our actions in them were totally predictable, totally unproblematic, then we could program our lives to avoid situations and actions in situations we do not like. But, of course, life is not totally predictable; life is always partially problematic. Our own feelings, thinking, and actions are problematic because we cannot totally predict what situations will arise. We therefore must always remain open to changing situations. We must adapt partially to concrete situations as they arise or emerge, independently of our earlier feelings, perceptions, thoughts, or anticipation of situations and actions.

The behavorial biologists have once again presented what seems to be the best general explanation of the problematically situated nature of life. Consider once again the lowly stickleback, whose response to the degree of light, heat of the water, and other stimuli in its environment determines whether or not eggs will be laid (and fertilized). The stickleback's complex reproductive behavior has evolved interdependently with its environment to endow it with the greatest chance of transmitting its genes successfully. If the water is too cold, the eggs will die. If the male does not act in just the right way in relation to the female's behavior, fertilization fails to occur. Suppose the stickleback were programmed to *not* react to one or more of the stimuli in their environment, for example, if the stickleback were programmed to always act as if the water were not hot enough to lay the eggs. What happens? Once in a while, as a matter of luck, it will be hot enough for the eggs to hatch and the offspring survive. But most of the time the delicate requirements of life will not be met, and the stickleback will die off in a few generations.

An alternative way of dealing with these problems would be to make the stickleback's situations unproblematic. In that way the stickleback would not have to worry about the natural situations that emerge. How would that be done? It could be done only by making all future situations completely predictable and then programming the stickleback's actions to meet exactly the situations that will arise. That is, if the stickleback could predict exactly when the water will be warm enough, the light of day long enough, when the female will appear and do just the right things, and so on, then it could fertilize at the precise time. Perhaps nature might logically have selected genes in terms of their ability to predict future situations and, thence, to program organisms to act in infinite chains of actions that do not depend directly on concrete situations.

But that is not what happens. Why? There seem to be two possibilities. Either nature is inherently partially unpredictable—inherently partially problematic—or nature is so complex that predicting concrete situations correctly would necessitate the capacity to process immense amounts of information—so immense that no form of life thus far evolved can do it. Whatever the reason, the fact is that future situations and the relations between present situations and behavioral responses and their consequences are always partially problematic for animals and these problems are most successfully solved by dealing directly with the concrete situation that does emerge. Life is situated because it is problematic, and it is problematic because it is situated. Or, life is both partially situated and partially problematic because, for whatever unknown reason, behavior that can change according to the situation at hand is the most adaptive (genetically successful).

Those who deny a fundamental continuity between forms of animal life and human life may also deny that human life is partially problematic and situated. They might assert, for example, that the distinction between human life and animal life is that human life is *transcendent;* it seeks to transcend its situation, to act in accord with values that are independent of the situation at hand. As they would rightly point out, the human being has a greater ability to predict and control natural situations than the stickleback precisely because the human being, with vastly greater abilities to process information about the world, can predict what will happen. This does make humans more *trans-situational* than other animals (an important point we shall consider in the next section of this chapter). But this ability never allows people to act successfully without dealing with the situations as *partially* problematic and, thus, partially acting according to the exigencies of a current situation. The only known human beings who act totally "out of situation," that is, who act always in the same programmed way, are the Don Quixotes. Don Quixotes always find evil windmills to attack in the same way. And what happens when Don Quixotes always perceive the same things in the world, always interpret them the same way, always act in the same ways—always feel, think, and act independently of the concrete situations they face? They meet disaster very quickly. Those who do not take into consideration the partially problematic nature of reality and adapt their feelings, thinking, and actions to concrete natural situations are "absolutists." Absolutists who merely talk absolutely, which is, after all, quite common, may succeed quite well. Those who act absolutely quickly meet disaster. That, presumably, is why all of our studies of human beings in everyday life reveal them to be almost always unabsolutist—or absolutist talkers and unabsolutist actors! People who are truly absolutist are normally already labeled mental patients and are said to be "acting out of situation"—that is, without regard to the situation or to the problems it poses.

The Partially Trans-Situated and Partially Ordered Nature of Life

We have emphasized that life is only partially situated and problematic. As we shall see in Chapters 5 and 6, there has been a tendency for some sociologists of everyday life to react against the extreme of structuralism, in which life is seen as totally unsituated and unproblematic, by going to the opposite extreme of seeing life as totally situated and totally problematic.

Life is a matter of degree. Some things are highly problematic and situated, while others are highly unproblematic and unsituated (or trans-situated). Consider, for example, those forms of behavior which are almost completely programmed in the human being. These are the simplest forms of reflexes, such as the prehensile reflex by which our feet tend to grasp something that exerts a moderate and general stimulus. It is an almost completely unproblematic and unsituated form of behavior, an automatic behavior. Because it is almost always adaptive to human beings to grasp the ground surface and, thus, to balance themselves on their feet, we have evolved a reflex that leads the feet to grasp the surface on which we are walking. Yet even that behavior is not totally programmed. If the stimulus is "sharp," then another and opposite reflex will supersede it (that of suddenly collapsing and retracting the foot). Some reflex actions, therefore, are dependent upon the stimulus of a situation. Of course people can choose to walk on very sharp objects that injure the feet, to override an instinctive reflex. Situations do occur in which it would be more adaptive to accept injury to the feet than to avoid it. Thus, all higher animals are able to abstract themselves from concrete situations, that is, to partially transcend the concrete situations they face in order to achieve some future situation: we can partially abstract ourselves from our injured feet perhaps to achieve greater safety. But, of course, when we do so we almost always do it with very cautious concern for the concrete situation in order to minimize the injury and maximize the chances of getting through safely without permanent maiming.

It is easy in everyday life to observe ourselves going through all degrees of problematicness and situatedness in feeling, thinking, and acting. Sometimes we are very uncertain about whether we are in love. Other times we feel certain. Sometimes we are highly flexible and open to new ideas about a situation. Other times we insist on acting in only one way because "it is a matter of principle." People must constantly adapt to situations requiring varying degrees of problematic decision making.

Principles, absolute in theory, have a way of bending in concrete situations. We may feel "certain for ever," but new situations sometimes remind us of our old uncertainties or stimulate new ones. The sociologist of everyday life must be concerned with *how* problematic and *how* situated individual and social life are, not with one extreme or the other, since these extremes are almost nonexistent.

The Social Construction of Meanings and Paths of Action

Because meanings and actions are partially problematic, individuals must construct (or create) concrete meanings and actions for the concrete situations that emerge in their everyday lives. The more problematic the meanings and actions, the more creative or constructive the work they must do. Some meanings and paths of action in some situations are almost totally shared and routinized. For example, members of our society almost always put on clothes that hide their sex organs before appearing in any public setting. This is one of the most shared and routinized patterns of action in our society. Nevertheless, there are people who deviate from this norm. Individuals do in fact have choices to make about whether they appear nude or clothed. Small children exercise this choice rather freely, causing parents to do a great deal of constructive work to convince children to wear clothes. Moreover, a great amount of constructive work goes into clothing and dressing, including that which "reveals by first hiding and then emphasizing" the clothed sex organs. (For discussions of the social meanings of nudity and clothing, see König, 1973; and Douglas and Rasmussen, with Flanagan, 1977).

Other meanings and paths of action are extremely problematic. Most sexual matters are quite problematic for the members of Western societies, but of course the degree varies greatly with individuals and from one group to another. Some of the rules might be very clear for some people, but feelings have a distinct tendency to go in different directions from the rules, causing many people to make highly creative interpretations of the rules and not infrequently to create deviant paths of action for themselves (see Douglas, 1980).

Most of the meanings we impute and most of our actions are made up more or less of the problematic. Most of the words we use in conversations have shared meanings within our particular social group for any concrete situation we face. But some words and many statements made by people are experienced by others as problematic, forcing others to consciously set about constructing the meanings for them. We do this by asking questions ("What do you mean by that?"), by giving answers, by qualifying and explaining, by interpreting, by inferring, and guessing.

Most of our everyday lives are lived in roughly the same way we cook something. That is, there are certain basic rules of cooking (use heat or microwaves to cook) that are almost universally shared and largely unproblematic. There are certain other shared meanings—pepper is hot, for example—and shared paths of action related to these which are not very problematic—such as always go easy on the pepper. There are also general sets of meanings and rules and paths of action that can be put together in relatively unproblematic ways to make up *recipes for living* in most of the concrete situations that emerge in our lives. Like any cooking recipes, these everyday life recipes give us certain pat or largely unproblematic *stocks of knowledge* (see Schutz, 1962, and Altheide, 1977) and rules. But they do not eliminate the problems involved in living, especially those involved in living well. We still must be very careful to put knowledge together in the right way, always taking note of the special properties of the concrete situation we face. (On hot days the bread dough will rise more easily than on cold days, so. . . . But just how hot is today? And will the humidity or breeze make a difference?) As anyone who has ever cooked knows, cooking remains a rather problematic thing for everyone, and even the best cook can spoil the simplest dish by burning it, oversalting it, undercooking it, or doing many other things that have problematic, unintended consequences. Even the most careful and wise construction cannot eliminate all problems or missteps that bring disaster. Life's concrete situations are partially constructed in accord with our recipes for living, but they always remain partially open, uncertain, problematic, and situated. Moreover, the rapid pace of change and conflict in Western societies today have made life far more problematic. Many more individual constructions of meanings must be made to avoid disasters.

The Differences among the Major Theories of the Sociology of Everyday Life

Basic ideas distinguish the perspective of the sociology of everyday life from the structural perspective, which is the traditional perspective of sociology. The rest of this book will be concerned primarily with explaining the details of the theories of everyday life and with the development of the ideas that further distinguish each of the theories. To prepare for the rest of the book, we will present a brief overview of each of the theories and the major relations among them.

Figure 1–1 gives us a general picture of the relations among the five theories presented in this book. They fall into roughly two major categories: those closely related to the symbolic interactionist theories of Cooley and Mead, and those closely related to the phenomenological analyses of Husserl and Schutz. Dramaturgy and labeling theory were largely derived from symbolic interactionism, so they share with it a

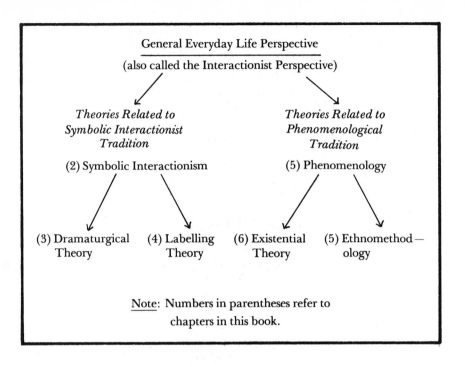

FIGURE 1–1. Basic Relations among the Sociological Theories of
Everyday Life (*Note that phenomenology and ethnomethodology are treated in one chapter because
ethnomethodology developed out of phenomenology.*)

general view of the social world as rather highly shared and symbolic.
Existential theory and ethnomethodology are both historically related to
phenomenology; they tend to see the world as far more problematic and
situated. These two differences in orientation are less marked and less
important than differences between the five special theories.

Symbolic Interactionism (see Chapter 2). Symbolic interactionists believe that the social world is constructed out of a shared symbolic universe by individuals using shared symbols in concrete interactions. They
place great emphasis on the ways in which individuals are taught by
significant others (individuals important to them) to share symbols and
the ways symbols lead to common patterns of actions. They also see the
learned symbols of the self—that is, self-images—as very important in
determining what individuals do. In an oversimplified way, one could
say that individuals taught to think of themselves as "tough" or "aggressive" will do aggressive things, so they are much more apt, for example,
to get involved in the activities of violent gangs. (Some sociologists use

the general term "interactionism" to mean "symbolic interactionism.")

Dramaturgy (see Chapter 3). This theory is probably the most completely derived from symbolic interactionism, although it is distinct enough to require a separate name. Dramaturgists believe that social actions are performances enacted for the purpose of creating or eliciting shared symbolic meanings, especially eliciting certain positive self-images. Individuals act like respectable citizens in public settings in order to get people to think and say they are respectable. Dramaturgy, then, is concerned predominantly with analyzing the self-presentations or appearances of people in public. Dramaturgists believe that people carefully manage these appearances—they act in order to get the "right" billing—that is, the "right" shared symbols *imputed* to them (said about them). Dramaturgists believe that social performances must be carefully managed, even planned, in everyday interactions, and that social actors normally support each others' presentations to produce effects they both desire.

Labeling Theory (see Chapter 4). Labeling theorists agree with the symbolic interactionists that people must share a symbolic universe, that they are taught to do this, that this influences their actions, and that of course all of this must be done through social interaction. Labeling theorists point out that there are certain important realms of society in which individuals and groups come into conflict over their symbolic definitions of each other. In some situations individuals (usually officials) try to control others or to treat them as rule violators. Labeling theorists generally believe that the most important labelers, those with the greatest effects on individuals' lives, are the official agencies of control such as the police and the courts. Most labeling theory assumes a high degree of sharing of symbolic meanings and sees little problem in constructing meanings.

Phenomenology and Ethnomethodology (see Chapter 5). Phenomenologists are much more concerned with the ways in which individuals construct in their own consciousness the meanings of things. They see the social world as ultimately made up of many more individual constructions than do the symbolic interactionists, dramaturgists, or labeling theorists, although they agree that interaction is fundamentally important in producing these constructions. They are much more concerned with the complex forms and problems of how social meanings are constructed.

Ethnomethodology, which was originally derived from phenomenology, comes the closest of all the special theories to being a different perspective entirely. It is predominantly concerned with the analysis of social accounts (body language and linguistic statements, for example), especially with the analysis of the ways in which individuals speak to each other in everyday life to appear rational. It overlaps a great deal with linguistics and psycho-linguistics. Unfortunately, ethnomethodology is sometimes used to refer to almost any sociological study of everyday-life interactions, and even the ethnomethodologists often disagree over what the term connotes. When used in this book it usually means the study of linguistic accounts, such as how individuals convince each other that someone is or is not deviant, a drug addict, or what not.

Existential Theory (see Chapter 6). The existential theorists differ from the phenomenologists and other interactionists in seeing perceptions and feelings (anxiety, dread, love, hate, and envy) as the ultimate goals and well-springs of social meanings and actions. They see meanings as much more problematic than even most phenomenologists do. Existentialists see a big gap between public life and private realities. The social world to them is necessarily full of conflict and individuals are much more on their own because of all this in constructing their own world. They see social order as highly problematic in our complex modern societies. They are very much concerned with the rise of technology and bureaucracy, modern institutions that try to dominate and repress the emotional needs of human beings. Their fundamental concern with "brute being" (the animal base of human life) has led to a progressive synthesis of the sociology of everyday life with behavioral biology.

In the following chapters we will examine each of the five theories of everyday life in detail. In each chapter we begin with some consideration of the origin of the theory. Then we present the more detailed ideas that distinguish the theory from the others and document the research that the theorists believe support those ideas. Finally, we present the criticisms of the theory under consideration and present the rebuttals most often given by those who believe the theory is true. We have also tried to give some idea of how a particular theory is likely to evolve in the near future, although we of course recognize how problematic such predictions are.

References

ALTHEIDE, DAVID. *Creating Reality*. Beverly Hills, Calif.: Sage Publications, 1977.

DAWKINS, RICHARD. *The Selfish Gene*. New York: Oxford University Press, 1976.

DOLHINOW, PHYLLIS, ed. *Primate Patterns*. New York: Holt, Rinehart, and Winston, 1972.

DOUGLAS, JACK D. *The Social Meanings of Suicide*. Princeton, N.J.: Princeton University Press, 1967.

DOUGLAS, JACK D. *American Social Order*. New York: The Free Press, 1971.

DOUGLAS, JACK D. *Investigative Social Research.* Beverly Hills, Calif.: Sage Publications, 1976.

DOUGLAS, JACK D. *Existential Sociology,* with John M. Johnson and others. New York: Cambridge University Press, 1977.

DOUGLAS, JACK D., and PAUL K. RASMUSSEN, with CAROL ANN FLANAGAN. *The Nude Beach.* Beverly Hills, Calif.: Sage Publications, 1977.

DOUGLAS, JACK D. *Creative Deviance and Social Change.* (available in mimeo), 1980, forthcoming.

EIBL-EIBESFELDT, IRENAUS, and WOLFGANG WICKLER. "Ethology," *International Encyclopaedia of the Social Sciences.* vol. 5. New York: Crowell Collier, 1968.

KÖNIG, RENE. *A la Mode.* New York: The Seabury Press, 1973.

LIPSET, SEYMOUR MARTIN. *The First New Nation.*

PARSONS, TALCOTT. *The Social System.* New York: The Free Press, 1951.

SCHUTZ, ALFRED. *Collected Papers.* The Hague: Martinus Nijhoff, 1962.

VAN LAWICK-GOODALL, JANE. *In the Shadow of Man.* New York, 1971.

WILSON, EDWARD. *Sociobiology.* Cambridge, Mass.: Harvard University Press, 1975.

2

Symbolic Interactionism

Peter Adler
Patricia A. Adler

Symbolic interactionism, the first and most widespread of the sociologies of everyday life, represents an important historical break from traditional macro-structural theories of sociology. Although this perspective is not without ideological antecedents in related disciplines such as philosophy, economics, psychology, and history, no major sociological paradigm is so little influenced by the natural sciences as a model for the study of society. Interactionism rejects the scientific method (prior formulation and testing of hypotheses); organismic analogy (likening society to the human body); holistic conceptions of the universe; cause-and-effect models and universal laws; goals of predicting behavior; the use of mathematical and statistical techniques; and the reverent attitude toward the ideal of scientific objectivity.

Departing from sociology's first proclaimed theory, positivism and its subsequent refinements, symbolic interactionism approaches the study of the social world from the concrete, tangible perspective of human beings and the everyday reality they perceive. Taking their goal as describing and understanding (rather than predicting) human life,

The authors wish to thank Peter K. Manning and Joseph Gusfield for helpful comments and insightful clarifications of the history of symbolic interactionism.

interactionism's progenitors sought to focus on the dynamic processes of reality rather than solely on the framework within which behavior functioned. Their creation is a loose body of ideas that can be utilized to study the empirical world without imposing a preconceived order upon it.

By building theory from a base in the real world, interactionism holds true to its most direct philosophical ancestor: pragmatism. No study of symbolic interactionism would be complete without an examination of this philosophical position, the first to emerge from a distinctly American heritage. Common to both interactionism and pragmatism is a grounding in the American experience of individualism, growth, and change.

The Pragmatists

As a relatively young country, America depended chiefly on her European ancestors for leadership and guidance in the academic and intellectual spheres. In the mid-nineteenth century this orientation was finally challenged by a group of philosophers who expounded a doctrine that gained international repute. *Pragmatism,* with its emphasis on the direct, uncomplicated, and efficient, was an almost inevitable outgrowth of the spirit of early America. Several historical factors contributed to the background that fostered pragmatism's development: 1) *science* and the scientific method in the nineteenth century enjoyed great prestige and influence in society; 2) in philosophy, *empiricism,* which emphasized the significance of experience, dominated thinking; 3) Darwin's theory of *biological evolution* was becoming accepted and applied to the social sciences; and 4) the *pluralism* of American society was cherished as a part of our *democratic ideal.*[1] Pragmatism remains the most important philosophical conviction to emerge from our country.

Charles Sanders Peirce (1839–1914)

Raised in a scientific family and academic milieu, Peirce spent his early life pursuing a career in logic and the physical sciences. His ideas on philosophy developed as a sideline and did not become the dominant thrust of his work until the late 1870s. The development of a *semiotic,* a general theory of signs, was his initial interest. Combining impressions about human thought and the uses of language, Peirce proposed that communication between people rested on a *sign relation.* How can we make our intended meanings clear to others, he asked, without pointing to the concrete objects we are discussing? According to Peirce, signs are commonly understood language symbols that mediate between the sender of the message and its interpreter, evoking similar thoughts, objects, or gestures in the minds of both parties.

Scientific analysis, Peirce felt, could be used as a tool for promoting the linguistic and conceptual clarity of signs. He therefore contributed a technique for determining meaning and solving problems (problems serve as the inspirational impetus to scientific inquiry), rather than elucidating any clear hypothetical philosophy or doctrine of truth.

The exception to this is Peirce's *doubt-belief theory of inquiry*. Feeling more comfortable with a stable set of beliefs than with feelings of doubt, human beings naturally strive to establish behavioral habits. Once thoroughly ingrained, habits become equivalent to beliefs, thereby keeping the individual in a satisfied, pleasant state, free from the chaos of doubt. Beliefs continue to perform this function as long as they "work" for the person; once they no longer achieve the desired results, new beliefs replace them. Peirce makes no attempt to reconcile varying beliefs of different people; his pragmatism sees no such need. Meanings and beliefs can fluctuate from person to person and situation to situation. The *pragmatic maxim* specifies how one arrives at such meanings and beliefs:

> . . . in order to ascertain the *meaning* of an intellectual conception one should consider what *practical consequences* might conceivably result by necessity from the truth of that conception; and the sum of these consequences will constitute the entire meaning of the conception.[2] (*Emphasis added*)

Peirce does not view meaning, then, as deriving from qualities inherent in objects; rather, he equates meaning with the behavior objects display in each situation. This is the original definition of pragmatism as conceived by its founder.

William James (1842–1910)

Peirce's ideas might have remained buried in obscurity were it not for his contemporary and good friend, William James. Emerging from an intellectually and philosophically eminent family,[3] the young James pursued interests spanning science, art, philosophy, and religion. Concentrating on multiple careers for much of his early life (as Peirce did), James began in the natural sciences and medicine, moving to philosophy at the turn of the century. His version of pragmatism varied considerably from Peirce's, causing the latter to experience much chagrin. Many of the divergences between these two interpretations can be traced to their differences in background and orientation. James was grounded in classical British empiricism and became very interested in developing the field of individual psychology, two areas detested by Peirce. And while Peirce's schooling in logical mathematics and physics led him to demand the establishment of causal relationships, James's humanistic orientation was satisfied with much weaker connective statements, focusing on obtaining general understanding. The particularity of the individual's experience was James's unit of analysis, in contrast to Peirce's more generic, universalistic bent. "James may have been anticipated by Charles Peirce and revised by John Dewey, but [he] was unquestionably the central figure in the pragmatic movement." [4] And it was actually William James who provided the first solid material for what was to become a symbolic interactionist framework.

Among James's humanistic convictions was the importance of subjectivity in the social world. Objects are found in scientifically pure and sterile form only where humans do not exist, where individuals are unable to make judgments or conceptions about them. Once a human being enters the scene, an image of the object is created in the mind, endowing the object with particular shades of significance and transforming it into an *idea*. Because its practical value may diminish, an idea is always subject to replacement.

The following is James's conception of the development of new opinions:

> The individual has a stock of old opinions already, but he meets a new experience that puts them to a strain. . . . The result is an inward trouble to which his mind till then had been a stranger, and from which he seeks to escape by modifying his previous mass of opinions. [5]

Although he draws upon Peirce's doubt-belief theory of inquiry and his adherence to practicality as a significant determiner of meaning, James is more use-oriented (rather than behavior-oriented) than his predecessor. The process of forming new opinions James describes above was the crux of the *pragmatic method*: each person evaluates ideas by the relative success of their potential use, and if these definitions "work" well, then they are good.

The pragmatic method was the first portion of James's theory; the second and major part was his *pragmatic theory of truth,* which he states as:

> Ideas (which themselves are but parts of our experience) become true just in so far as they help us to get into satisfactory relations with other parts of our experience. [6]

James expands Peirce's pragmatic maxim by postulating that beliefs that work are equivalent to truth. (Peirce only carried this line of reasoning to explain meaning.) James later explained this radical position more carefully, differentiating between *subjective truth* and *objective,* or *abso-*

lute, truth. Transmuted into a relative condition, truth becomes roughly equivalent to a very good–very bad continuum:

> True is the name of whatever proves itself to be good in the way of belief, and good, too, for definite assignable reasons.[7]

Ultimately, the "truth relation" (conception of reality) becomes something that is constructed by individuals and evolves continually according to its usage value rather than being anchored to a permanent definition.

By symbolic interactionist standards, some of James's more significant ideas reside not in his pragmatic volumes but in his psychological works. His magnum opus, *Principles of Psychology* (1890), presents his theories on the development of children. James traces the roots of adult behavior to the infant's earliest impulses and unsatisfied needs. Originally unaware of suitable resolutions, the infant follows blind instincts—acts without clear goals. As the child matures and develops a memory, he or she learns to relate means to ends. Patterns and habits then arise, enabling the child to function in the world. Because humans are adaptable, they can amend their habits whenever it becomes practical, as in the formation of new opinions.

At a certain stage the child begins to identify objects as "me" or "mine." James calls this the "awareness of being" or having a *self.* Of the four varieties, the material self, spiritual self, pure ego, and the *social self,* only the last was selected by Symbolic Interactionists as highly significant. This social self refers to an individual's reflection of himself or herself, not only his or her physical and emotional states but all his or her possessions, tangible or abstract. Due to the diversified and complex nature of life, the "me" has many roles:

> Properly speaking, a man has as many social selves as there are individuals who carry an image of him in their mind . . . he has as many different social selves as there are distinct groups of persons about whose opinion he cares.[8]

In order to view oneself objectively, the presence of others is necessary. Society thus has direct input into the formation of each individual. Once matured, the person is capable of exercising free will and affecting the course taken by himself or herself and others. A mutual interdependence is posited between each individual and society.

The portion of the self known as "I" is much more difficult to define. If the "me" is the self viewed as an object, then the "I" is the portion that does the viewing—the subject. This essence lies beyond situational consciousness, at the base of identity. Referred to as "the thinker," the "I" has a permanently lodged position in the self. Taken together, the "I" and "me" achieve the quality of *sameness* for the self from day to day and *connectedness* from role to role; they function to determine the feeling of self the individual has.

In both the breadth of his concern and depth of his inquiry, James's work must be considered seminal. His outstanding contributions encompass both the natural and social sciences. He is best remembered for his elaboration of pragmatic thought, for refining the loose body of Peirce's unrecognized ideas into a cogent system.

John Dewey (1859–1952)

Raised in the quietude of Vermont's mountains, John Dewey, the great American educational and social reformer, was a thoroughly New England man. Plunging into the world of academic philosophy in his undergraduate years at Johns Hopkins University, Dewey initially advocated the holistic and organic doctrine of Hegelian idealism. He gradually came to question many of his early beliefs, however, becoming convinced that all of life was not homogeneous and unified, but unintegrated, often conflictful, and heterogeneous. This pluralistic view of society occasioned his espousal of a complex view of humanity and the universe, in which he focused on each individual experience as the necessary unit of analysis. Like James, Dewey rejected grandiose hypothesizing about the inner workings of nature in favor of the search for a useful perspective to examine and gain understanding of the social world. The logic of Peirce's approach appealed to him, though, and true to his dialectical origin Dewey attempted a synthesis of Peirce's and James's ideas.

Dewey's version of the pragmatic maxim substitutes the idea of "warranted assertion" for James's more radically subjective truth and Peirce's view of meaning. People operate on the basis of a particular warranted assertion as long as it is useful to them. Reformulation of a previous assertion is not occasioned by doubt, as in Peirce's theory, but by conflict. Upon experiencing a "felt difficulty," people attempt to achieve a resolution.[9] By studying the nature and content of warranted assertions, the researcher can discover common norms and rules underlying human behavior.

During his residence at the University of Michigan (1884–1894), Dewey made the acquaintance of his most influential colleague, George Herbert Mead. Like his esteemed friend, Dewey came to see humanity, the social world, and the physical universe as interconnected and inseparable. No discussion of human beings should exclude the social world that both determines and is determined by them. Comparing humans to animals, Dewey and Mead saw a fundamental evolutionary similarity, differentiated only by a greater degree of complexity in humans. What separates the developing human child from lower species is the ability to use language to achieve higher levels of conceptualization and active internalization [10] of society's ideals.[11] Communication, then, holds the key to the developing self and its relationship with the surroundings. Knowledge, meaning, and the core of psychosocial evolution are located in the individual's interactional experience.

All mental activity is seen as processual by Dewey. This can be illustrated by comparing Dewey's description of *habit* with James's. For James, habit connoted mindless, repetitive behavior, sometimes in opposition to the better interests of the individual. But Dewey saw each action as building on the last, whereby people learn from their previous experiences. Every new action is part of an emergent process of habit formation. This leads to a conception of the mind as processual rather than structural.

Dewey's legacy to sociologists lies in his pluralistic analysis of American society; his emphasis on the significance of reflective experience in shaping human life and altering the social world; his emergent or processual view of human nature and his early work, along with Mead, in trying to promote the field of sociology and broaden its base to encompass psychological elements.

Early Interactionists

The philosophers discussed above were clearly influential in building a symbolic interactionist stance through their contributions of meaning as grounded in experience, scientific ideals, creative emergence, and development of the child through a symbolic social process. These ideas were significantly refined and broadened by the subsequent and concurrent work of thinkers outside the realm of philosophy.

Charles Horton Cooley (1864–1929)

Born in the university town of Ann Arbor, Michigan, Cooley was an unhealthy and shy child from birth. He evidenced early a predilection toward introspection and solitude that was to become central to both his life and work. Although he lived as a recluse with his family, Cooley's application of philosophy and other disciplines helped earn him one of the first prestigious positions at the University of Michigan's fledgling sociology department.

Fundamental to Cooley's ideology was the importance of subjectivity. Following James and other idealists, he saw the locus of reality as situated within the individual's mind. Society and its institutions are considered "mental habits," abstract concepts within the mind of its members. This definition makes an understanding of the subjective interpretations and perspectives of social actors fundamental. Cooley employed his own technique of *sympathetic introspection* to reflect on the meanings that might exist in the minds of his subjects. "It employs the dramatic experience of the investigator through his own ideas or feeling of the "I" as actor in the situation." [12] This methodological tack, used by James for formulating his psychological humanism, was refined and made famous by Cooley.

In contrast to many of his predecessors and successors, Cooley was sensitive to the role of emotion in human behavior. He did not sharply separate ideas from sentiment, impulses, and feeling, the non-rational aspects of humans. This stress on the affective quality contributed to a more realistic and rounded view of human nature.

Darwin's evolutionary influence also manifests itself in Cooley's conception of the development and socialization of individuals within the group. Cooley emphasizes both hereditary and environmental factors. The infant, who is born devoid of a "self," possesses an uncanny ability to learn, primarily through gestural and later linguistic communication. The people who immediately surround the newborn constitute his or her *primary group* and are of central importance in the process of developing a social self. Often considered Cooley's most significant contribution to sociology, *primary relationships* are those face-to-face associations characterized by a strong *we-feeling*. Interaction with these early significant others is the key to the youngster's successful maturation into a social being. Due to their malleable nature, infant human beings are effectively shaped by primary groups: the "nurseries of human nature." Awareness of other selves thus precedes the individual's awareness (or even possession) of his or her own consciousness.

Once the child secures some measure of control over its immediate surroundings, the *I-feeling* (the sense of self) is born. The self-identity of each individual, an enduring creation, evolves next. Finally, a person reaches the position from which he or she can successfully imagine how he or she appears to others.

Socialization now complete, the child starts to anticipate the actions and thoughts of others. Each member of society is credited with the ability to engage in their own sympathetic introspection, ascribing their characteristics and feelings onto others. From this point unfolds the sharing of states of mind, which forms the basis of the bonds comprising the material facts of society (considered basically mental constructions by Cooley). Cooley's theory of child development leads up to the notion of the *looking-glass self*. This concept, central to his theory, encompasses three dimensions: 1) people make a self-presentation and try to imagine the impression formed about themselves by others; 2) people imagine some judgment of their self-presentation; and 3) people experience an emotional reaction to this perceived evaluation.

Cooley subscribed to the organic conception which, as we saw with Dewey, considers all elements of human nature as functionally interconnected pieces of a whole. Interaction is the tissue that binds all these highly diverse units into a whole. Although Cooley showed how people are born into a social world that shapes them, he followed his pragmatic predecessors in subscribing to the belief in individuality and freedom. The eminent capacities of humans for personal choice, valuation, and the exercise of will allows us to shape in part both the tempo and direction of our world.

Cooley compiled his perspective from assorted bits and pieces of ideas. Sympathetic introspection, the method by which he evoked and resolved the critical questions of human nature, was highly regarded by his peers and has had a profound effect on future generations. His perceptions of human development, the primary group, and the looking-glass self, are his most remembered contributions.

William Isaac Thomas (1863–1947)

Born in Virginia, the son of a rural southern preacher, Thomas pursued an academic career in English and foreign studies before turning his interests to the social sciences. Invited by Albion Small, chairman of the new sociology department at the University of Chicago, Thomas became one of Chicago's first graduate students and was offered a position on the faculty shortly thereafter. Arriving at Chicago in 1893, Thomas found and came to be influenced by the strong center of pragmatism thriving there. Critical to his work, as to the work of all members of this philosophical coterie, was a rejection of any pre-conceived, overarching set of rules or statements, favoring instead an articulated approach and method for discovering the particularities of each unique setting. Thomas began his career with a somewhat cognitive orientation but turned toward a more interpretive sociology that suggested probabilities and made inferences rather than created general laws or rigid behavioral models. Like his pragmatic colleagues, Thomas was disposed toward an active view of the individual. His notion of socialization took the empirical world as existing prior to the birth of an individual but not totally determinate of the individual's outlook. Surrounded by a primary group, the infant develops through the interactive process, until as an adult he or she possesses the capacity to exert an influence over the society.

Other pragmatic strains are uncovered in Thomas's impressions of both personal and social change. Stable habits (in Dewey's emergent, not James's static, terms) provide people with a feeling of equilibrium. As habits are called into question by contradictory evidence, a crisis arises. Reconsideration of habits is thus forced, usually leading to new habits or beliefs. This can occur both within the individual mind or for the society as a whole. Thomas thus conceived of society as processual and of the human organism as fluid and evolving.

Taking the individual as his fundamental unit of analysis, Thomas continued the subjective orientation of his precursors. He became concerned with the attitudes and values people came to formulate about the social objects and social world surrounding them. Many interpretations, he felt, were affected by the context or situation in which exposure to social objects and contact with the social world were made. The unique reaction and evaluation a person makes of objects and actions are highly colored by what Thomas called one's *definition of the situation,* or subjective perspective. The ensuing definition of the situation depends on the nature of beliefs possessed by each individual. Thus, the famous Thomas theorem: "If men define situations as real, they are real in their consequences." [13]

The *situational approach,* Thomas's major interest, was utilized in *The Polish Peasant in Europe and America* (1918–1920), a magnum opus Thomas coauthored with Florian Znaniecki. A multi-year, multi-volume undertaking, this systematic research focused on the micro level of sociology, on concrete human lives. The *Polish Peasant* dealt with the integration and assimilation of Chicago's largest ethnic community into the dominant culture. It concluded that mediating social institutions such as Polish churches and newspapers were positive rather than negative influences within this subculture. Instead of removing the Poles from the mainstream of American life, as outsiders imagined they were, these community organs helped maintain solidarity and order, reduced criminal behavior, and eventually served as agents of assimilation into the broader way of life. To arrive at these findings, the authors applied their situational approach to both macro and micro levels of analysis. At the macro level, this included culture, norms, and social codes, while the micro part of the study included considerations of factors pre-existent in the individual, of environmental stimuli, and of the subjective perceptions and evaluations formed by the individuals involved.

The implications of this method were significant and lasting. Both objective (i.e., environmental) and subjective (i.e., perceptual) phenomena were deemed relevant and worthy of research. (Up to this point social scientists had examined one or the other phenomenon exclusively.) Statistical, demographic, and other objective methodological techniques began to be employed with subjective probes. Thomas studied human documents, for example, in order to gain subjective insights; he collected many letters and diaries written by Polish immigrants to get a view of their life and thoughts from their perspective.

In Blumer's (1939) important critique of the *Polish Peasant,* these subjective techniques are lauded as major advancements in methodology that yield an intimacy for the researcher with his or her subjects. Blumer also commends the sensitive theoretical approach taken and the way Thomas's methods are utilized to respect both the empirical world and the theory from which they are derived. But the groundwork is laid for the criticisms of subjective methods that remain unresolved to this day: how can human document analysis be freed from dependence on the researcher's interpretive competence? Further, can generalizations be made with confidence from subjective data?

George Herbert Mead (1863–1931)

The central figure associated with the symbolic interactionist perspective is George Herbert Mead. Although he never applied this label to his theoretical outlook, in his teachings and thoughts the complete body of ideas that began with pragmatic philosophy finally came together and crystallized. Mead's inspirational effect on many colleagues and students gave impetus to the movement that was the first break from the classic European absolutist theories of individuals and society.

A product of New England, Mead left Massachusetts to attend college at Oberlin. After working with William James and Josiah Royce to earn his graduate degree at Harvard, Mead followed the traditional pattern of studying abroad where he pursued philosophy, psychology, and the idealism of Wilhelm Wundt. After a year's position at the University of Michigan, he was brought to the University of Chicago by his good friend Dewey. Eventually he became chairman of the philosophy department, remaining at Chicago until his death.

In a profession where books are the core tools of the trade, it is unusual that Mead published not a single volume during his lifetime. Several articles were printed, but he was apparently content with delivering lectures and interacting with colleagues. So unfinished was his work that a number of his students assembled their collected class notes and combined them into a series of books that were published posthumously (see especially Mead, 1932, 1934, 1936, and 1938). The result of this state of affairs is unfortunate: since few of Mead's publications were written by him, each version is somewhat colored by problems of interpretation.[14]

Mead's actual work is a labyrinth of incomplete impressions. His perception of the universe emphasizes a dynamic tension between the polarities that comprise the fabric of our everyday lives and are never resolved. Many of the basic questions that plagued Mead concern the nature of the human mind, human knowledge, human selfhood, and human morality.[15]

Society

Focusing on the individual as his unit of analysis, Mead locates the social world and social interactions among people as the center of reality (not the individual mind as James and Cooley posited). This social environment exists prior to birth and must be effectively communicated to the child by the primary group. Language, the key to Mead's theory, is the medium through which all knowledge passes and through which human development occurs. Society, however, does not stamp its mark on a passive individual helpless to reciprocate; once mature, the person becomes capable of effecting social change through his or her own actions. Mead's image of social order envisions a consensual world, which rests on the basis of real, shared meanings. The intersubjectivity allowed by the shared meanings lends an aura of stability to a universe that is in continual flux.

Following Darwin's biological and evolutionary orientation and pragmatism's behaviorism,[16] Mead operated from within a phylogenetic framework: humans and animals, although differentiated by complexity, are conceived as structurally similar. Lower species gesture to each other, but this is only stimulus-response type of behavior, without reflective or symbolic thought. Animals frequently have little or no control over their actions because they are governed by instinct. "Conversations of gestures," Mead's term for this superficially reactive behavior, are best exemplified in his famed example of a dog fight: the growling, baring of teeth, and nipping of one dog automatically elicits corresponding behavior from the other—but not because of any underlying symbolic meaning. The second dog is incapable of reflecting on the hostile intentions of the first because he is biologically unequipped to do so, reacting instead with a fixed-action pattern of response to the initial stimulus. These surface interchanges lack the type of meaning achieved by humans.

Mead, with inspiration and collaboration from Dewey, advanced linguistic interpretations to the symbolic plane. In contrast to lower species, human communication operates on the basis of symbolic interchange, of which there are verbal and nonverbal varieties. When a gesture or phrase evokes the same meaning for the receiver as it does for the sender, a *significant symbol* has been used. Most human interaction takes the form, not of gesture, but of significant linguistic interchange.[17] Humans can develop significant symbols because of the complexity of their vocal apparatus. According to Mead, each word is part of a language system, representative of an entire cultural tradition. As children learn to talk, the meanings and values of their entire culture are transmitted through language.

If a gesture or symbol is significant, it has meaning. The function of meaning is a practical one; its role in the universe is to "work" for people (James's version of the pragmatic maxim), to achieve desired ends by successfully predicting the behavior of others from the meanings of symbols they use or infer.

Development
of the Self

At birth, humans, like animals, are instinct-motivated, unreflective creatures. Before symbolic interaction can occur, they must develop a *self*. Mead's impressions about the nature of a self draw heavily upon James's and Cooley's, extending beyond their conceptualizations.

Genesis of the self occurs through communication, through the social interaction process. At birth the infant is incapable of grasping any significance from its surroundings. When not behaving instinctually, it engages only in meaningless imitation of the adults in its world. Development progresses through a series of stages beginning with *play,* wherein the child practices taking the roles of different significant people (mother, father, friend, teacher). One at a time the child orients his or her actions toward these roles and begins to conceive of himself or herself through the eyes of an other. This is the first step toward building a self.

Advancing to the *game* stage, the child acquires enough sophistication to engage in a formalized game with rules. Moving from handling a single role, he or she now is faced with the necessity of playing several roles at once. He or she must be able to anticipate the behavior of others, to cast himself or herself into their roles in order to play his or her own. Next, the child must advance from taking each role simultaneously to abstracting several roles into one. This conglomeration of roles comprises the *generalized other,* or child's internalization of the composite views of a group or society. By taking this role, the now socialized child can view his or her own behavior in light of society's expectations, completely approaching himself or herself as an object. Socially desirable (or controlled) behavior is maintained through each individual's successful anticipation of norms. Here, then, is a picture of how people come to take themselves as objects in the course of developing a self, and learn the process of *role-taking*.

Again following James's lead, Mead isolated two components of the self, the "I" and the "Me." Earlier in this chapter we noted the subject/object distinction that James attributed to these two parts of the self and which Mead's characterization follows. But Mead goes into more detail, citing the "I" as the impulsive, non-deterministic aspect of the individual and the "me" as the more controlled, socially conscious aspect of personality. The "I" acts with an opinion of the self as a unified whole, while there exists a separate "me" for each of the individual's roles and social groups. A dynamic internal process is thus envisioned, whereby people actively engage in conscious behavior involving themselves and others. Mead uses a "stimulus-*organization*-response" model to highlight the thinking character of humans, rejecting the simple stimulus-response formula of behaviorism.

Two implications of Mead's view of the self concern the *selectivity* and *reflectivity* encompassed in the mental process. His theory suggests that through our unique perceptions we react selectively to portions of the environment, giving each individual, each situation, and each insight a slightly different perspective. We also utilize our reflective nature to continually engage in an internal dialogue, plotting out possible scenarios and courses of action that can be modified or revised at any time toward the culmination of a social act. Within each person Mead envisioned a society in miniature, a little parliament with conflicts, debates, evaluations, and decisions. None of these processes are accessible to observation, yet Mead assigns them crucial import and considers them worthy of study. His subjective view of private character accounts for individuality (particularly the "I"); it allows for our inherent capacity to exercise free will and encounter chance.

Mind

Mind, for Mead, like Dewey and Cooley, is an ongoing process, not a static structure. By producing and receiving significant symbols, particularly linguistic ones, meaning is made and interpreted by humans. Mind is not judged to be merely an inner psychic world, but rather a mode of behavior that involves interaction through language symbols and commences only when presented with a problem [18] in a particular setting.[19] Reflective thought is thus tied to problem solving.

Another unique feature of the mind, according to Mead, is its accumulation and storage of personal history. While old group ties or events may recede into the less significant portions of memory, they are never forgotten. They allow the individual to learn from past experiences. Every situation is approached from a novel position by humans due to the constantly emerging quality of mind and the way it changes and develops.

Objects

We can now see the difference Mead intended when Blumer (1966) wrote that although people *react* to stimuli, they *act* toward objects. Objects, as previously noted, derive meaning not from an ontological definition, but, as the pragmatists felt, from their function. This can vary as the actor varies his or her perspective. For example, a tree can be a place of refuge in the rain, a source of fire in the cold, a potential shelter, a barrier between people, or an aesthetic object to the nature lover. Objects are colored by our perceptions and plans of action toward them, thereby becoming endowed with elements of subjectivity. They are largely shared, however, due to the common usage humanity makes of them.

The Act

In addition to the individual, the single act is a basic unit of study for Mead. As Cooley did, Mead thought each act of an individual begins and ends in equilibrium. He postulated four stages as comprising a complete act: impulse, perception, manipulation, and consummation These stages may be of varying duration, for once an action is launched it may not yield its final consequences for a considerable length of time. And any event in between the impulse and consummation of an act may become relevant to the ultimate evaluation and resolution of that act. In addition to completed acts, Mead speaks of collapsed acts, blocked acts, automatic acts, incipient acts (attitudes), and other complex concepts that further define and refine varieties of human behavior.

Time

Mead's dynamic theory of time extends into many of his other concerns. Reality is always grounded in a *present* [20] that the individual is experiencing. The *past* is something previously known as a present but which can never be viewed in exactly the same way because of knowledge we have acquired in the meantime. Every present, however, is rooted to the past from which it arose. Similarly, the *future*, bound to the present, has no meaning when it is severed from it. Thus, Mead's conception of the present is highly influenced by the past leading up to it and the future growing out of it.

Mead's seminal thought draws upon many traditions and perspectives that were flourishing in the stimulating center of intellectual creativity at the University of Chicago. Implanted firmly in the center of the symbolic interactionist movement, influencing and being influenced by almost all of the early interactionists, Mead's theory encompasses elements of pragmatism, behaviorism, biological evolutionism, relationalism, and idealism.

The Chicago School

Central to the birth of interactionist ideas is the University of Chicago, which brought together prominent thinkers from all over the world to create a stimulating and dynamic intellectual center. Given the magnanimous sponsorship of John D. Rockefeller, each new department chairperson was unencumbered in his search to secure the most eminent assemblage of faculty. A community of scholars arose whose mutual respect and influence extended across department and disciplinary lines.

Pragmatism, the first social science movement to take root there, was followed closely by the nascent doctrine of symbolic interactionism. William I. Thomas in sociology, Mead in philosophy, John Watson (behaviorism) in neuro-psychology and Edward Sapir in linguistic anthropology all combined to give fruitful ideas to symbolic interactionism. When Thomas left the University in 1918, his protege Robert E. Park emerged as the leader of the new movement.

Park brought to his career in sociology a colorful and varied background. Trained in Europe and America under Dewey, James, and Georg Simmel, after completing his Ph.D. in 1904 Park spent several years as a political speechwriter, activist, and investigative journalist. Shortly after his mentor, Thomas, left, Park introduced a *field work orientation* to the Chicago School that inspired a plethora of empirical studies that sought to "get inside" various aspects of Chicago life and analyze them sociologically. Louis Wirth's *The Ghetto* (1928), Frederick Thrasher's *The Delinquent Gang* (1927), Harvey Zorbaugh's *The Gold Coast and the Slum* (1929), and Clifford Shaw's *The Jack-Roller* (1930) were published in the 1920s when the Chicago School began to flourish and develop the naturalistic investigative technique of *participant-observation*.

Park and his young colleagues Ernest Burgess and Roderick McKenzie created a perspective out of their empirical studies of the city known as the *ecological* or *social disorganization* school of urban sociology. This model posited several concentric rings emanating from the downtown urban areas of major cities. Each ring served as an informal geographic boundary separating distinct class and ethnic groups. Aside from the very rich residing in the core circle, the central parts of the city were filled with the poorest and most recent immigrants, becoming increasingly assimilated as one progressed outward to the affluent suburbs. Social disorganization and deviance increased as one moved back toward the inner city.

When Park retired in 1929 and Mead passed away in 1931, a new generation of field work and interactionist-oriented students took their places. Everett Hughes continued in Park's tradition of field work, guiding another decade and more of studies "from the inside." Herbert Blumer assumed Mead's position as leader and defender of the as yet unnamed theoretical perspective. (It was Blumer who finally gave Symbolic Interactionism its name.) Other influential leaders of this second generation of interactionists were Burgess and Wirth who maintained the ecological school. These four carried the eminence of the sociology department of the University of Chicago through the 1930s and 1940s.

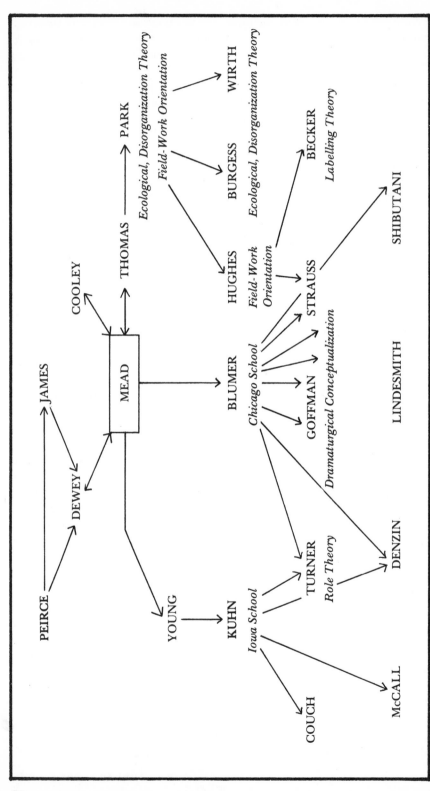

FIGURE 2–1. Genealogy of Symbolic Interactionism

By the late 1940s and early 1950s this generation began to disperse, marking the end of the era of Chicago sociology, as many other departments ascended to national stature with prominent faculties. Students trained during the last period formed a third generation of sociologists of the Chicago School, but they were geographically scattered and formed different movements or theories deriving from symbolic interactionism. Particularly noteworthy among the third generation are Erving Goffman (the dramaturgical conception; *see* chapter 4); Howard Becker (labeling theory; *see* chapter 3); Anselm Strauss; Ralph Turner (role theory); Alfred Lindesmith, Tamotsu Shibutani, and others.

Application of Symbolic Interactionist Theory

Addiction and Opiates (1947): Alfred R. Lindesmith. To illustrate how Mead's theories were put into practice, let us examine Lindesmith's investigation of addiction, a classical empirical study undertaken from the perspective of symbolic interactionism. Having received his graduate degree in 1936 from the University of Chicago, Lindesmith accepted a faculty position at Indiana University whence this research was conducted.

When Lindesmith began his study of opiate use, current theories pointed to the pleasure and ecstacy of the drug habit as the primary motivating factors leading to addiction. Lindesmith, however, became convinced that it was not positive but negative reinforcement that kept people tied to narcotics. Addiction, he found, is a "learned process": only those individuals who make a mental connection between the cessation of agonizing withdrawal symptoms and repeated use of the drug move on to habituation. He speaks of addicts becoming "trapped against their will by the hook of withdrawal." [21] Finally, he documented a profound attitudinal and behavioral change that overcomes an individual as he or she moves from the role of a normal, healthy person into a deviant mode.

Through case study research, Lindesmith sought to probe the essential nature of the self. He became convinced that the difference between a human's and an animal's potential reaction to opiates is the human ability to comprehend language symbols and to make causal connections. Young children, without a fully developed self, will not become addicts because they cannot engage in introspection or respond to complex linguistic structures.[22] In contrast, the adult drug user, who can perceive linguistic and conceptual interchanges, may become sensitized to changing attitudes toward him or her through reflectively *taking the role of the other*. A turnabout may thus be effected as the individual applies the wider group's terms to himself or herself and adopts their views.[23]

Lindesmith's approach utilized the *analytic induction technique* developed by Znaniecki (1934). This method involves the creation of a universal theory intended to fit all cases. By searching for contradictory examples that would force reformulation, Lindesmith hoped to refine his theory until all possible deviations were included. Forced to reconstruct his hypotheses of addiction three times to fit the emerging data, he acknowledges that the ultimate explanation may be as yet undiscovered and beyond the range of social science.[24] Crucial to the method of analytic induction, then, is an identification of causal relationships, rather than a descriptive analysis of motivation. Taken as a whole, Lindesmith's research is deterministic in its emphasis on a single, identifiable type of experience that is the same for all individuals in a situation. It also encompasses elements of behaviorism, evolutionism, and pragmatism.

Branches of Symbolic Interactionism

In examining the state of symbolic interactionism today, we find multiple strains. Part of the reason for this lack of unanimity is the paradigm's long oral tradition. Since Mead put few of his ideas into writing it became necessary for students and colleagues to verbally communicate these theories among themselves; this gave rise to misinterpretations, variations in emphasis, and contradictions over certain points. The posthumous publication of Mead's work by his students did not fill this void with a clear and comprehensive statement of theory but tended to produce a chaos of interpretation.

For our purposes we will identify three resulting branches of symbolic interactionism: 1) the *Chicago School,* led by Herbert Blumer; 2) the *Iowa School,* with its progenitor Manfred Kuhn; and 3) the *dramaturgical conceptualization* of Kenneth Burke and Erving Goffman (discussed in chapter 4). These three branches have in common an interest in micro sociology; a concern for the degree of free will in the human condition; a commitment to the study of social interaction for investigating the meanings of everyday life; and an acceptance of viewing the world from the member's perspective. Beyond these commonalities, the various branches diverge in their ideas.[25] We will now consider in some detail the Chicago and the Iowa schools and the theoretical perspectives they espouse.

Herbert Blumer: The Chicago School

Receiving his graduate training at the University of Chicago during the early 1920s, Blumer was very much influenced by Ellsworth Faris (an early interactionist), Park, Thomas, Cooley, Dewey, and, most especially, Mead. His early career was so outstanding that upon Mead's death in 1931, it was Blumer whom everyone acknowledged as heir to the position of leadership. Commencing teaching in 1925, Blumer continued in that role as a dominating force, molding several generations of graduate students. When he finally left Chicago in 1952 to accept the department chair at the University of California, Berkeley, an entire heritage followed and blossomed on the West Coast. He remains there to the present day.

Provided with the groundwork of an existing philosophy, Blumer contributed a great deal toward pragmatism's evolution into the sociology of symbolic interactionism. Ideas only implicit in the work of his predecessors were expanded in original directions. Blumer's sociology contained more phenomenological influences than Mead's, emphasizing the negotiated order of interactions and shared meanings. Blumer also gave Thomas's situational approach an increased significance: subjective definitions of the situation impinging on each encounter became of greater relevance for study. Some of the positivism inherent in Mead's philosophy was abandoned by Blumer, orienting symbolic interactionism less toward the discovery of general behavioral laws and more toward discovery of the nature of the empirical world. A shift away from the causal model of action ensued, bolstered by a less deterministic image of human beings.

Finally, Blumer incorporated the field-work orientation of the Chicago School into symbolic interactionism, replacing sympathetic introspection with the method of participant-observation. Although he conducted few empirical studies, Blumer stressed the need to ground and continually reformulate hypotheses by testing them in the concrete, everyday world. Interactionist researchers were to maintain the integrity of their data by studying the data in their situational and temporal contexts.

Six "root images," [26] or basic premises about human nature and social life, were posited by Blumer as theoretical guides to aid in the discovery of everyday life.

Human society or *human group life* (the first "root image") [27] refers to any interaction involving at least two actors engaging in ordinary activities or pursuing a continual course of action. Broader notions such as *culture* and *social structure* are derived directly from this root image: culture is created out of what people do, their patterns of behavior, values, and myths. Social structure is formed by the interpersonal relationships that arise during the course of everyday life. Society is comprised of humans fitting together their respective "lines of action," thereby creating social organization.

Human social interaction (Blumer's second "root image") is the phenomena of people interpreting each other's acts and anticipating each other's behavior, in an effort to coordinate their activities. Interaction for Blumer is not a process wherein abstract factors or roles come together and play against each other. Rather, interaction occurs between real people; any reduction to smaller parts or greater forces does not correspond to concrete reality. Social interaction is the foundation out of which human beings and their conduct originate. Likewise, *symbolic* and *non-symbolic interaction* are relevant to this root image, comprising "the use of significant symbols" and "the conversation of gestures." People learn to interpret each other's roles in both a specific sense (the actual person involved) and a generic sense (the generalized other). Mutual understanding of role-taking is indispensible to the communication process.

Beyond people, *objects* (the third "root image") form the building blocks of our world. Physical objects are solid matter, items such as houses, dirt, or cars. Social objects are less tangible and involve a conceptual relationship, such as, friends, children, or politicians. The third type of objects are abstract objects, higher constructs such as morality, the criminal justice system, or religious doctrines. All of these objects have meaning for people who use them. Human behavior, as each individual subjectively perceives it, determines the meaning of objects. Three essential premises are associated with this ascription:

> The first is that human beings act toward things on the basis of the meanings that these things have for them. . . . The second premise is that the meaning of such things is derived from, or arises out of, the social interaction that one has with one's fellows. The third premise is that these meanings are handled in, and modified through, an interpretive process used by the person in dealing with the things he encounters.[28]

Meanings are social products that can be changed when the interactional setting so suggests. This is because *the human being as an actor* (the fourth "root image") is a perceptive creature, involved in a continual interpretation of interacting with his or her self. The self is not inborn but socially developed. Blumer accepts Mead's processual analysis of evolution, noting the play stage, game stage, and eventual internalization of the generalized other. Once a person has learned to view himself or herself as an object, he or she becomes capable of *reflectivity*: of carrying on an internal dialogue with himself or herself. The attribute of reflectivity is a unique characteristic of humans, fundamental to their understanding of the world, and differentiating them from animals. Human beings, as highly complex organisms, continually re-assess their situation and behave as best they can in a world that cannot be depended upon to remain simple and constant. This repudiates the behavioral supposition of an actor passively responding to stimuli. Instead of reacting, the individual puts forward lines of action that amount to instant innovations.

To permit this unique performance, *human action* (the fifth "root image" that Blumer postulated) must be recognized as rational behavior. People's interpretations are crucial to an understanding of their behavior. We act by using self-indications (inner reflections) to think and organize the nature of the social world around us. Symbolic interactionism refutes the stimulus-response model and argues for a model of stimulus-organization-response as the pattern of human thought. Collective action and individual behavior are analyzed equally well by this model.

Completing the presentation, Blumer concludes with a consideration of *interlinkage of action* (the sixth "root image"). An examination of joint action must include the sum of individual actions as well as the unique character of the interaction between the actors—those social bonds that arise in fitting together lines of action. Thus, joint action and those human groups that come together to interlink their acts are the proper focus of study for symbolic interactionists.

Human life is both stable and changing. Stability is maintained by social norms, channelling patterned behavior into expected and socially acceptable routes. Much of life follows this path and thus the symbolic interactionists presuppose a commonality of pre-established meanings. The status quo is thus ensured through this inter-generational transmission of social meanings.

But human behavior is not totally static or normative; otherwise there would be no war, no individuality, and no advancement of civilization. First, new situations arise that have no precedent. As we move through the life cycle, decisions and crises peculiar to various ages are encountered. Each day we learn new things through exposure to new knowledge and different situations. Second, each instance of joint action must be re-aligned anew. Some days a group can pick up where it left off, but this is not always possible. New players ask to be admitted into the game or old ones fail to show up and adjustments must be made. The situation must be constantly renegotiated, possibly affecting the outcomes. Finally, any action arises out of a background of experience that is changed each time a new encounter is added to the repertoire. Mead's temporal thesis, which asserts that all acts remain inseparable from their historical past, is thus preserved.

Blumer's Methodology. To carry out these theoretical goals, Blumer delineated some research strategies. By methodology, he referred to the entire scientific quest, not merely a selected phase of data collection. This endeavor must form an integrated and unified whole that respects both the theoretical orientation and the obdurate character of the empirical world.[29]

Two specific modes of inquiry are depicted by Blumer. During exploration, the researcher familiarizes himself or herself with the topic through immersion in the setting, focusing on relevant data, and determining the relations between people. Interpersonal sensitivity is essential as the sociologist strives to be continually aware of how his or her presence and subjective interpretations may affect the findings. A range of qualitative methods are applicable to this stage of research, which ultimately yields a *descriptive depiction.*

Following data gathering is the *inspection phase,* when analysis begins. The substantive findings then undergo intensive scrutiny, being combined to form generalizations that eventually attain the level of formal theory. These two components—description and inspection— combine to produce a *naturalistic investigation.* Blumer's methodology stresses harmony between social science and the empirical world. By using the characteristics of a situation to suggest the methodological approach most suited, the symbolic interactionist can generate a truer understanding of human group life.

Although Blumer actually made few sojourns into the field to utilize his perspective, his colleagues and students generated many excellent empirical studies using his methodology. The following are two studies that exemplify a symbolic interactionist approach of the variety developed by Blumer and his Chicago School.

Boys in White (1961): Howard S. Becker, Blanche Geer, Everett Hughes and Anselm Strauss. A leading group of interactionists, Becker et al., approached their research project as a team, spending two years submerged in the setting. The effect of medical school on students (beyond the simple transfer of knowledge) served as an initial guiding question for the research. Young men fresh out of college, filled with naive idealism about how they were going to save lives, were observed throughout their years of medical school and internship until they left the medical education system. The authors looked upon them initially as "boys in white," the uninitiated men who wore the medical uniform, but for whom this covering was merely superficial. As the medical students became increasingly immersed in the situation, they were gradually socialized into the roles of medical student, intern, and doctor.

As a social-psychological study, the evolution of student ideology and culture became the crux of the findings. It was unexpectedly discovered that students have considerable control over their own behavior. Although their position was compared with that of prisoners in total institutions, the study showed that they can achieve autonomy by setting their own guidelines for the degree and direction of effort. The medical students did this by weighing the pragmatic value of immediate goals such as getting through school or pleasing the faculty against long-range goals such as alleviating human suffering. Usually the medical students opted for the former. Conflicts with the faculty over practical instead of purely academic orientations were also informally resolved in the student's favor by their seizing opportunities to pursue clinical experience and medical responsibility.

According to symbolic interactionist methodology, the research was undertaken without any preconceived hypotheses. Unstructured techniques (without a formal interview questionnaire) prove particularly valuable at the beginning of such endeavors; Becker and Geer (1960) thus developed the approach of asking questions such as "what's happening here?". Their primary purpose was descriptive or phenomenological, but after a lengthy period their analysis began to develop and closely followed the discovery of new data. Naturalistic methods such as participant-observation worked best, permitting freedom in the hospital to ask questions at any time. Formal interviews with faculty, students, and administrators were later added to these more casual ones. Methodological operationalizations of symbolic interactionism included taking member's perspectives as highly consequential. The researchers assumed that all parts of the school system would be functionally interrelated and so inseparable for the purposes of analysis. They maintained a sufficiently loose format so that key, but unexpected, emphases could emerge.

Several main themes were pursued by the authors, all congruent with symbolic interactionisms's major concepts. Among these is the concept of *emergence*. Becker et al.'s model of the actor assumes the kind of human flexibility that permits adaptability to distinctly different situations and forces existing for freshmen, advanced medical students, and clinical interns. *Shared meanings* also became evident as the power and extent of student culture was perceived. A collective perspective and collective action developed out of the everyday problems faced by students. Surrounding these shared students' meanings is the perspective of the entire social organization. The medical school was conceptualized as an "organization of collective forms of social actions." [30] Thus, this study represents a processual analysis of an organization, which traditionally has been structurally approached.

Thomas's *definition of the situation* served as another major *tool* for examining both immediate (micro) and long-range (macro) perspectives of students. The authors observed a conflict between the idealism of the long-range goal of helping humanity and the cynical realism of the immediate goal of getting through school, which was pragmatically resolved by shelving future aspirations to concentrate on present necessities. Students' practical tasks of pleasing faculty and anticipating professors' desired behavior required that they be competent at role-taking and flexible enough to adapt their attitudes and actions to achieve desirable ends. This was accomplished in the classic manner of "making indications to their selves" (the inner dialogue), projecting a multitude of scenarios, and "ignoring possible lines of action which appear preordained to fail or unworkable, discarding those which may cause conflict—in short, choosing the action which seems reasonable and expedient." [31] This is the interactionists' pragmatic view of behavior.

Boys in White is a classic symbolic interactionist study. It is a clear utilization of a Meadian perspective that allows the true nature of the empirical setting to guide the researchers' emerging and developing formulations.

Stations of the Lost (1970): Jacqueline P. Wiseman. Of still a later generation of Blumer's graduate students is Wiseman, studying with him during his Berkeley rather than Chicago years. Receiving her degree during the 1960's, she is now a professor at the University of California, San Diego.

Winner of the C. Wright Mills award, *Stations of the Lost* is considered an important contribution to the literature on skid row alcoholics. One of the features that makes this work particularly cogent is Wiseman's use of many groups' perspectives to show the radically different attitudes held by the participants she studied. Her work suggests part of the reason why conventional treatments designed to "cure" the skid row inebriate have such little success. But that was not the purpose of her undertaking. Consistent with symbolic interactionist goals, an illumination of the insider's views was the original aim of the research.

Wiseman discovered what she termed the "loop" and its "stations," a group of institutions that support, treat, or attempt to rehabilitate alcoholics and return them to society. By continually moving from station to station, a skid row inhabitant can live free for an almost indefinite period. The camaraderie and continuous success with which these people managed to obtain food, shelter, and clothing from institutions without having to quit drinking made life enjoyable for these alcoholics and provided a measure of security and safety. The more frustrated group of people in the skid row neighborhood are the agents of social control who staff the institutions, having sometimes sincere, yet often hypocritical attitudes. Wiseman describes several of these stations and shows the conflicting realities that exist for the various groups, while penetrating the "fronts" that they put up for each other.

Aside from her substantive findings, the interesting and important aspects of Wiseman's research pertain to her research strategy and operationalization of concepts. In her methodology the notion of emergence appears. That is, the unfolding of her research plans illustrates the various changes and revisions of the study as it progressed. Initially Wiseman envisioned her project as an attempt to gain a member's perspective on skid row life, but when it was discovered that few men actually remain on skid row for long, the study's focus was widened to include the institutions they frequented outside of skid row. As more and more stations emerged, Wiseman categorized them, limiting her attention to the exemplary ones. In discussions with individuals from social agencies, Wiseman perceived a decided contrast between their view and that of the skid row members. The final change in the study design included a contrasting of perspectives between what had by then clearly emerged as two groups.

Wiseman followed the methodological prescriptions outlined by both Blumer (1969) and Becker and Geer (1960). She followed unstructured exploratory techniques, free of initial preconceptions (such as those often contained in hypotheses), by more structured interviewing, as significant data emerged and showed connections. These were augmented continuously with frequent participant-observation work.

Of chief concern in Wiseman's study is the nature of human group life. People fitting their lines of action together—such as people on skid row combining their panhandling resources to buy a communal bottle of wine—make up these groups. Social interaction occurs not between forces but among human beings. Human group life is also processual; new situations and social factors occur to make life different as time passes. The skid row dwellers learn from their own experiences and from those of their friends just as the agents do—sooner or later some tricks will become exposed and will no longer work successfully. The definition of the situation, also highly meaningful in this book, is exemplified by the skid row inebriate's cleverness in assessing each surrounding before deciding how to behave.

Without a self, personal history would be impossible for the human as a social actor. Through self-indication, Wiseman's subjects formulate plans of action: sob stories and demeanor may vary, depending on their perception of the other's attitude (be it a Christian-missionary or the police). Skid row habitués know that society (the generalized other) condemns them, but they do not internalize this reflection or apply it to their self-identity.[32] This tenacity is attributed to a jovial self-image due to human beings' mind process: the uniquely human stimulus-organization-response mentioned in our earlier discussion.

A final operationalization of symbolic interactionism theory is the portrayal of *multiple realities* instead of an absolute, objective truth. Wiseman shows the conflicting perspectives held by each group yet does not attempt to reconcile them or determine which perspective holds the ultimate validity. Her implicit conclusion about why government policies and social "cures" have failed is that they stem from the beliefs and the value system of agents from the greater society. This suggests that only programs grounded in the social meanings and definitions that are significant for the alcoholics can be effective.

Manfred H. Kuhn: The Iowa School

An important strain of interactionism, albeit not dominant, the Iowa School is almost synonymous with the late Manfred Kuhn. Distinctively different in interpretation and methodological preference from Blumer, significant similarities still justify placing Iowans within the same general rubric of symbolic interactionism. Douglas (1970), for example, sees the "phenomenological interactionism" of Blumer and the "behavioral interactionism" of Kuhn as conflicting but parallel strains of the same theory. Kuhn, however, considers his changes so great that he relinquishes any claim to the symbolic interactionist name, calling his work *self theory*. Qualifying the fundamental divergence between his sociology and that of his predecessors, Kuhn cites the work of Cooley, Dewey, and Mead as "a body of conjectural and deductive orientation," while referring to his own efforts as "a derivative but developing set of generalizations, tested by empirical research." [33] Thus, Kuhn's intention is to generate a specific set of hypotheses about the social-psychological nature of individuals in society.

Kuhn's exposure to symbolic interactionist ideas came indirectly, rather than from the principal theorists themselves. While a graduate student at the University of Wisconsin he studied under Kimball Young, a University of Chicago scholar who had been trained by Mead, Thomas, and Sapir. Young had derived an interest in attitudes from Thomas, and Sapir had oriented him toward the study of linguistics and how the structure of an entire culture could be contained within its language. Receiving his doctorate in 1941, Kuhn finally settled to teach at the State University of Iowa where a center for his ideas developed.

Kuhn respected the work of Mead but sought to resolve some of the ambiguities resulting from the oral record left by Mead and the subsequent interpretations. Kuhn found Mead's handling of the question of determinism—the degree to which human nature can be considered relatively unfree and predictable by cause-effect relationships independent of one's will—particularly unclear. This confusion rested, according to Kuhn, on definitional problems surrounding the "I" and the "me." And intimately tied to this definitional vagueness was the difficulty of operationalizing potentially obscure terms. Finding the indeterminate variables linked to impulse and the "I" the hardest to test concretely, Kuhn oriented his theory toward a greater emphasis on the "me." Thus Iowan symbolic interactionism adopts a deterministic slant through its concentration on the self as a study of "me's"—the various roles and images one has of oneself.

For Kuhn, the ideal of social science is to achieve a universal similarity of methods, whereby uniformity and replicability are achievable. He desired to create generic laws that would extend to all humans in different situations. To this end, one of his first undertakings was the creation in 1950 of an analytical tool for the investigation of the self. The Twenty Statements Test (TST) asks the respondent to create twenty answers to the simple question, "Who am I?". In contrast to survey research, which provides a closed-ended and limiting set of answer categories, the TST is open-ended, allowing the nature of the self to emerge unfettered.[34]

Kuhn notes that interactionists employ indirect methods such as participant-observation or asking informal questions for inferring significant attitudes. He suggests that this roundabout procedure may not be necessary; people will honestly volunteer information about their innermost selves when questioned directly. A definition of the self is attained through the TST. We each achieve self-identity by taking the role of the other and discovering the other's attitude toward us. The self, then, consists of a set of attitudes and internalized roles (the "me's").

Society, for Kuhn, precedes the individual and contains a number of constants that are gradually made known to people as they become capable of learning them. Of special import is language, the only reality we experience that embodies within it the nature of an entire culture. Cultural notions within language are not thrust upon the actor in a stimulus-response sense of passive internalization, but are learned through the individual's role-taking, where he or she actively comes to see both the world and himself or herself through the eyes of specific and generalized others.

Objects comprise the social material of reality (including the self as an object). Meanings become associated with objects on the basis of their behavior. Behavior also is related to attitudes, which are defined by Kuhn as "plans of action." Thus Kuhn shared with behaviorism the desire to infer causal social-psychological relationships from external manifestations of actors; he did not seek to "get inside their heads," as the more strict practitioners of symbolic interactionism would. He considered covert facets of personality fundamental, but tried to make them surface through the use of the TST.

Building loosely on the reflection of primary groups as "nurseries of human nature" (Cooley's idea), Kuhn became vitally concerned with the "significant other" [35] or "reference group." [36] The individuals who are instrumental in affecting how self-conceptions arise and change are those who are emotionally or psychologically relevant to the individual. Former judgments about the significant other have always been too categorical. To amend this problem, Kuhn (1964b) proposed the concept of the *orientational other*: that set of persons which the individual defines as truly meaningful. The locus of a person's orientational other determines the attitudes about himself or herself that he or she will internalize. Thus, the syllogism underlying the Iowan's work: orientational others determine self-attitudes; self-attitudes determine behavior; hence, if we know the orientational other of a given person we can *predict* his or her behavior.

Comparing Kuhn to Blumer, it becomes clear that "while Blumer's image of man dictates his methodology, Kuhn's methodology dictates his image of man." [37] A man torn by several conceptual conflicts, Kuhn had high ideals about how his efforts would improve symbolic interactionism, but his methodological beliefs frequently stood at odds with his theoretical commitments. Such is the case with the structural-processual dilemma. Kuhn acknowledged Mead's view of the individual as a dynamic, changing actor, yet his instrument, the TST, captured a temporally static image of individuals. Thus, this method relegated to minor status such crucial elements of social-psychology as emergence, personal history, future visions, and varying self-attitudes.

Kuhn's legacy lies in his attempts at operationalizing ambiguous assumptions of Mead's thought and in the questions he raised about important theoretical misunderstandings. His untimely death in 1963 left it in the hands of his students to continue the tradition and further resolve the issues. To date no one has emerged to finish his work.[38]

"Self Conceptions and Others: A Further Test of Meadian Hypotheses" (1970): E. L. Quarentelli and Joseph Cooper. An examination of the type of empirical research generated by Manfred Kuhn may shed more light on the nature and concerns of the Iowa School of interactionism.

Quarentelli and Cooper's study cannot be understood without first mentioning a previous work by Miyamoto and Dornbusch (1970). This earlier research inquired into the nature of self-conceptions by considering dimensions of personality and physical attractiveness. Subjects were asked first to record their own self-conceptions and then estimate how they felt significant others (who were chosen by the researchers, not themselves) thought of them. The actual ratings by the significant others completed the research design. Findings suggested a higher correlation between how people conceived of themselves and how they believed others thought of them than between what they perceived that others felt and the reality of those others' opinions. Miyamoto and Dornbusch concluded that people are more accurate in taking the role of the generalized other than in perceiving how specific others feel.

Quarentelli and Cooper attempted to replicate and further this investigation. They posited three goals: (1) to add to the empirical base of interactionism; (2) to incorporate a sensitivity to temporality [39] into their study, and (3) to clarify the nature of the self. Working with dental students, they asked questions similar to those posed in the earlier study to their subjects at the beginning of each academic year (four times). Moreover, others from a specific variety of roles (friends, family, fellow dental students) were selected, covering what was hoped to be a full range of friends and acquaintances. As before, the subjects were asked to rate their self-concepts and how they thought the specific others felt. The specific others completed the same form as well. Recognizing a shortcoming in previous research, Quarentelli and Cooper sought to establish a processual image of personality. Lastly, a more precise operationalization of the generalized other was one final and expected result.

As was found in the previous study, the perceived attitudes of others were closer to self-conceptions than to the actual sentiments of others. This suggested that the intuited, not the factual, response of the other is more significant in creating self-attitudes. Further, this correlation remained the same over four years of studying the same group, indicating that people came no closer to approximating the actual beliefs of others after knowing them for awhile. Self-concept was also found to be more a function of an individual's interpretations of the generalized other than of the genuinely held attitudes of the generalized other.

Given the intricacy of the research design and the multi-variable analysis, surprisingly few theories or substantive findings have been generated by this and other such studies. The problem of static images still remains; although temporal complexity was attempted, Quarentelli and Cooper still presented a series of frozen instants removed from their historical and situational contexts. Approaches of the Iowa School are to be commended for their attempts to focus on creating methodological accuracy and rigor, but this should not be at the expense of a dynamic and fluid model of the human actor.

Critiques of Symbolic Interactionism

Currently, symbolic interactionism is a loose body of theories that encompasses several conflicting and occasionally competing interpretations. Yet despite their differences, interactionists continue to affiliate as part of a larger network tied to the traditions of several seminal thinkers.

Criticisms of symbolic interactionism have been raised from several perspectives. The major ones will be presented here, along with rebuttals where they have been offered. Critiques from the perspective of everyday life sociologists will be offered first, followed by those from structural, Marxist, and other macro sociologists.[40]

Critiques within the Sociologies of Everyday Life

Numerous terms and concepts are considered unclear or are used inconsistently by Mead (and Blumer where he follows his mentor's usage). Citing the oral tradition of Mead's work as partly responsible for this confusion and variance in interpretation, Kuhn emphasizes problems in formulating strict definitions of the relations between the self and other (i.e., of self-consciousness and the generalized other). Functional roles assigned to the "I" and "me" are frequently contradictory, leading to differences in interpretation about the relative determinism of humans. Denzin (1970b) acknowledges Kuhn's misgivings about the fundamental vagueness inherent in the term *self,* presenting many unsolved problems for its operationalization. Meltzer (1967) adds to the list of confusing terms such uncertain notions as impulse, role-taking, mind, meaning, symbol, gesture, object, and attitude.

Methodological difficulties have also plagued interactionism. Mead gave scant consideration to this topic. The technique of sympathetic introspection proffered by James and Cooley proved inadequate for all situations. Thomas and Znaniecki's life history method, combining the structuralists' previously developed objective approach with their own subjective one, laid the groundwork for the later work of Blumer. It was Blumer, though, who finally presented a cogent and thorough statement on methodology, attempting to cover all aspects of sociological inquiry. Many have argued that Blumer's methods were hard to follow or replicate because of their over-reliance on the sociologist's intuition in "getting inside the subjects' heads." Kuhn especially saw this methodological approach as problematic. The difficulties of operationalization took first precedence in Kuhn's work, as he sought to rectify the conceptual inconsistencies and form a scientifically precise set of hypotheses about the self.

Several academicians have pointed to symbolic interactionism as possessing many substantive omissions. Mead's theory makes no reference to the unconscious aspects of self or human life. The Freudian suggestion, that our psyche has a subconscious component housing knowledge and memories hidden from direct access, is a seemingly valuable perception of human functioning. Further, social and historical forces may be at work that are not readily apparent to the actor, yet are highly influential. While the actor may not be consciously aware of submerged and structural forces, they often are relevant to human life. More important, the role of emotion is almost totally ignored by interactionism, since the current thinkers never followed the leads of James and Cooley. Although many have bemoaned this over-rational model of the actor (Meltzer, 1967; Brittan, 1973; Garfinkel, 1967), few have applied the idea of an emotional being.[41] Movements such as existential sociology [42] (see chapter 6) and the sociology of the absurd [43] have surfaced recently, attempting to deal with affective and irrational tendencies on a theoretical level.

Finally, several writers have called attention to interactionism's over-emphasis of certain key concepts. Emergence has received repeated focus from all but the Iowa School of interactionists. This skewed orientation may direct theoretical formulation toward change, to the detriment of a stable and structural model of the actor. Mead's theory is viewed as socially based: out of the bonds of social interaction, human beings and their society emerge. Hence, the role of individual consciousness and innate psychological and biological drives may be underemphasized. Mead's assumption of shared meanings and its implications for a consensual base has been questioned and considered problematic by phenomenologists, ethnomethodologists, and existential sociologists. Finally, the importance of meaning may be over-valued, yielding an image of the actor as excessively rationalistic and reflective. Anticipating this problem, Dewey pointed out that the majority of human actions are non-reflective and automatic, unconcerned with symbolic significance. Many of these criticisms have some merit and have been remedied in the works of various individual practitioners of symbolic interactionism.

Critiques outside the Everyday Life Tradition

We now consider some of the more trenchant critiques of interactionism from several outside viewpoints.

One of the most prominent criticisms of symbolic interactionism is that it contains an *astructural bias*. Popularized by Alvin Gouldner (1970; Zeitlin, 1973; and Reynolds and Reynolds, 1973), this idea claims that interactionism ignores the influence of greater social organization and social structure on the individual by concentrating on micro sociological concepts. Specifically, Horowitz suggests that "the amount of mechanical activity and behavioral response to organizational pressures and institutional constraints is either left out or reinterpreted into terms more amenable to personality." [44] Thus, symbolic interactionism posits a freer, more open universe than the one we actually experience. A measure of truth exists in this assertion. Blumer suggests that we view large-scale organizations and institutions not as systematic wholes but as a "diverse array of participants occupying different points in the network, engaged in their actions at those points on the basis of using given sets of meanings." [45] Thus Blumer directs our attention away from a simple framework of society toward the processes occurring within that framework. Maines (1977), however, denies this astructural allegation and outlines the ways social structure and social organization are included in analyses of symbolic interactionists.

A related criticism says interactionism is *ahistorical* and *noneconomic* in character (see Block, 1973; Garfinkel, 1967; Gouldner, 1970; Reynolds and Reynolds, 1973; Ropers, 1973; Smith, 1973; and Zeitlin, 1973). Symbolic interactionism is said to be incapable of explaining historical or institutional factors. Its practitioners lack a proper understanding of forces greater than the individual or ones of which the individual may be unaware. It cannot be denied that interactionism focuses on the social-psychological factors in our everyday lives; its interest is not in the abstract social forces that exert influence on the greater society. Historical and economic trends may indeed be significant; to the extent that they are reflected in the social meanings and social processes surrounding the individual, they are significant objects of symbolic interactionist study. No theoretical perspective thus far, however, deals with all types and levels of analysis. Just as interactionism is limited in interpreting macro dimensions, so structural sociologies tend to neglect the importance of the interacting human actor and the way major trends affect concrete reality.

We now address the *bias of emergent theory* as proposed by Joan Huber (1973a,b). When a sociological approach does not specify logically related hypotheses and presuppositions for a given setting, the individual researcher must observe the scene and permit theoretical formulations to emerge from the data. Huber criticizes symbolic interactionism for its departure from standardized norms of the scientific method: it uses no hypotheses for testing, nor does it determine causal variables or universal laws. Her main criticism can be summarized in two points: (1) the initiation of inquiry devoid of hypotheses amounts to the "atheoretical simplicity of a blank mind"; [46] and (2) this absence of theory forces the researcher to rely on his or her own perceptions of the situation, introducing bias and destroying objectivity.

Blumer (1973) responded to these allegations, indicating that borrowing from its pragmatic ancestors, interactionism conceives of sociological inquiry as beginning not with a "blank mind," but with some problem to solve or elucidate. Once in the empirical world, the researcher formulates generalizations, questioning them and using various empirical evidence to examine that world. Huber's critiques are valuable in the sense that symbolic interactionism's essence involves a purposive departure from traditional theories. However, by refusing to make prior specific hypotheses about research findings and openly acknowledging and encouraging the use of subjective understanding in sociological investigation, symbolic interactionism has attempted to permit sociologists to ground themselves in the reality of the empirical world rather than being blindly wedded to some absolute theory.

A final critique suggests that symbolic interactionism is culturally limited, valid only for the contemporary American actor. To the extent that Mead's model of the reflective actor is based on American cultural norms of interaction and personality, this may be true. Symbolic interactionism, however, may be less vulnerable to this charge than other theories that posit definitive structural models of the individual and society. Further research in other cultures would serve interactionist theory well.

Symbolic Interactionism Today

Symbolic interactionism, the largest and most important form of the sociologies of everyday life (most others have been directly or indirectly recipients of its influence), has been examined here from a historical and critical framework. Primary focus has been on the Chicago and Iowa schools of interactionism, the two main strains. Taken as a whole, this perspective holds great promise for the future. Still a young theory, its influence has spread slowly over the past half-century. Only recently has it begun to receive serious critiques and attention from established, older theories. Many young people have been exposed and attracted to pursuing interactionist approaches to the social world. Within this country numerous centers of interactionism are thriving, although there are significant differences between sub-branches and between geographic regions. (Symbolic interactionism is considered by many to be the "ideology of the Midwest," and somewhat different from West Coast versions.[47]) Interactionism also has clusters of practitioners abroad, particularly in England, Europe, and Japan.

Recent contributions of symbolic interactionism range in nature and focus from highly theoretical treatments that re-examine the basic propositions of the founders to fundamentally empirical works, interested in studying specific types of human behavior and analyzing them. Ongoing changes in both society and individuals necessitate a continual re-evaluation of the full spectrum of our surroundings so that neither theory nor empirical assumptions grow stale.

Two examples that illustrate the richness of modern symbolic interactionist concerns and approaches are Zurcher's (1977) *The Mutable Self* and Wright's (1978) *Crowds and Riots.* Zurcher stands in the classic social-psychological tradition of studying the self. Building primarily on the roots of Kuhn's self theory, Zurcher works with four key components of self-concept: physical self, social self, reflective self, and oceanic self. While these images of humans were suitable in a more stable era, today's world is characterized by "ephemeral social anchorages" and rapid social change. Zurcher proposes the possibility of a mutable self, where the individual "achieves autonomy by learning to shift modes of self-reference" so as to cope most effectively with the fluctuations of varying situations. This book offers theoretical creativity and an insightful analysis of the important changes occurring in the individual and society.

Wright's book serves as a useful contrast by following another strong symbolic interactionist tradition: participant-observation studies of group life. Through a multitude of observations made in crowd situations, Wright offers insight into how multiple perspectives on a single reality are born. For example, what one group considers a "night of terror" appears more to others as a "festive spirit of one giant Christmas party." Wright's concern is with how people fit their lines of action together to create spatial or group forms. His analysis of collective activity illuminates group dynamics from an insider's perspective not previously available. His work provides a spatial delineation and analysis of the forms and tones commonly taken by crowd interaction.

These works and many other contemporary ones are carrying on the spirit, vigor, and distinctive concerns that made symbolic interaction the originator of the new humanistic sociologies of everyday life.

Notes

1. Charles Morris, *The Pragmatic Movement in American Philosophy* (New York: George Braziller, 1970), p. 5.

2. Charles Hartshorne and Paul Weiss (eds.), *The Collected Papers of*

Charles Peirce, (Cambridge, Mass.: Harvard University Press, 1931–1958), Vol. 5, paragraph 9.

3. The James household was often the seat for discussions and debates among such literary greats as Ralph Waldo Emerson and Oliver Wendell Holmes. Although the elder James's transcendental and romantic humanitarianism never fully appealed to William, its problems and foci remained close to his interests.

4. Morton White, *Pragmatism and the American Mind* (New York: Oxford University Press, 1973), p. 31.

5. William James, *Pragmatism: A New Name for Some Old Ways of Thinking* (New York: Longmans Green, 1907), p. 50.

6. Ibid., p. 49.

7. Ibid., p. 59.

8. William James, "The Social Self," in *Social Psychology through Symbolic Interaction,* by Gregory Stone and Harvey Farberman, eds. (Waltham, Mass.: Xerox Publishing Co., 1970), p. 374.

9. This process originates only upon perception of a problem, which is reminiscent of Peirce's notion of science and Mead's conception of "mind," discussed later in this chapter.

10. We do not mean to imply that Dewey adhered to a stimulus-response model of internalization of behavior. Indeed, he took this as a polemical nexus and sought strenuously to avoid falling into behaviorist pitfalls.

11. This emphasis on language is a direct result of Mead's influence on Dewey while they were both at Michigan. Many of Dewey's ideas about the development of children stem from his productive association with the creative mind of G. H. Mead.

12. Roscoe C. Hinkle, "Charles H. Cooley's General Sociological Orientation," *Sociological Quarterly* 8, Winter 1967, p. 10.

13. William I. Thomas and Dorothy S. Thomas, *The Child in America,* (New York: Alfred A. Knopf, 1928), p. 571.

14. A remarkable and fresh exception to this sorry state of affairs is the selected original papers of Mead, edited and with an introduction by Anselm Strauss (Mead, 1956).

15. Morris, *The Pragmatic Movement,* p. 8 suggests these four concerns.

16. The pragmatists drew upon behavioristic psychology that emphasizes that one should infer human intelligence from outward displays of activity.

17. Mead was oriented toward the study of language and gestures through the exposure he had to the German idealism of Wundt.

18. Mead's view of minded behavior is similar to Peirce's and Dewey's view of science: scientific inquiry does not occur every time the scientist does something; only when he is faced with a problem does the scientific act begin. Thus Mead expands to all mental activity what his predecessors had ascribed to scientific inquiry alone.

19. Morris, *The Pragmatic Movement,* pp. 126–127.

20. Following Bergson, Alexander, and Whitehead, Mead differentiates between objective and subjective, or "inner" time. Because of this latter type

there are many possible presents to which he refers: the "specious present," "knife-edge present," "larger present," "pulses of the present," etc.

21. Alfred Lindesmith, *Addiction and Opiates* (Chicago: Aldine, 1968), p. 9.

22. Ibid., p. 194.

23. This use of the notion of taking the role of the other clearly involves the individual accepting society's definition of him *after* that definition has been applied through language symbols. Lindesmith's study is obviously a precursor to the labeling theorists who built on this and other works.

24. Lindesmith, *Addiction and Opiates*, p. 10.

25. See Meltzer, Petras, and Reynolds (1975) for a more complete discussion of these break-downs into sub-varieties.

26. These root ideas can be found in most of the lectures Blumer delivers and in his central statement on theory and method (1969). The order in which Blumer organizes and presents them is used here.

27. We do not intend here to elucidate the entirety of Blumer's theory. He adopted a position essentially similar to Mead's, although with changes of emphasis. To avoid further redundancy we will handle his concepts in somewhat less detail, eliminating the points on which he and his mentor obviously converge.

28. Herbert Blumer, *Symbolic Interactionism* (Englewood Cliffs, N.J.: Prentice-Hall, 1969), p. 2.

29. Ibid., p. 24.

30. Howard S. Becker, Blanche Geer, Everett Hughes, and Anselm Strauss, *Boys in White* (Chicago: The University of Chicago Press, 1961), p. 32.

31. Ibid., p. 442.

32. This study can then be taken as an empirical refutation of labeling theory's central contention that the powerless deviant must accept and internalize society's vision of him or her. Wiseman's alcoholics stand by the values of their peculiar subculture and steadfastly refuse to allow society's morals to affect them in any way.

33. Manfred H. Kuhn, "Major Trends in Symbolic Interaction Theory in the Past Twenty-five Years," *Sociological Quarterly* 5, Winter 1964, p. 70.

34. Ironically, Kuhn's vision of methodological requirements necessitated the categorization of these answers by the researcher for the purpose of analysis, introducing obvious biases into the resultant data.

35. Harry Stack Sullivan introduced this term, using it in loose correspondence to Mead's notion of the "other." Kuhn liked this expression but considered it too general for his purposes.

36. The "reference group" was conceived by Herbert Hyman in 1942 and used in various psychological senses. This idea was first used in sociology in 1950 when Merton and Kitt employed it in a study of American soldiers. It too was rejected by Kuhn.

37. Bernard N. Meltzer and John W. Petras, "The Chicago and Iowa Schools of Symbolic Interactionism," in Tamotsu Shibutani (ed.), *Human Nature and Collective Behavior,* (Englewood Cliffs, N.J.: Prentice-Hall, 1970), p. 14.

38. This is not to say that no prominent and creative sociologists have arisen from within Kuhn's tradition. Norman Denzin, George McCall, and J. L. Simmons have all made significant contributions to symbolic interactionism and Ralph Turner, with his closely related role theory, is one of the most creative and systematic thinkers of modern sociology.

39. The researchers here refer to Kuhn's frustrated attempts at introducing a time dimension into his work, acknowledging his recognition (in theory) of a processual self.

40. We would like to acknowledge a debt to Meltzer, Petras, and Reynolds (1975) who supplemented our own findings with an excellent discussion and organization.

41. Some exceptions to this include Goffman, 1967; Gross and Stone, 1964; and Hochschild, 1975.

42. See especially Douglas, 1976; Douglas and Johnson, 1977; Manning, 1973; and Johnson, 1975.

43. Stanford Lyman and Marvin Scott, *A Sociology of the Absurd* (New York: Appleton-Century-Crofts, 1970).

44. Irving Louis Horowitz, "Review of Howard S. Becker's Sociological Work: Methods and Substance," *American Sociological Review,* 36, June 1971, p. 527.

45. Blumer, 1969, *Symbolic Interactionism,* p. 19.

46. Joan Huber, "Symbolic Interactionism as a Pragmatic Perspective: The Bias of Emergent Theory," *American Sociological Review,* 38, April 1973, p. 282.

47. This point was suggested by Peter K. Manning in a personal communication.

References

BECKER, HOWARD S. *Outsiders.* New York: The Free Press, 1963.

BECKER, HOWARD S. *The Other Side.* New York: The Free Press, 1964.

BECKER, HOWARD S. "Whose Side Are We On?" *Social Problems.* Winter 1967.

BECKER, HOWARD S. *Sociological Work.* Chicago: Aldine Publishing Co., 1970.

BECKER, HOWARD S. and BLANCHE GEER. "Participant Observation: The Analysis of Qualitative Field Data." In Adams and Preiss (eds.), *Human Organization Research.* Homewood, Ill.: Dorsey Press, 1960.

BECKER, HOWARD S.; BLANCHE GEER; EVERETT HUGHES; and ANSELM STRAUSS. *Boys in White.* Chicago: University of Chicago Press, 1961.

BERNSTEIN, RICHARD J. *John Dewey.* New York: Washington Square Press, 1966.

BLEWETT, JOHN, ed., *John Dewey: His Thought and Influence.* New York: Fordham University Press, 1960.

BLOCK, FRED. "Alternative Sociological Perspectives: Implications for Applied Sociology." *Catalyst* 7, Winter 1973.

BLUMER, HERBERT. "An Appraisal of Thomas and Znaniecki's The Polish Peasant in Europe and America." *Social Science Council Bulletin* 44, Critiques of Research in the Social Sciences, I, 1939.

BLUMER, HERBERT. "What Is Wrong with Social Theory?" *American Sociological Review* XIX, 1954.

BLUMER, HERBERT. "Attitudes and the Social Act." *Social Problems* 3, October 1955.

BLUMER, HERBERT. "Sociological Analysis and the Variable." *American Sociological Review*, XXI, 1956.

BLUMER, HERBERT. "Society as Symbolic Interaction." In Arnold Rose (ed.), *Human Behavior and Social Process*. Boston: Houghton Mifflin, 1962.

BLUMER, HERBERT. "Sociological Implications of the Thought of George Herbert Mead." *American Journal of Sociology*, LXXI, 1966.

BLUMER, HERBERT. *Symbolic Interactionism*, Englewood Cliffs, N.J: Prentice-Hall, 1969.

BLUMER, HERBERT. "Action vs. Interaction." *Society* 9, April 1972.

BLUMER, HERBERT. "Comment on Symbolic Interactionism as a Pragmatic Perspective: The Bias of Emergent Theory." *American Sociological Review* 38, December 1973.

BLUMER, HERBERT. Speech given at Pacific Sociological Association meetings, San Diego, California, March 25, 1976.

BRITTAN, ARTHUR. *Meanings and Situations*. London: Routledge and Kegan Paul, 1973.

BURKE, KENNETH. *A Grammar of Motives*. New York: Prentice-Hall, 1945.

COLLINS, RANDALL, and MICHAEL MAKOWSKY. *The Discovery of Society*. New York: Random House, 1972.

COOLEY, CHARLES H. *Human Nature and Social Order*. New York: Charles Scribner's Sons, 1902.

COOLEY, CHARLES H. *Social Organization*. New York: Charles Scribner's Sons, 1909.

DAVIS, FRED. *Passage Through Crisis*. Indianapolis: The Bobbs-Merrill Co., 1963.

DAVIS, FRED. *Illness, Interaction and the Self*. Belmont, Calif.: Wadsworth Publishing Co., 1972.

DENISOFF, R. SERGE; OREL CALLAHAN; and MARK LEVINE, eds., *Theories and Paradigms in Contemporary Sociology*. Itasca, Ill.: Peacock Publishing Co., 1974.

DENZIN, NORMAN. *The Research Act*. Chicago: Aldine Publishing Co., 1970a.

DENZIN, NORMAN. "The Methodologies of Symbolic Interaction: A Critical Review of Research Techniques." In Gregory Stone and Harvey Farberman (eds.), *Social Psychology through Symbolic Interaction*. Waltham, Mass.: Xerox Publishing Co., 1970b.

DENZIN, NORMAN. "Symbolic Interactionism and Ethnomethodology." In

Jack D. Douglas (ed.), *Understanding Everyday Life*. Chicago: Aldine Publishing Co., 1970c.

DEWEY, JOHN. "The Reflex Arc Concept in Psychology." *Psychological Review* 3, July 1896.

DEWEY, JOHN. "The Need for Social Psychology." *Psychological Review* 24, 1917.

DEWEY, JOHN. *Human Nature and Conduct*. New York: Henry Holt, 1922.

DEWEY, JOHN. *Experience and Nature*. New York: W. W. Norton, 1925.

DOUGLAS, JACK D. *Understanding Everyday Life*. Chicago: Aldine Publishing Co., 1970.

DOUGLAS, JACK D. *Investigative Social Research*. Beverly Hills, Calif.: Sage Publications, 1976.

DOUGLAS, JACK D., and JOHN M. JOHNSON, eds., *Existential Sociology*, New York: Cambridge University Press, 1977.

FELDMAN, W. T. *The Philosophy of John Dewey*. New York: Greenwood Press, 1968.

GARFINKEL, HAROLD. *Studies in Ethnomethodology*, Englewood Cliffs, N.J.: Prentice-Hall, 1967.

GLASER, BARNEY and ANSELM STRAUSS. *The Discovery of Grounded Theory*. Chicago: Aldine Publishing Co., 1967.

GOFFMAN, ERVING. *The Presentation of Self in Everyday Life*. Garden City, N.Y.: Doubleday, 1959.

GOFFMAN, ERVING. *Interaction Ritual*. Garden City, N.Y.: Doubleday, 1967.

GOULDNER, ALVIN. *The Coming Crisis of Western Sociology*. New York: Avon Books, 1970.

GROSS, E., and GREGORY STONE. "Embarassment and the Analysis of Role Requirements." *American Journal of Sociology* 60, July 1964.

GUSFIELD, JOSEPH. *Symbolic Crusade*, Urbana, Ill.: University of Illinois Press, 1963.

HALL, PETER. "A Symbolic Interactionist Analysis of Politics." *Sociological Inquiry* 42, 1972.

HARTSHORNE, CHARLES, and PAUL WEISS, eds., *The Collected Papers of Charles Sanders Peirce*, V. I–VIII, Cambridge, Mass.: Harvard University Press, 1931–1958.

HICKMAN, C. A. and MANFRED H. KUHN. *Individuals, Groups and Economic Behavior*. New York: Dryden Press, 1956.

HINKLE, ROSCOE C. "Charles H. Cooley's General Sociological Orientation." *Sociological Quarterly* 8, Winter 1967.

HOCHSCHILD, ARLIE R. "The Sociology of Feeling and Emotion: Selected Possibilities." In Marcia Millman and Rosabeth Moss Kanter, *Another Voice: Feminine Perspectives on Social Life and Social Science*, Garden City, N.Y.: Anchor Books, 1975.

HOROWITZ, IRVING LOUIS. "Review of Howard S. Becker's Sociological Work: Methods and Substance." *American Sociological Review*, 36, June 1971.

HUBER, JOAN. "Symbolic Interactionism as a Pragmatic Perspective: The Bias of Emergent Theory." *American Sociological Review* 38, April 1973a.

HUBER, JOAN. "Reply to Blumer: But Who Will Scrutinize the Scrutinizers?" *American Sociological Review* 38, December 1973b.

JAMES, WILLIAM. *Principles of Psychology,* 2 Vols. New York: Henry Holt, 1890.

JAMES, WILLIAM. "Does 'Consciousness' Exist?" *Journal of Philosophy, Psychology and the Scientific Method,* I, 1904.

JAMES, WILLIAM. *Pragmatism: A New Name for Some Old Ways of Thinking.* New York: Longmans, Green, 1907.

JAMES, WILLIAM. "The Social Self." In Gregory Stone and Harvey Farberman (eds.), *Social Psychology through Symbolic Interaction.* Waltham, Mass.: Xerox Publishing, 1967.

JANDY, EDWARD C. *Charles H. Cooley.* New York: Octagon Books, 1942.

JOHNSON, JOHN M. *Doing Field Research.* New York: Free Press, 1975.

JUNKER, BUFORD. *Field Work.* Chicago: University of Chicago Press, 1960.

KANTER, ROSABETH M. "Symbolic Interactionism and Politics in Systematic Perspective." *Sociological Inquiry* 42, 1972.

KUHN, MANFRED H. "Major Trends in Symbolic Interaction Theory in the Past Twenty-five Years." *Sociological Quarterly* 5, Winter 1964a.

KUHN, MANFRED H. "The Reference Group Reconsidered." *Sociological Quarterly* 5, Winter 1964b.

KUHN, MANFRED H. "Self-Attitudes by Age, Sex and Professional Training." In Gregory Stone and Harvey Farberman (eds.), *Social Psychology through Symbolic Interaction.* Waltham, Mass.: Xerox Publishing Co., 1970.

KUHN, MANFRED H., and THOMAS S. McPARTLAND. "An Empirical Investigation of Self-Attitude." *American Sociological Review* 19, February 1954.

KUHN, THOMAS. *The Structure of Scientific Revolutions.* Chicago: University of Chicago Press, 1962.

LINDESMITH, ALFRED. *Addiction and Opiates.* Chicago: Aldine Publishing Co., 1968.

LINDESMITH, ALFRED, and ANSELM STRAUSS. *Social Psychology.* New York: Holt, Rinehart and Winston, 1968.

LOFLAND, JOHN. *Deviance and Identity,* Englewood Cliffs, N.J.: Prentice-Hall, 1969.

LOFLAND, JOHN. *Analyzing Social Settings.* Belmont, Calif.: Wadsworth Publishing Co., 1971.

LOVEJOY, ARTHUR O. *The Thirteen Pragmatisms.* Baltimore: The Johns Hopkins Press, 1963.

LYMAN, STANFORD, and MARVIN SCOTT. *A Sociology of the Absurd.* New York: Appleton-Century-Crofts, 1970.

MAINES, DAVID. "Social Organization and Social Structure in Symbolic Interactionist Thought." *Annual Review of Sociology* 3, 1977.

MANIS, JEROME, and BERNARD MELTZER. *Symbolic Interaction,* Boston: Allyn and Bacon, 1967.

McCall, George, and J. L. Simmons. *Issues in Participant Observation,* Reading, Mass.: Addison Wesley, 1969.

Mead, George Herbert. *The Philosophy of the Present.* Edited by A. E. Murphy. Chicago: Open Court, 1932.

Mead, George Herbert. *Mind, Self and Society.* Edited by C. W. Morris. Chicago: University of Chicago Press, 1934.

Mead, George Herbert. *Movements of Thought in the Nineteenth Century.* Edited by M. H. Moore. Chicago: University of Chicago Press, 1936.

Mead, George Herbert. *The Philosophy of the Act.* Edited by C. W. Morris. Chicago: University of Chicago Press, 1938.

Mead, George Herbert. *On Social Psychology.* Edited by Anselm Strauss. Chicago: University of Chicago Press, 1956.

Meltzer, Bernard. "Mead's Social Psychology." In Jerome Manis and Bernard Meltzer, *Symbolic Interaction.* Boston: Allyn and Bacon, 1967.

Meltzer, Bernard, and John Petras. "The Chicago and Iowa Schools of Symbolic Interaction." In Tamotsu Shibutani (ed.), *Human Nature and Collective Behavior,* Englewood Cliffs, N.J.: Prentice-Hall, 1970.

Meltzer, Bernard; John Petras; and Larry Reynolds. *Symbolic Interactionism.* London: Routledge and Kegan Paul, 1975.

Mills, C. Wright. *Sociology and Pragmatism.* New York: Oxford University Press, 1966.

Miyamoto, S. Frank. "Self, Motivation and Symbolic Interactionist Theory." In Tamotsu Shibutani (ed.), *Human Nature and Collective Behavior.* Englewood Cliffs, N.J.: Prentice-Hall, 1970.

Miyamoto, S. Frank, and Sanford M. Dornbusch. "A Test of Interactionist Hypotheses of Self-Conception." *American Journal of Sociology* LXI, March 1956.

Morris, Charles. *The Pragmatic Movement in American Philosophy.* New York: George Braziller, 1970.

Natanson, Maurice. *The Social Dynamics of G. H. Mead.* Washington, D.C.: Public Affairs Press, 1956.

Petras, John, and Bernard Meltzer. "Theoretical and Ideological Variations in Contemporary Interactionism." *Catalyst* 7, Winter 1973.

Quarentelli, E. L., and Joseph Cooper. "Self-Conceptions and Others: A Further Test of Meadian Hypotheses." *Sociological Quarterly* VII, Summer 1966.

Reynolds, Larry. "Interactionism, Complicity and the Astructural Bias." *Catalyst* 7, Winter 1973.

Reynolds, Larry, and Bernard Meltzer. "The Origins of Divergent Methodological Stances in Symbolic Interactionism," *Sociological Quarterly* Spring 1973.

Reynolds, Larry, and Janice Reynolds. *The Sociology of Sociology.* New York: David McKay, 1970.

Ropers, Richard. "Mead, Marx and Social Psychology," *Catalyst* 7, Winter 1973.

Rose, Arnold. *Human Behavior and Social Process,* Boston: Houghton Mifflin, 1962.

Rose, Arnold. "A Summary of Symbolic Interaction Theory." In R. Serge Denisoff, Orel Callahan, and Mark Levine (eds.), *Theories and Paradigms in Contemporary Sociology,* Itasca, Ill.: Peacock Publishing, 1974.

Schatzman, Leonard, and Anselm Strauss. *Field Research,* Englewood Cliffs, N.J.: Prentice-Hall, 1973.

Shaskolsky, Leon. "The Development of Sociological Theory in America —a Sociology of Knowledge Interpretation." In Larry Reynolds and Janice Reynolds (eds.), *The Sociology of Sociology.* New York: David McKay, 1970.

Shaw, Clifford R. *The Jack Roller.* Chicago: University of Chicago Press, 1930.

Shibutani, Tamotsu, ed., *Human Nature and Collective Behavior.* Englewood Cliffs, N.J.: Prentice-Hall, 1970.

Smith, Dusky Lee. "Symbolic Interactionism: Definitions of the Situation from H. Becker and J. Lofland." *Catalyst* 7, Winter 1973.

Stone, Gregory and Harvey Farberman, eds., *Social Psychology through Symbolic Interaction.* Waltham, Mass.: Xerox Publishing, 1970.

Thomas, W. I. *On Social Organization and Social Personality.* Chicago: University of Chicago Press, 1966.

Thomas, W. I., and Dorothy S. Thomas. *The Child in America.* New York: Alfred A. Knopf, 1928.

Thomas, W. I., and Florian Znaniecki. *The Polish Peasant in Europe and America,* vol. I–V, Chicago: University of Chicago Press, 1918–1920.

Thrasher, Frederick. *The Gang.* Chicago: University of Chicago Press, 1928.

Tucker, C. W. "Some Methodological Problems of Kuhn's Self Theory." *Sociological Quarterly* 7, Summer 1966.

Weber, Max. *The Methodology of the Social Sciences.* New York: Free Press, 1949.

White, Morton. *Pragmatism and the American Mind,* New York: Oxford University Press, 1973.

Whorf, Benjamin Lee. *Language, Thought and Reality.* Cambridge, Mass.: MIT Press, 1956.

Wirth, Louis. *The Ghetto.* Chicago: University of Chicago Press, 1928.

Wiseman, Jacqueline P. *Stations of the Lost.* Englewood Cliffs, N.J.: Prentice-Hall, 1970.

Wright, Sam. *Crowds and Riots.* Beverly Hills, Calif.: Sage, 1978.

Zeitlen, Irving M. *Ideology and the Development of Sociological Theory.* Englewood Cliffs, N.J.: Prentice-Hall, 1968.

Zeitlen, Irving M. *Rethinking Sociology.* New York: Appleton-Century-Crofts, 1973.

Znaniecki, Florian. *The Method of Sociology,* New York: Rinehart, 1934.

Zorbaugh, Harvey. *The Gold Coast and the Slum.* Chicago: University of Chicago Press, 1929.

Zurcher, Louis. *The Mutable Self.* Beverly Hills, Calif.: Sage, 1977.

3

The Mask and Beyond: The Enigmatic Sociology of Erving Goffman

ANDREA FONTANA

Erving Goffman has constructed a sociology to examine and analyze how individuals present themselves to others and how they influence each other in their face-to-face interactions.[1] Goffman shows the inherent conflict in our social world between individuality and its social forms of communication. The struggle of individual life against social forms can be seen in the very act of breaking silence and uttering words. In so doing we become individuals in our own right and we emerge from anonymity. But in order to break the silence we must rely on social forms that were there before us, such as language, manners, and gestures, which we merely borrow for the occasion. We are cast into the roles that we play, that others have played before us, and that others will play after us. In short, in the very act of becoming individuals we lose our individuality.

Concern for forms is at the core of Goffman's sociology. His work must be understood in this light: If life is only expressable through forms, we must look at these forms, at how the members of society go about creating and sustaining a day-to-day life in conflict with the forms but that is only apprehendable through them. Goffman studies how the self both expresses itself and is constrained by its roles, which are its vehicles of social expression.[2]

Goffman's writings to date will be examined here by dividing them into four stages: his early dramaturgical works; a second stage that poses deep existential questions about a personal self; a third stage in which he portrays alienation as pervading every level of daily life; and a final stage (to date) in which Goffman shifts the focus of his work from the self to the props that allow the self to express itself.

Beyond Symbolic Interactionism

Goffman's sociological approach to everyday life does not lack antecedents, as claimed by some.[3] Rather, it follows various trends already existing in sociology, psychology, philosophy, and theater.

Goffman can be considered in some ways a symbolic interactionist, as noted in chapter 2, but he is the most enigmatic major follower of that approach, so difficult to categorize in fact that he deserves individual consideration. Following the lead of George Herbert Mead, Goffman focuses upon the self as a concept defined by others. Goffman pays particular attention to the forms that members of society use to convince others about their presentation of self. As do most symbolic interactionists, Goffman has little concern for methodology and, while he draws his data from observations of the daily interactions among members of society, he shows little concern for systematic consideration of empirical data.

Goffman differs from Mead in that he does not assume that the members of society present themselves to others in an unproblematic way. Instead, presentations of self are a very problematic enterprise, as each individual has to choose among various alternatives, often not clearly or rationally understood. This view of the self clearly differentiates Goffman from the other two major disciples of Mead, Manford Kuhn and Herbert Blumer. Blumer in fact considers Goffman a misguided follower of Mead; in referring to Goffman's work he says:

> Human interaction, as Mead emphasized it, consists fundamentally of efforts of the participants to grasp what each other is doing or plans to do and then to direct one's own act in the light of this knowledge. Instead, to treat face-to-face interaction as though it consists of efforts to create and sustain personal impressions is to misrepresent its true nature.[4]

Blumer considers human beings as straightforward, honest, and cooperative participants in the construction of social order, while Goffman focuses on how people manage the impressions they make on others.[5]

Blumer takes for granted that the self can be unproblematically defined by individuals in interaction. Therefore Blumer can be described as concentrating on interaction as a social process.

Goffman feels that society does not afford us the luxury of being self-assured. The fragmentation and relativization of values and the estrangement from one's workplace in modern bureaucracies lead human beings to act cautiously when confronted by others in public settings. People are unsure of those who are unfamiliar, those who may in fact harm them at any time.[6] Individuals trapped in this kind of society must place primary attention on their presentation of self in everyday, public settings. They must foster personal impressions that will be seen as normal by others. The (fragile) appearance of normalcy allows social order to go on, as people attend to their business without being alarmed by the presence of others.

Goffman, then, looks at the ways in which members of society manage their self presentations. He focuses not so much on social interaction itself as on the individuals who are interacting. Goffman is concerned with the *self as a social process*—communicating, receiving, and interpreting information about social actors.

By viewing life as a theater and human beings as social performers, Goffman assumes a *dramaturgical perspective.* In this approach, Goffman is well within the sociological tradition of role theory, which employs the metaphor of the theater to elucidate its concepts. Role theory says that individual behavior is shaped by social expectations, constraints, rewards, and punishments imposed by others. The performing individuals therefore understand and regulate their performance in terms of the others. According to role theorists, social performances bear a striking similarity in comparable situations, regardless of who the performers are.[7] Role theorists have emphasized the normative aspect of human life; they aim at discovering the shared social constraints that regulate people's performances.

Although Goffman is well aware of the normative constraints on individuals, he turns role theory inside out by focusing on the performers themselves, not on the normative social constraints. Above all, he differs from the symbolic interactionists and especially from the structural role theorists by focusing on the ways performers try to hide from others behind socially acceptable masks:

> Every new inmate learns to dog-face, that is to assume an apathetic, *characterless* facial expression and posture when viewed by authority. The dog-face is acquired easily when everyone freezes or relaxes into immobility. The face is that typical of streets, of social occasions, of all concealment. Relaxation comes when inmates are alone: there is an exaggeration of the smiling effervescence of the "friendly" party. The face that is protective by day is aggressively

hardened and hate-filled by night against the stationed or pacing guard. Tensity and dislike follow assumption of the face, guards react with scrupulous relaxedness, holding the face "soft" with an effort often accompanied by slight trembling of hands.[8]

The above quote contains important features of the dramaturgical ideas presented in Goffman's work: the mask we put on for the appropriate audience and the silent features of interaction that present us to others before we utter a single word.

The Presentations of Self

The Presentation of Self in Everyday Life (1959) [9] is Goffman's earliest published book, and many of his subsequent writings are elaborations of it. *Behavior in Public Places* (1963) is a closely related work that elaborates on the first book and focuses more on the shared norms and strategies of self-presentations in public settings. Goffman begins his work on the presentation of self by looking at *performances,* seen as the activities attended to by a performer during an interaction. Performances affect the participation of other individuals in the interaction. His analysis of performances begins by considering the sincerity or cynicism involved in social performance. The two are seen as ends of a continuum rather than dichotomous choices. There are of course difficulties involved in separating sincere from cynical elements in a performance in order to place the performance on a continuum, since the two elements are often inextricably intertwined.

This mixture of sincerity and cynicism in our presentations of self accompanies us throughout our lives. It may lead us more toward cynicism as the sincere belief in what we do diminishes, as, for example, in the case of young medical students who progressively change an idealistic, sincere belief in their profession to a cynical one.[10] But this mixture of sincerity and cynicism may also lead us toward increasing sincerity, in the sense that we may come to believe in what we had regarded a cynical performance, thus creating a fusion of self and mask: [11]

In a sense, and in so far as this mask represents the conception we have formed of ourselves—the role we are striving to live up to—this mask is our truer self, the self we would like to be. In the end, our conception of our role becomes second nature and an integral part of our personality. We come into the world as individuals, achieve character, and become persons.[12]

Performers act by presenting a front; a *front* consists of the expressive resources used during a performance. Fronts incorporate the features of setting, appearance, and manner. *Setting* is the physical location in which the interaction occurs, including all of the props needed (such as furniture and lighting) to convey the desired impression. *Appearance* refers to one's personal front—clothing, hair style, facial expression, and insignia of rank. *Manner* concerns the way one presents oneself—meekly, aggressively, politely, rudely, and so on. Coherence is usually expected among the three features of interaction, but it is not always present or even desired.

Paramount to the success of one's performance is the *dramatic realization* of it. Individuals must make their activities significant to others by a skillful presentation and by fullfilling the expectations of the others. A vivid example of the very important presentational aspect of everyday life is furnished by Tom Wolfe's character, a fellow named Chaser, who instructs his friends on how to "mau mau" the bureaucrats at the Office of Economic Opportunities in San Francisco:

> "Now don't forget. When you go downtown, y'all wear your ghetto rags . . . see . . . Don't go down there with your Italian silk jerseys on and your brown suede and green alligator shoes and your Harry Belafonte shirts looking like some supercool tooth-pick-noddin' fool . . . you know . . . Don't anybody give a damn how pretty you can look . . . You wear your *combat* fatigues and your leather pieces and your shades . . . your *ghetto* rags . . . see. And don't go down there with your hair all done up nice in your curly Afro like you're messing around. You go down with your hair *stickin' out* . . . and *sittin' up!* Lookin' wild! I want to see you down there looking like a bunch of wild niggers!" [13]

Chaser is obviously aware of the importance of living up to the expectations of the bureaucrats and of acting out a role to realize it dramatically.

This setting can be divided into a *front region* and a *back region*. The analogy of the theater is clear: the lighted proscenium is the front region. The wings are the back region in which the actors await their turn to perform and where all the stage props are hidden from the audience. The setting is of extreme importance both in the theater and in everyday life in determining the credibility and success of a performance. Certain means are employed to convey a desired dramatic effect:

> Take the scene of the banquet in *Macbeth*. Every line is a straight line, every angle is a right angle. All form is reduced to a barbaric severity. But the two rectangular windows in the background through which the cold Northern stars glitter are narrow and tall—so unimaginably tall that they seem to touch that sky of doom. The torches turn the rough brown of the primitive walls to a tarnished bronze. Only on the rude table lie splashes of menacing

yellow. There is something barren and gigantic about the scene—a sinister quiet, a dull presage.[14]

Emotion, according to Goffman, can only be conveyed by the setting, which is as integral a part of the interaction as the spoken dialogue.

Goffman thinks of *human interaction* as basically fragile and easily disrupted. Disruptive elements of human interaction include *discrepant roles* that do not fit the given framework of teams of performers and audience. Another disruptive element is communication out of character, that is, communication that does not fit with the official impression the individual attempts to convey. Discovery of communications out of character or of discrepant roles by the audience disrupts a performance.

Goffman calls *impression management* the ability of interactants to save the show by carrying out the interaction despite the presence of disruptive features.

> Even if you are placed next to some one with whom you have had a bitter quarrel, consideration for your hostess, who would be distressed if she knew you had been put in a disagreeable place, and further consideration for the rest of the table which is otherwise "blocked," exacts that you give no outward sign of your repugnance and that you make a pretense, at least for a little while, of talking together.
>
> At dinner once, Mrs. Toplofty, finding herself next to a man she quite openly despised, said to him with apparent placidity, "I shall not talk to you—because I don't care to. But for the sake of my hostess I shall say my multiplication table. Twice one are two, twice two are four—" and she continued on through the tables, making him alternate them with her. As soon as she politely could she turned again to her other companion.[15]

Goffman says that his use of dramaturgical metaphors is but a vehicle to point out the constructed nature of social interactions. Goffman stresses the fleeting nature of the self. The self is not a solid structure but a movable perspective, a process that evolves with the presentation and credibility of various performances.[16] This is the irony within Goffman's early thought: the self can only find expression in its performances and thus imprisons within itself whatever other elements it is unable to present in its performances but which constitute the total sum of an individual. These unseen elements remain imprisoned inside the mask that faces the outside world, that copes with others. Thus, in the early dramaturgy of Goffman the self is defined by its presentational forms. It is knowable only through the masks it puts on, locking its other elements in what may be considered an innaccessible back region of the self.

Beyond the Mask:
The Naked Self

In his early works Goffman presented a self that was oriented toward others, to the extreme of sacrificing one's sincerity in favor of social approval. But in some of his work, most notably in *Asylums* (1961),[17] he shows the attempts of human beings to break away from their performing selves, away from selves defined by others. Goffman uses total institutions—places in which individuals lead a regimented life while isolated from the wider society—in order to show how a self can go beyond the official definitions imposed upon it by society.

At first sight total institutions would be the last place one would look for the blossoming of an individual self. Goffman shows how institutions socialize the recruits who enter them, whether they be prisoners, mental patients, or army trainees. In total institutions the new members are cut off from other realms of life. They often are strictly subjected to a new official "definition of the situation" by the staff. The total institution therefore provides an experimental ground in which it can be seen how much the human self can be changed, how much a self can be molded by social forces.

Various spheres of life are collapsed together in the total institution. Individuals are forced to live in the constant company of others under a tightly regulated schedule. Individuals entering the total institution must undergo a series of changes aimed at stripping away the roles they held in their life outside the institution. Personal possessions and clothing are discarded because they constitute a tie to previous roles. Hair is usually shorn to reduce differences in looks. The new clothing issued is usually drab and baggy, reducing individuals to amorphous lumps wrapped in colorless robes.

After these initial socialization processes, a series of public degradations of the self follow, usually in the form of "obedience tests," to ensure the new member's submission. In the total institution of the military, these tests often take the form of a public ceremonial display in front of the other recruits:

> He marched down my side of the hut, checking the beds. Little Nobby, taken by surprise, had one boot on and another off. Corporal Baker stopped. "What's the matter with YOU?" "I was knocking out a nail which hurts my foot." "Put your boot on at once. Your name?" He passed on to the end door and there he whirled around, snorting, "Clarke." Nobby properly cried, "Corporal" and limped down the alley at a run (we must always run when called) to bring up stiffly at attention before him. A pause, and then curtly, "Get back to your bed." Still the Corporal waited and so must we, lined up by our beds. Again, sharply, "Clarke." The performance was repeated, over and over, while the four files of us looked on, bound fast by shame and discipline. We were

men, and a man over there was degrading himself and his species, in degrading another.[18]

Having broken down the will of individuals by defiling the very aspects that made them self-respecting adults in the outside world, a new process of socialization begins. It is aimed at making a member of an institution out of an individual stripped of any selfhood. In the military a recruit begins a new career by going through a proper sequence of changes within the established framework of that total institution. According to Goffman, the selfhood the recruits develop there is not their own but evolves from the rules and controls of the institution. The new self is not so much controlled by the institution as it actually "belongs" to the institution that defines it.[19]

Members of total institutions, then, must accept the official definition of self given them by the institution and comply with the expectancies of the role in which they are cast, be it mental patient or army trainee. They must do so in order to successfully complete the period of rehabilitation or training and get out of the institution. A recruit should be nothing but a mask created by its maker, the institution.

There are ways in which military recruits resist the attempt to crush their individuality through official socialization. Goffman refers to these ways of preserving selfhood as secondary adjustments.[20] These adjustments do not openly challenge the definition of the situation provided by the staff. Secondary adjustments are minor, secret adaptations expressed in acts that defy the tightly structured rule system of the institution. An example of such acts is the hoarding of personal possessions forbidden by the rules—"a red comb, a different kind of toothbrush, a belt—these things are assiduously gathered, jealously hidden or triumphantly displayed." [21] Secondary adjustments can take other forms, such as muttering discontent at the officials' orders or obeying these orders in such a way as to show contempt for or detachment from the rules. Patients may feign senility and spit on the floor in convalescent centers [22] or pretend to be deaf and dumb, such as Chief Bromden did in *One Flew Over the Cuckoo's Nest*.[23] These acts may seem trivial, but they are not. They are the only ways in which patients can express their personal selves, selves distinct from the official self demanded and expected by the institution. In these small, furtive actions the naked self hides. It is a naked self because it is all that is left after the institution has stripped away the social self.

The attempt to retain some personal self through secondary adjustments may be misunderstood by the authorities. While secondary adjustments are used by patients in order to defy the definition of self provided by the authorities, these adjustments may be seen as confirming the official definition of the patients:

Acts of hostility against the institution have to rely on limited, ill-designed devices, such as banging a chair against the floor or striking a sheet of newspaper sharply so as to make a sharp explosive sound. And the more inadequate this equipment is to convey rejection of the hospital, the more the act appears as a psychotic symptom, and the more likely it is that the management feels justified in assigning the patient to a bad ward.[24]

This is a tragic image of human beings who struggle in vain to push away the mask that authorities forcibly impose on them. Patients succeed in asserting some personal selves in what Goffman refers to as "the cracks," "the damp corners," and "the little ways in which we resist the pull." [25] These small acts of resistance are more than mechanisms of defense; they constitute the naked self, a self hidden by the mask, a self unafraid of social sanctions and unashamed of social disappointment.

The self beyond the mask, however, can find expression only in desperate situations. A vivid example of an individual who does not want to conform to the definition of self and life furnished by the institution is Ken Kesey's character, Randle Patrick McMurphy, the patient who openly defied the institutional system, who in the face of the overwhelmingly cool sadism of Big Nurse completely "dropped the mask." He threw aside all vestige of social pretense and physically attacked Big Nurse:

> Only at the last—after he'd smashed through that glass door, her face swinging around, with terror forever ruining any look she might ever try to use again, screaming when he grabbed for her and ripped her uniform all the way down the front . . . only at the last . . . did he show any sign that he might be anything other than a sane, willful, dogged man performing a hard duty that finally just had to be done, like it or not.[26]

Human beings show their true selves when they are cornered, when the institutional, social, or dramaturgical masks can no longer be sustained in front of the mounting, pressing day-to-day adversities or oppressions of life. Then the individual's outer cover, just like a wax mask exposed to a hot flame, begins to melt under the heat of daily pressure, finally revealing underneath the dripping wax a face, a face which, freed from the oppressive cover, gives vent to that life which has been for so long denied. The life explodes violently, it shouts, it laughs, it cries, as McMurphy does:

> He gave a cry. At the last, falling backward, his face appearing to us for a second upside down before he was smothered on the floor by a pile of white uniforms, he let himself cry out. A sound of cornered animal . . . when he finally doesn't care anymore about anything but himself and his dying.[27]

A desperate person may show a naked self, but society is there to squelch these attempts to assert oneself and break the bonds of institutional rules.

McMurphy pays the price, as his desperately sane behavior is used as an example of dangerous madness: "The ward door opened and the black boys wheeled in this gurney with a chart at the bottom that said in heavy black letters, MCMURPHY, RANDLE P. POST-OPERATIVE. And below this was written in ink, LOBOTOMY." [28]

But even after such a ruthless reprisal, the self cannot be completely controlled by the authorities, and McMurphy's fellow patients refuse to recognize this hulking red-haired vegetable as their old friend. In denying McMurphy's identity, they turn aside the institutional definition of the situation, they deny Big Nurse, who is the personification of the establishment, the pleasure to use McMurphy as an example of what rebellion may bring about. In their denial of McMurphy's new institutional mask, his mates suffocate life out of this body from which life has already gone.

A Cautious Self

After having shown the deep anguish of human beings in their attempt to retain a personal self free from society's normative constraints, Goffman returns to his favorite theme—the behavior of the self in the presence of others and in response to others. This concern, present in all of Goffman's work written after *Asylums,* is best shown in *Relations in Public* (1971).[29] In this work Goffman no longer stresses a dramaturgical perspective but relies on an ethological one. *Ethology* is the study of animals in their natural settings. Goffman focuses on our modern society, especially our immense, colorless, odorless, faceless cities, and looks at the dangers threatening human beings in their daily lives.

There is a shift of concern from earlier works in *Relations in Public.* Goffman still describes social interaction as upheld cooperatively, but his emphasis is on the fragile nature of interaction. The others in an interaction are no longer "friends" to be relied upon, but strangers whom we are forced to trust. We are forced since we live in such close proximity with strangers and must share many territories with them, turn our backs on them, knowing that they might assault us and harm us.[30] Therefore, our trust is a cautious one; we are always ready to flee.

Goffman begins by using the metaphor of the individual as a vehicular unit in the traffic of our cities—a rather fragile "pilot" walking about as a pedestrian in the downtown city streets. Pedestrian traffic flows rather freely. The fact that people avoid colliding with each other indicates that there is mutual trust and expectancies among strangers in the streets.

Another important element considered by Goffman is that of territoriality. Goffman examines the territorial claims staked out by individuals in the city. These spatial claims are various, as are the expectations attached to each claim. When the expectations are not met, someone encroaches on someone else's claimed territory and a territorial offense occurs. Individuals adapt to various contingencies in order to avoid committing a territorial offense. Given the crowded conditions of the cities, participants will often take painstaking care not to violate territorial rules:

> For example, urinals in public toilets in America bring men very close to each other under circumstances where, for a period of time, they must expose themselves. In such places considerable care is taken in regard to eyes lest privacy be violated more than necessary.[31]

Interchanges, in Goffman's terminology, are the rituals that people (called performers) engage in when confronted with each other, even briefly. Interchanges show civility and the desire to uphold the "sacredness" of the interaction. They can be of a supportive nature, such as returning a greeting or acknowledging a courteous gesture. Goffman also refers to *remedial interchanges.* When someone violates a social norm in our society, they usually try to make acceptable what could be interpreted as an offensive act by apologizing.

Even given the problematic ways of understanding and coping with social interaction, Goffman says there is a remarkable cultural uniformity in the little ways in which individuals comment and act upon what could be seen by others as discrepant behavior. It is also remarkable that individuals feel compelled to do something to remedy an act that may make the continuation of the interaction troublesome. The others expect offending parties to engage in remedial work and become indignant when they refuse to do so:

> The case of a man charged with driving 110 mph on an E. Bay Freeway (the arresting officer testified he had to go 130 to nail him). "And why were you doing 110?" the judge inquired. "Because," replied the driver, "my car won't go any faster." This so infuriated the magistrate that he bopped the defendant on the head with his gavel—so hard that the wise guy went to the hospital.[32]

When individuals confront each other face to face they treat each other differently according to the relationship that exists between them. If a previous relation exists, the participants communicate signs that indicate the ties between them. Goffman refers to these indications as "tie-signs." For instance, in meeting one's wife one may kiss; in meeting a friend one may smile broadly; but in meeting perfect strangers one may safely ignore them.

In the essay "Normal Appearances," [33] the fulcrum of *Relations in Public,* Goffman employs the ethological metaphor of human beings as animals. As animals do, human beings "go about their normal business," but they are always on the alert for signs of danger. Individuals behave normally as long as their "safety zone" (*umwelt*) is not encroached upon. If it is invaded, then human beings, like animals, either flee or get ready for battle. For example, on a crowded sidewalk an individual will have a concern to avoid collisions, and this ordinarily will involve attention to the immediate layer of persons encircling him or her. However, on an otherwise empty street at night the individual can find that the appearance of a pedestrian a half a block away can be a matter of concern.[34]

Individuals must also be concerned with presenting to others a normal appearance, in order not to arouse suspicion or fear. This preoccupation with presenting a normal appearance can be manipulated by individuals to exploit a situation. For example, robberies, kidnappings, and other crimes are committed under the pretense of acting normally. Given that routine behavior may hide treachery, the concept of normal appearance as one in which no immediate danger is present becomes inadequate. Individuals must be suspicious at all times.

We are but wild beasts in a jungle, ready to spring at all times. Presentation of self to others is still our paramount concern but interaction has become very thin ice in a society in which safe presentations may hide danger. The ice is thin and may break at any time but, doomed to our way of life, we go on skating.

Constructing Social Reality

Goffman no longer looks directly at the self in *Frame Analysis* (1974),[35] but rather attempts to look beneath the self, to see what supports it. Until this book, Goffman spoke as if everyday reality was a given, and on that basis had engaged in various analyses of the self. In *Frame Analysis* Goffman steps back from everyday reality in order to examine its assumptions. He does not, as he did in his earlier works, painstakingly scrutinize the props of individual performers on the stage of life. In *Frame Analysis* Goffman focuses on the props that hold the stage of life together. Are these props solid pillars? Williams James (*see* chapter 2) and Alfred Schutz (*see* chapter 5) distinguished multiple realms of reality,[36] but they singled out everyday reality as the paramount one that solidly anchors other realities to the real world.

In *Frame Analysis*, Goffman tries to see just how solid this paramount reality is. Goffman begins this work with a basic idea contributed by Harold Garfinkel (*see* chapter 5). Garfinkel looked at the methods by which social performers create and sustain social order. He did this by dissecting the daily social routines that unconsciously provide the foundations of reality.* (For example, if a person enters a toilet marked "ladies" and is not questioned by the women already inside, this very routine action of going to the toilet sustains the reality of "being a

---

* The meaning of this will be made clear in chapter 5.

female" for that person.) Goffman goes one step beyond Garfinkel. Rather than examine the routines that sustain reality for social performers within a social situation, he looks at the elements that create the social scene itself. For example, notice the elements by which the husband creates a social scene of insanity in the following quote:

> *Dear Abby:* My husband is trying to make me, and other people, think I am insane. He takes things out of my drawers, hides them, and then after I have searched the house for days, he puts them back in their original places and tries to tell me they were there all the time. He sets all the clocks ahead, and then sets them back until I am so confused I don't know what time it is! He calls me vile names and accuses me of terrible things like going with other men.[37]

Goffman examines how the social scene is maintained, how it changes, what its parameters are, how it can be constructed, how it can be manipulated, and how it can collapse.

The sociological inspiration may be Garfinkel, but, as Goffman readily admits, Pirandello is the master of showing how social reality is constructed. In the "theater of the absurd" of Pirandello,[38] realities are layered upon each other, intertwined, and confused to the point that the paramount reality is no longer a clear, solid entity.

Another influence on these ideas is Georg Simmel. Simmel viewed social reality as an invisible web that binds humanity together. Goffman believes that there is, in the end, a solid, obdurate reality ("you need to find places for cars to park and coats to be checked, and these had better be real places. . . ."[39]). However, the whole of reality is not, for Goffman, a granite monolith, but a fish net full of holes. We ourselves fill in the holes by constructing social scenes, and then are duped by our own construction into seeing the loose mesh of net and social construction that fills the holes as a solid wall. We *reify*, or take as concrete reality "out-there"—what we ourselves have constructed out of social meanings.

To use another metaphor, Goffman looks at everyday reality as if it were an onion: layer upon layer of thin substance is stripped away. What happens to reality under such close scrutiny? Its foundations prove to be very fragile. But we believe everyday social reality to be solid, to be paramount, and precisely because we believe it, it becomes our paramount reality.

How does Goffman explain the self in *Frame Analysis?* He returns once again to the theme of *The Presentation of Self in Everyday Life.* We are all social performers who construct our lives in a dramaturgical fashion. But Goffman no longer considers the dramaturgical approach as a metaphor to help us elucidate social interaction. Acting is the very stuff of life in *Frame Analysis,* not acting according to a written script, but acting by piecing together the situated fragments of everyday life.

In *The Presentation of Self in Everyday Life* Goffman implied that beneath the socially constructed self there was an "inner" self. His later works described the "naked" self that exists behind the officially prescribed public self. In *Frame Analysis,* Goffman presents us with a much more desolate view of the self. After Goffman has peeled the layers of the onion which is the self, he finds no "core" inside it.

An Enigmatic Sociology for an Enigmatic Life

Goffman has developed his work in a very enigmatic fashion. In his early writings his thought vacillated between emphasizing a view of individuals as self-willed coordinators of their own lives and a view of individuals as helpless figures governed by social norms. In his first works, Goffman went from a strong emphasis on society controlling human beings to the claim for a personal self (in *Asylums*), to a view that human beings must guard their evanescent selves against a threatening society. All of these trends are present in all of Goffman's work. What we have done here is to show when Goffman's emphasis shifted. The simultaneous presence of these trends in his thought reflects the constant struggle between the individual and society—the struggle of individual life against the very social forms it helps to create and sustain.

Goffman does not look at the relationship between human beings and society as a clearly defined one in which a person either controls completely or not at all. Awareness of this complex relationship leads Goffman to show the self as a changing element, as a process, but a process confined within a normative, structured society. The result is a very enigmatic sociology that defies categorizations and portrays an enigmatic, multifaceted life.

Goffman has attempted to show how human beings construct their daily lives. He has done this not by looking at the results of social interactions, but by examining the very features that sustain the construction of interactions. He has looked at the props needed to sustain the performance of life. For Goffman, these features go beyond a verbal construction of reality; they go beyond language, which Goffman sees as only a part of the presentation of self. Spoken words in themselves may not indicate at all what is going on in the interaction; a performance comprises many other elements, such as dress, mannerism, facial expression, and spatial distance.[40] Thus, for instance, to sustain the reality of a love scene two lovers must do much more than say "I love you." Their eyes, hands, and bodies must all speak of love.

Goffman's work is ironic but its irony is not an amoral way of playing with the world. Instead, it is a way to understand the world; the thrust of Goffman's work is expressed in no better words than those of Martin Esslin:

. . . the need to confront man with the reality of his situation is greater than ever. For the dignity of man lies in his ability to face reality in all its senselessness; to accept it freely, without fear, without illusions—and to laugh at it.[41]

Goffman's Sociology Today

There are no heirs apparent to Goffman's sociology, but there are numerous sociologists who have followed in his footsteps. It would be impossible to enumerate all of them. In order to provide a general vision of the future of this kind of sociology, we shall present here three young sociologists who have brilliantly carried on in Goffman's style.

Murray Davis has followed Goffman in scrutinizing the self very closely. His book, *Intimate Relations* [42] analyzes presentations of the self in private situations. Davis notices that in American society performances for various audiences are fragmented, so that we find it hard to pull together the various pieces and call our presentations a self. In order to portray ourselves as a whole person, we resort to intimate relations with an audience of one. We are able to assume a unique identity only in the loving reflection of our intimate partner. Ironically, in so doing we abandon ourselves wholly to the other and lose ourselves in this unison. Thus, the moment we recognize our total self, we also lose it.

Davis also presents the problems inherent in intimate relations. Performances at close range are hard to sustain, since the cracks that go unseen from afar become fully visible at close range. Therefore, an intimate relation has continuous small crises that must be resolved to avoid the major crisis of "splitting up." Davis examines the various ways in which individuals become intimate and how they lose intimacy. In a creative analysis, Davis uses Goffman's approach to explore more intimate territories of human relations.

Sherri Cavan is another follower of Goffman. In her book, *Liquor License,*[43] she reports her study of bars in San Francisco, "time out" places in which the members of society may drop their social masks and relax. In bars people do things that they would not do in other settings because here they are supposedly not accountable in the future for their behavior there:

There were about nineteen people in the bar. A couple in their late thirties were dancing in the middle of the room. The woman began to posture in a mock-seductive way in front of the males along the bar, pulling her dress up above her stocking tops and the like, occasionally saying in an unserious tone of voice, "Oooo, aren't we awful!" But no one paid much attention to her.[44]

In a final Goffmanian twist of irony, Cavan asks if we are really free to drop our masks in a "time out" setting or whether we must play at being relaxed, because people will remember how we behaved and may use that information against us.

David Sudnow's *Passing On*[45] brings the study of the self into a medical ward of the modern hospital. Sudnow is concerned with the meaning of death as constructed by the members of the setting (the hospital). He looks for the routines that create, define, and sustain the meaning of death for the members in the hospital setting.

Sudnow examines both the differences in settings and the presentations of self of the various members and the daily routines around which the daily lives of those who fight the Grim Reaper revolve. He discovers that the hum-drum of routinized events in a hospital demystifies and dehumanizes everything. In this case death loses its mystery and patients lose their humaness. The self becomes dulled by too many "repeat performances."

Goffman has inspired a new generation of sociologists. Murray Davis's excursus beneath the facade that we project to others examines the self in a close, delicate context. Sherri Cavan's study of social interaction in bars questions whether we can ever relax and drop our social mask. David Sudnow's study of hospitals shows us how the self becomes dulled by routinization to the point that the sacred becomes profane.

The Self and Sociology

Goffman's work on presentation of self, the skillful management of one's front, and the successful performance in front of an audience, have all been severely criticized by a number of sociologists. Harold Garfinkel criticized Goffman's notion of a self. In his study of a transsexual,[46] Garfinkel looks at the self as a fragile entity continuously changing and gaining acceptance in the interaction. Agnes, the transsexual in the study, is considered a woman because her interactional performance is convincing and accepted by the members of society. The acceptance of a performance, which is exhibited through daily routines, allows for the recognition of selves. For instance, the daily routines of helping Agnes put her coat on, open the car door for her, and hold her by the arm while crossing the street are all recognitions of her female status. According to Garfinkel, these recognitions of the self are dependent on the situation and the interactants; Goffman's trans-situational rules for performing in front of others are therefore inadequate. They are static rules that fail to define a continuously changing self.

Carol A. B. Warren and Barbara Ponse defined the self differently from Goffman. In their study of the gay world,[47] they view the presentation of self as a manipulated self whose aim is to convince the audience, regardless of the sincerity of the performance. According to Warren and Ponse, Goffman's self need not be a true one. In their study they found that gay individuals usually present a public self that is stigmatized by society and does not represent their true self. Gay people's true self, or *existential self* as the authors call it, lurks beneath their official veneer and is not a calculated set of rules, but a primordial "feeling" self. Consequently, gay individuals are faced with a continuous conflict within themselves. They have to incessantly negotiate between their official self, constrained within societal bounds, and their existential self, which wants to express the freedom of choice of the individual, regardless of societal bounds.

Another sociologist, Alvin Gouldner, is concerned with the morality of Goffman's self. He sees Goffman's aim as that of teaching people how to cope with an existing social order by using unscrupulous and devious means that ignore established moral values.[48] While Gouldner admits that Goffman places human beings at the center of the picture (after they have been tagged for so many years as mere cogs in the great machine of society), Gouldner sees Goffman's individuals as "tricky, harassed little devils" [49] who have lost any sense of morality. "For Goffman what counts is not whether men *are* moral but whether they *seem* moral to others." [50]

Garfinkel is correct that the self changes and gains acceptance in social interaction. However, it is also true that the routines used by members of society to be accepted by others are remarkably similar from situation to situation. Goffman examines the ways in which the self gains acceptance in different situations, in order to gain a trans-situational understanding of the self. Garfinkel and Goffman are not really at odds; they are just looking at different things.

Gouldner and Warren and Ponse, and the others see Goffman's work as leading to a cynical or amoral view of the self and society. Goffman's critics say that his sociology deals only with forms of life and teaches individuals how to manipulate situations to their advantage. Given Goffman's initial premise (taken from Georg Simmel [51]) that life is only expressable through forms, how else could one develop a self if not by using those forms known as roles, by performing in the forms of wife, mother, lover, teacher, athlete, or scientist in front of others? This is the irony of life: as one emerges from anonymity by breaking the silence and speaking in the quest toward individuality, one thereby surrenders to pre-established forms. The performers have one by one "moved center stage, first to tell us who they uniquely are and then, as they keep talking, to reveal that they are nobody in particular." [52]

Goffman has not ignored the role of the hierarchy of existing values. He has merely pointed out their ineluctable existence in our midst and has argued that our actions support their existence. Goffman's sociology is not amoral, as charged by Gouldner. Goffman's sociology is really an attempt to reveal how the difference between a sincere performance and a cynical one is very problematic since performances depend on successful management. If the performer conveys an impression of sincerity, then for all practical purposes that performance is sincere, for it has convinced us. Therefore, *we exist in a world of social constructions rather than one of absolute standards.*[53] We are indeed "merchants of morality"[54] for Goffman, but only as performers, since as performers our obligation is not to morality but to a successful presentation of our self. But since our presentation is aimed at satisfying the audiences composed by the various groups of society, the performance takes on a moral tinge even if it may not have been morally intended. In other words, we may play at being moral to satisfy others, and in so doing we turn a cynical performance into one of moral import.[55]

We must protect interaction since it is through interaction that we present ourselves to others and achieve a self. We must get along with others, whether we like it or not. To Goffman humans are not amoral beings launched on a quest of self-aggrandizement; rather, they are moral beings concerned with the welfare of other interactants. Goffman's sociology is a *sociology of cooperation* in which masks are used to project pleasing images to the community. Quoting Durkheim, Goffman said that "the human personality is a sacred thing; one does not violate it nor infringe its bounds, while at the same time the greatest good is in community with others."[56] Instead of being masters of intrigue we are individuals constrained and restrained by a society that denudes us of any personal self-image, and that carefully delineates the bounds within which we may operate.

Goffman has pointed the way to the understanding of the social construction of performances that create the self. Others influenced by Goffman have used his theories to understand the actions of human beings and to determine what constitutes a self. If one accepts the basic premise of Goffman's work—that life is but a variety of forms—the self may be unknowable. In Goffman's terms, the self also becomes a form, an elusive social mask that we all wear.

Notes

1. Erving Goffman, *The Presentation of Self in Everyday Life* (New York: Anchor Books, 1959), esp. p. 15.

2. See also Stanford Lyman and Marvin Scott, *A Sociology of the Absurd,* (New York: Appleton-Century-Crofts, 1970).

3. See, for instance, Richard Sennet, "Two on the Aisle," *New York Times Book Review,* Nov. 1, 1973.

4. Herbert Blumer, "Action vs. Interaction," *Transaction* 9, p. 52.

5. Cf. Herbert Blumer, "The Methodological Position of Symbolic Inter-actionism," in *Symbolic Interactionism: Perspective and Method* (Englewood Cliffs, N.J.: Prentice-Hall, 1969); and Erving Goffman, *Presentation of Self.*

6. See Erving Goffman, *Relations in Public* (New York: Basic Books, 1971), esp. p. 302.

7. See Bruce Biddle and Erwin Thomas, *Role Theory* (New York: John Wiley & Sons, 1966), esp. p. 4.

8. Erving Goffman, *Behavior in Public Places* (New York: The Free Press, 1963), p. 28.

9. Goffman, *Presentation of Self.*

10. See Becker, Howard; Blanche Geer; Everett Hughes; and Anselm Strauss, *Boys in White* (Chicago: University of Chicago Press, 1961). For a detailed account of this work *see* chapter 2.

11. See Goffman, *The Presentation of Self.*

12. Robert Park, in Goffman, *The Presentation of Self,* pp. 19–20.

13. Tom Wolfe, *Radical Chic & Mau-Mauing the Flak Catcher* (New York: Bantam Books, 1971), p. 120.

14. Ludwig, Lewisohn, in Theodor Hatlen, *Orientation to Theater* (New York: Appleton-Century-Crofts, 1962), p. 241.

15. Emily Post, quoted in Goffman, *Behavior in Public Places,* p. 172.

16. See Goffman, *The Presentation of Self,* pp. 252–253.

17. Erving Goffman, *Asylums* (New York: Anchor Books, 1961).

18. T. E. Lawrence, in Goffman, *Asylums,* p. 35.

19. Goffman, *Asylums,* p. 168.

20. Ibid., p. 55.

21. Cantine and Rainer, in Goffman, *Asylums,* p. 307.

22. See Andrea Fontana, *The Last Frontier* (Beverly Hills, Calif.: Sage Publications, 1977).

23. Ken Kesey, *One Flew Over the Cuckoo's Nest* (New York: Signet, 1962).

24. Erving Goffman, *Asylums,* p. 306.

25. Ibid.

26. Ken Kesey, *Cuckoo's Nest,* p. 267.

27. Ibid., p. 267.

28. Ibid., p. 269.

29. Erving Goffman, *Relations in Public.*

30. Ibid., p. 329.

31. Ibid., p. 59.

32. Herb Caen, in Goffman, *Relations in Public,* p. 174.

33. Erving Goffman, *Relations in Public.*

34. Ibid., p. 255.

35. Erving Goffman, *Frame Analysis* (Cambridge, Mass.: Harvard University Press, 1974).

36. Ibid., p. 3.

37. Ibid., p. 461.

38. For an excellent secondary source spanning all of Pirandello's works, see Walter Starkie, *Luigi Pirandello* (Berkeley, Calif.: University of California Press, 1965).

39. Erving Goffman, *Frame Analysis,* p. 1.

40. See Edward Hall, *The Hidden Dimension* (Garden City, N.Y.: Anchor Books, 1969).

41. Martin Esslin, *The Theater of the Absurd* (New York: Anchor Books, 1969), p. 377.

42. Murray S. Davis, *Intimate Relations* (New York: The Free Press, 1973).

43. Sherri Cavan, *Liquor License* (Chicago: Aldine Publishing Co., 1966).

44. Ibid., p. 75.

45. David Sudnow, *Passing On: The Social Organization of Dying* (Englewood Cliffs, N.J.: Prentice-Hall, 1967).

46. Harold Garfinkel, in *Studies in Ethnomethodology* (Englewood Cliffs, N.J.: Prentice-Hall, 1977).

47. Carol A. B. Warren and Barbara Ponse, "The Existential Self in the Gay World," in Jack D. Douglas and John M. Johnson (eds.), *Existential Sociology* (New York: Cambridge University Press, 1977).

48. See Alvin Gouldner, *The Coming Crisis of Western Sociology* (New York: Avon Books, 1970).

49. Ibid., p. 383.

50. Ibid., p. 383.

51. Cf. Georg Simmel, *The Conflict in Modern Culture and Other Essays* (New York: Teachers College Press, 1968).

52. Richard Poirier, *The Performing Self* (New York: Oxford University Press, 1971), p. 8.

53. See Goffman, *The Presentation of Self,* esp. p. 71.

54. Ibid., p. 251.

55. Ibid., p. 251.

56. Emile Durkheim, in Goffman, *The Presentation of Self,* p. 69.

4

Labelling Theory and Everyday Deviance

Joseph A. Kotarba

> This [labeling theory] is a large turn away from older sociology which tended to rest heavily upon the idea that deviance leads to social control. I have come to believe that the reverse idea, i.e., social control leads to deviance, is equally tenable and the potentially richer premise for studying deviance in modern society (Lemert, 1967: v).

The development of the sociologies of everyday life, particularly symbolic interactionism, has been marked by shifts in theoretical and methodological emphases. As we have seen in chapters 1 and 2, the traditional view of society as a *structural* order existing independently of its members to shape and constrain their behavior has been abandoned in favor of viewing social reality as a *creative process*. People interact creatively to align their paths of interaction, to find meaning for life, and to construct social order. The sociologists of everyday life do not assume that social order determines how individuals live and act; rather, they study how individuals collectively construct and destroy social orders (see Douglas, 1971: 1–6). The special area of sociology known as "deviance" or "deviant behavior" addresses this question by studying how rules are created and used to establish classes of normal and abnormal people and behavior, and the relation of deviance to social order.[1]

The principal writers within the tradition of symbolic interactionism, G. H. Mead and Herbert Blumer, have inspired others to study deviant behavior in order to see how it emerges in specific interactions. The outcome of this study has been the emergence of *labelling theory* or the *societal-reaction approach* to deviant behavior. As an outgrowth of symbolic interactionism, labelling theory embodies many of its strengths as well as a few of its weaknesses.

This chapter will sketch the predecessors of the labelling perspective, from the once-dominant structural-functionalists to Frank Tannenbaum and Alfred Lindesmith, two criminologists whose work anticipated the basic ideas of labelling. Second, the field-research tradition at the University of Chicago, which directly prefigured labelling theory and methods, will be discussed. Third, the basic concepts and propositions of labelling theory will be shown by using Becker's research on marihuana use as a clear example of their empirical application. Fourth, research on mental illness will be examined because it is an area where labelling theory has been most successfully applied. Fifth, the issues and criticisms surrounding labelling theory will be summarized, and some concluding remarks that demonstrate how labelling theory, despite its shortcomings, has led to some creative explorations into the everyday world of deviance.

Deviance and American Sociology

American sociologists have tried to explain deviant behavior using such concepts as social pathology, value conflict, social disorganization, and anomie (Rubington and Weinberg, 1971). The last two are directly relevant to the emergence of labelling theory. Social disorganization theory (as we shall see later) demonstrates the value of directly observing the contrasting themes of urban America, while the positivistic and scientistic approach of anomie theory became a suitable target for the proponents of labelling theory.

As sociologists became entrenched in the university during the early part of this century, they sought to establish their field as a "respectable science" modeled after the natural sciences. This led to a formal and systematic sociology that was epitomized by structural-functionalism, the dominant sociological paradigm of the past thirty years. As is true with all perspectives in sociology, functionalism is distinctive in its approach to questions of social order and deviance. Merton's paper on social order and anomie (1938) was the first major statement of functionalism. Merton argued that deviance has specific social causes that cannot be reduced to simple biological or psychological factors. This stance was similar to that of the social disorganization theorists, although Merton did go one step further by contending that social order is the result of people acting out the values they share by virtue of their participation in a *collective conscience* or *value consensus* (see Durkheim, 1964).[2]

Merton argued that a fundamental value held by all Americans is the achievement of success, which is usually measured in terms of money or material possessions. While most Americans can achieve success through legitimate, institutionalized means (e.g., education, job entree, job mobility), among the lower strata of society there is a disjunction between the cultural goal of success and the legitimate means of attaining it. Members of the lower class want to "make it" as much as anyone else, but because of poor education, prejudice, etc., they often are unable to gain success legitimately. Merton calls this disjunction between cultural goals and legitimate means "anomie." Persons for whom the feeling of anomie is strong will adapt to their situation in life in various ways, including becoming criminals and delinquents.[3]

Merton's theory is general and not specific, for it was intended to explain differences in general rates of deviance among social classes and not to explain the origin of specific deviant acts. Nevertheless, Merton's theory led to much supportive research; between 1955 and 1964, sixty-four research studies on anomie were published (Merton, 1964: 216). One of the best of these was Cohen's (1955) study of delinquent boys. Instead of thinking in terms of individual adaptations to values, Cohen focused upon group or subcultural adaptations. Working-class boys tend to form gangs that hold values antithetical to those of the middle class. Each gang has its own set of norms and statuses so that success within the context of the gang may be obtained by members, even if it is unobtainable within the larger society. Each boy learns how to be a gang member, and thereby a delinquent, by being socialized to reject middle-class values.

The anomie theory of deviance, with its variations and modifications, has been criticized for theorizing without regard for the realities of everyday life. In trying to explain all deviance with one simple theory, anomie theory draws heavily upon the intuition of the theorist, setting him up as an "omniscient sociologist" (Douglas, 1971: 34) who can dispense with actual research on deviance. Cohen, for example, believed that much of the delinquent boys' behavior, such as vandalism, is non-utilitarian, because it does not attain material success. As Douglas indicates (1971: 37–38), Cohen failed to investigate what meaning vandalism held for the boys, but simply imputed his own opinion. The boys might have used vandalism to develop in-group solidarity or to provide a means for status mobility within the group, both of which would be utilitarian in their context. How would anyone know without studying the boys directly through observation or interviews?

A distance between the theorist and his subjects accrues when easily obtainable sources of data are relied upon, especially official records and statistics, which are in themselves abstrations of actual behavior. These official sources of data are usually collected and processed by official agencies of control such as the police, courts, school districts, and welfare agencies. The purposes of the official agencies for developing data are often totally different from the sociologist's. Analyses of the construction of official data have shown that rates of deviance reflect at best only those deviant acts that are actually "caught," or registered.[4] And, since lower classes tend to be over-policed, their acts of crime tend to be overrepresented in the crime statistics. In addition, rates of crime by category may be rendered unreliable by plea bargaining and multiple indictments. Certain official categories of deviance such as suicide are especially unreliable since many cases are hidden because of religious or status considerations of families. By separating theory from the phenomenon in question, the structural-functional approach to deviance leads to theory construction that distorts the realities of the everyday world of deviance.

While structural-functionalism gained prestige in American sociology, other social scientists continued to study the interactional processes by which deviance becomes a social reality. Two criminologists were especially interested in how individuals came to be classified as "deviants." In one of the earliest works exploring the social creation of deviant definitions, Tannenbaum (1938) analyzed how a local community inadvertently forced certain boys down the path of delinquency.

In his textbook on criminology, Tannenbaum argued that there was a progression of conflict between the juvenile delinquent and the larger community, beginning with a disparity between the meaning of the juvenile's activities he himself holds and the meaning held by the community. Initially the juvenile sees his activity as a form of play or adventure. The community, on the other hand, sees his activity as a nuisance or as delinquency, and calls for official control. Gradually, the definition attributed by the community shifts from the evil of the act to the evil nature of the juvenile himself. In a short time, the youth senses that he is being singled out as different or bad. Eventually he may see himself as delinquent because that is the only identity he is permitted. A snow-balling effect takes place as the youth increasingly acts out his ascribed status, while the community increasingly reacts to his socially defined character and less to his actual behavior. Tannenbaum refers to this entire process as *tagging*, and the people around the delinquent tag him as bad whether they intend to help or punish him. Thus, tagging becomes the genesis of what sociologists later called labelling:

> The process of making the criminal, therefore, is a process of tagging, defining, identifying, segregating, describing, emphasizing, making conscious and self-conscious; it becomes a way of stimulat-

ing, suggesting, emphasizing and evoking the very traits that are complained of. If the theory of the relation of response to stimulus has any meaning, the entire process of dealing with the young delinquent is mischievous in so far as it identifies him to himself or to the environment as a delinquent person.

The person becomes the thing he is described as being. (Tannenbaum, 1938: 19–20).

Tannenbaum's concept of tagging was used in explaining a specific form of deviant behavior (juvenile delinquency) and therefore did not have the theoretical power that the proponents of labelling theory later claimed.

Another early work dealing with the phenomenon of labelling was Lindesmith's study of opiate addiction (1947). Lindesmith studied the process by which a person becomes aware that he is addicted to opiate drugs. His research led him to theorize that the meanings one ascribes to the self and behavior are formed through social interaction with significant others (*see* chapter 2). Lindesmith argued that addiction to opiates occurs when the user learns from other users to associate withdrawal symptoms with the absence of the drug. In other words, addiction is not an outcome of drug use, but of a social definition. A user learns that he is an addict when that label is given him by a significant other, usually another user. Lindesmith went on to call for a change in society's attitude toward the addict. He proposed that the addict be treated as a sick person, so that he may be placed under the care of doctors rather than the police.

The Return to the Teachings of the "Green Bible"

Influential labelling theorists such as Howard Becker, Kai Erikson, John Kitsuse, Edwin Lemert, Edwin Schur, Thomas Scheff, and Erving Goffman studied the actual social world of the deviants themselves in order to view deviance from their perspective.[5] They extended empathy to the deviant as the underdog in the morality game, the person they believed to be "victimized" by the forces of social control, the one who is "more sinned against than sinning" (Becker, 1967: 240). They also tried to achieve a more balanced picture of deviance by studying the labellers as well as the labellees.

What were the immediate sources of this new perspective? One source was the growing disenchantment among sociologists with the predominant structural-functionalist theory of deviance. Labelling theorists argued that it is absurd to believe that any reified notion of society actually causes deviance. The concept of anomie, for example, cannot explain why only certain members of the lower classes actually commit criminal acts while the vast majority do not. They chose instead to view society and social order as the cumulative result of on-going, face-to-face interaction.

While earlier writings such as Tannenbaum's and Lindesmith's demonstrated the theoretical premise of interactional analysis, the work of George Herbert Mead and Herbert Blumer placed specific emphasis on the *self* in sociological investigation. This allowed the later proponents of labelling to develop a theory of deviance that places a distinct moral worth on an individual who is otherwise stigmatized as immoral or criminal by agents of social control. As Blumer indicates:

> Symbolic interactionism provides the premises for a profound philosophy with a strong humanistic cast. In elevating the "self" to a position of paramount importance and in recognizing that its formulation and realization occur through taking the roles of others with whom one is implicated in the joint activities of group life, symbolic interactionism provides the essentials for a provocative philosophical scheme that is particularly attuned to social existence (Blumer, 1962: 73).

Another direct influence on labelling theory was the department of sociology at the University of Chicago, where the vast majority of the labelling proponents received their graduate training. When they demanded that their students go out and directly study the social world around them, the pioneers of that department set the direction for social research that was to dominate sociology until the emergence of structural-functionalism. Although trained after World War II, the labelling theorists were quite aware of their department's tradition, as exemplified by what was affectionately referred to as the "Green Bible." An early collection of essays which served as one of the first texts in sociology, the "Green Bible" was written by Robert Park and Ernest Burgess, two members of the sociology department at Chicago. The "Green Bible" was a call to sociologists to become personally committed to the phenomena they study:

> The first thing that students in sociology need to learn is to observe and record their own observations: to read, and then to select and record the materials which are the fruits of their readings; to organize and use, in short, their own experience. The whole organization of this volume may be taken as an illustration of the method, at once tentative and experimental, for the collection, classification, and interpretation of materials, and should be used by the students from the very onset in all their reading and study (Park and Burgess, 1921: 45).

Sociology at the University of Chicago during those early years was a vibrant and exciting enterprise. The city of Chicago itself was a teeming laboratory for the study of social processes; it provided the stark contrasts that were the hallmark of America's many burgeoning metropolises. Power and poverty and crime and civility were often separated by a few city blocks. If sociology was to become an established discipline, it would have to come to grips with the "whys" and "hows" of the urban mosaic. The pioneering sociologists at the University of Chicago sought to meet their professional and civic responsibilities by setting out to study and experience their social milieu, while urging their students to do the same. As one of these pioneers remarked:

> Leaders of the Chicago school were not afraid to urge their students to trust their feelings for a situation or an event, were not afraid to stress the role of insight, and to warn against a slavish devotion to figures, charts, graphs, and sterile scientific techniques (Wright, 1945: Introduction).

The energy of the Chicago School sociologists was matched by a desire to find solutions to the human misery in urban life. Thus, their field work was "undertaken by men who believed that social facts well presented would point the way to reform of the conditions and ways of living at or below the poverty line" (Hughes, 1962: xxxvii).[6]

The Chicago sociologists produced many books describing the social foundations of their city, including studies on ghetto life (Wirth, 1928), suicide (Cavan, 1928), juvenile delinquency (Shaw and McKay, 1931), and contrasts between the life styles of the rich and the poor (Zorbaugh, 1929). A dominant perspective in these works, *social disorganization theory*, is best represented by Thrasher's study of 1,313 gangs in Chicago (1927). Thrasher utilized the ecological framework to demonstrate how gangs develop only in certain zones of the city, especially those areas marked by extensive poverty and transiency. The gangs emerged spontaneously, maintaining internal organizations all their own. Thrasher argued that the cause of gang behavior cannot be traced to any specific psychological abnormality among members. On the contrary, gang activity commonly occurs where communities are too disorganized to provide constructive channels for the adventuresome spirit of youth. The majority of community members were first-generation immigrants who could not establish strong institutions of control to minimize delinquency and crime. Thrasher thus demonstrated how social disorganization within a community led to deviance.

Labelling theory was also a product of the times. The late 1950s and early 1960s were marked by growing social ferment. The Civil Rights movement, student dissent, and the growing awareness of poverty amongst plenty resulted in a shift of sympathy, especially among academics, to those people presumed to be oppressed by the more powerful "rule makers" and "rule enforcers." As young idealists in their own right, the labelling theorists fell into this trend. They were, however, wary of assuming too radical a position lest their politics corrupt their sociology:

> These dissenters [labelling theorists] were caught between the conflicting roles of detached scientist and committed citizen, and became politically strangled by their disenchantment with the status quo and their inability to accept the utopian myths that nurture revolution. They finally resolved this ethical and political conflict by a type of proletarian "cool," remaining occupationally secure in the academic world, while staying detached from its middle-class images and moralistic compulsions (N. Davis, 1975: 167).

This position of being a "rebel within the system" influenced the temperament and tone for much of the work of the labelling perspective. The world of deviance, with all its "romantic embellishments," was studied in depth, as dictated by the tenets of symbolic interactionism. By the same token, the subterranean world of the deviant could be enjoyed by association if not by commitment. As one critic of labelling theory put it:

> This group of Chicagoans finds itself at home in the world of hip, Norman Mailer, drug addicts, jazz musicians, cab drivers, prostitutes, night people, drifters, grifters, and skidders, the cool cats and their kicks. To be fully appreciated, this stream of work cannot be seen solely in terms of the categories conventionally employed in sociological analysis. It has also to be seen from the viewpoint of the literary critic, as a style or genre. . . . it prefers the offbeat to the familiar, the vivid ethnographic detail to the dull taxonomy, the sensuously expressive to dry analysis, naturalistic observation to formal questionnaires . . . (Gouldner, 1962: 209).

The General Theory of Labelling

The labelling theorists pursue a path of inquiry that represents the social world as it is experienced by the deviant actor. They have produced meaningful, if modest, generalizations describing the process of morality construction. The basic premise of labelling theory is deceptively simple: Deviance is not a quality intrinsic to any particular act or category of acts, but is a socially constructed, discrediting definition:

> Deviance is not a property *inherent in* certain forms of behavior; it is a property *conferred upon* these forms by the audiences which directly or indirectly witness them. The critical variable in the study of deviance, then, is the social audience rather than the individual actor, since it is the audience which eventually determines

whether or not any episode of behavior or any class of episodes is labelled deviant (Erikson, 1962: 11).

Labelling theory rejects the assumption maintained by the more traditional sociologies of deviance that the wrongness of an act is known by all societal members, including the sociologist. Consequently, searching for the etiology or causes of deviance is rejected in favor of searching for the processes by which certain acts come to be defined by society as deviant. The audience that Erikson mentions varies according to the type of deviant behavior in question. As we have seen, the audience for a juvenile delinquent is often the larger community or its social-control agents. For an opiate addict, it could be another addict. Ordinarily, we think of the audience of acts labelled as criminal as being the agents of social control. The audience involved in labelling non-criminal acts of deviance, such as homosexuality, is comprised of a *generalized other* (representing ideas commonly held within society) or a *significant other* (a significant person encountered in interaction) (Blumer, 1968).

Audiences do not arbitrarily define acts as deviant. They usually do so by invoking a rule. Although labelling theorists reject the normative paradigm of structural-functionalism as an explanation, they do feel that the creation of deviance occurs within a normative framework. Becker states this view in his definition of deviance:

> . . . social groups create deviance by making the rules whose infraction constitutes deviance, and by applying those rules to particular people and labelling them as outsiders. From this point of view, deviance is not a quality of the act the person commits, but rather a consequence of the application by others of rules and sanctions to an offender (Becker, 1963: 9).

Who makes the rules? The labelling theorists have mixed feelings about this issue. As true liberals, they contend that American society is essentially pluralistic, so that the creation of any rule is the result of interaction, negotiation, and compromise among vested interest groups. As Lemert argues:

> It is doubtful that . . . procedures for defining deviance can be laid to the creations of any one group, class or elite. Rather, they are the products of the interactions of groups (Lemert, 1974: 462).

Pluralism is readily observable in American society. The many ethnic and interest groups that make up our population each maintain specific sets of values. For the most part, members of these groups accommodate the values of the dominant group, but occasionally their group values are accepted by the society at large; for example, the successful lobby by blacks to have Dr. Martin Luther King's birthday designated an official holiday. Other special-interest groups that have prevailed in recent years include the anti-war groups that successfully redefined the war in Vietnam as immoral, the various women's groups that have successfully lobbied for liberalized abortion rights in many states, and the current taxpayers' groups that led to the passage of Proposition 13 in California.

The labelling theorists, however, do not go so far as to insist that the American society is egalitarian. A group must ultimately have political or economic power to enforce its views or values. As Becker (1963: 17) notes: ". . . people are in fact always forcing their rules on others, applying them more or less against the will and without the consent of those others." Becker is not saying that one elite, all-powerful group creates all rules in our society, but rather that most rules, whoever their sponsors are, rest on a foundation of power. In this light, it is understandable how rules are made by parents for children, by officers for enlisted men, and, to a lesser degree in recent times, by men for women.

Thus far, we have seen two aspects of labelling: 1) the perception and definition of the deviant act by an audience, and 2) the relationship of the act to a rule. In one of the early formulations of labelling theory, Becker (1963: 20) designated an analytical relationship between these two factors (*see* Table 4–1).

TABLE 4–1. TYPES OF DEVIANT BEHAVIOR

	OBEDIENT BEHAVIOR	RULE-BREAKING BEHAVIOR
Perceived as Deviant	falsely accused	pure deviant
Not Perceived as Deviant	conforming	secret deviant

The conforming and pure deviant types are self-explanatory. The false accusation is commonly referred to as a "bum rap," in which a person is blamed for a deviant action not actually committed. Secret deviance is especially interesting because it represents a situation where rule breaking occurs without being perceived by an audience. According to the general definition of deviance given by the labelling theorists, the secret deviant is not really deviant at all, for he or she is not labelled publicly. Becker does allow, however, for the possibility of *self-labelling* by the secret deviant. For example, people who are homosexual or who shoplift without being caught may label themselves as deviant, with similar effects.[7]

The effects of labelling can be manifold, including incarceration and social ostracism. Following the tradition of symbolic interactionism, the labelling theorists have concentrated on the effects of labelling on the self. Lemert (1967: 17) expressed this idea succinctly in distinguishing *primary deviance* and *secondary deviance*:

> Primary deviation is assumed to arise in a variety of social, cultural, and psychological contexts, and at best has only marginal implication for the psychic structure of the individual; it does not lead to symbolic reorganization at the level of self-regarding attitudes and social roles. Secondary deviation is deviant behavior or social roles based upon it, which becomes a means of defense, attack, or adaptation to the overt and covert problems created by the societal reaction to the primary deviation.

To be labelled deviant transforms one's self-conception from normal to deviant. To be labelled deviant is not merely to be accused of acting wrongly, but to be thought of as a person who habitually acts wrongly and is likely to do so in the future. It is to gain a new identity, a *stigma* (Goffman, 1962), and a *master status* (Hughes, 1945) that takes over the labelled person's other claims to status. Since this new identity is a negative one, the labelled person's options in life are limited, as in the case of a convicted felon who cannot get a job after release from prison. The continuous imputation of the deviant label strongly affects the process of socialization, both among adults and adolescents. Like the juvenile delinquent in Tannenbaum's study, the secondary deviant may come to believe that the negative identity imposed upon him from the outside is really what he truly is on the inside. Both the external constraint of identity and the internal constraint of a deviant self often lead to a career in deviance, for this may be the only viable option available to the accused.

Goffman (1962) uses the concept of a *moral career* to denote the sequence of personal adjustment to the devalued identity experienced by the stigmatized person. The individual undergoes two phases of a socialization process by which he learns society's standards, which indicate the consequences of possessing a particular label, and at some point also learns that he possesses the particular label.

Whether the individual learns of this difference early or late in life, the type of adjustment depends on whether the individual is discredited or discreditable (Goffman, 1962: 41–42). A *discredited person* learns to accommodate normals while at the same time developing relationships with others so afflicted. For example, a physically deformed person may either take advantage of the special opportunities for in-group participation (e.g., a blind person joining the local Lighthouse group), or he may reject others like himself because he thinks they exhibit dependency, defeatism, or low aspirations. On the other hand, if a discreditable person's differentness is not immediately apparent to others, as a homosexual's would not be, he may decide to embark upon a moral career whose objective is "passing" among normals to avoid being stigmatized. The concept of a moral career is also useful in understanding the stigmatization process that occurs with delinquents and criminals.

The Labelling Theory of Marihuana Use

An early but definitive empirical application of labelling theory is Becker's study of marihuana users (1963). As a former jazz musician, Becker was acquainted with many marihuana users even before smoking pot became widespread and open. Using his own experience, fifty extensive interviews with users, and an analytical induction framework (*see* chapter 2), Becker developed a typology of the processes of learning marihuana use. He argued that the effects of smoking marihuana are essentially psychological sensations that denote neither pleasure nor pain. Marihuana smokers must learn from others that these sensations are uniquely pleasurable. Becker delineated three steps in the process of becoming a regular marihuana user:

> No one becomes a user without (1) learning to smoke the drug in a way which will produce real effects; (2) learning to recognize the effects and connect them with drug use (learning, in other words, to get high); and (3) learning to enjoy the sensations he perceives. In the course of this process he develops a disposition or motivation to use marihuana which was not and could not have been present when he began use, for it evolves and depends on conceptions of the drug which could only grow out of the kind of actual experience detailed above (Becker, 1963: 58).

Social control is always present during the marihuana experience, for its use is illegal and severely punishable (much more so when Becker did his study than now). These social controls take three forms. First, there are legal restrictions on the supply of marihuana, as well as on its use. Second, the use of marihuana must be kept secret from significant others who may not value the unusual or bizarre behavior it often produces. Third, the simple use of marihuana, if discovered, may be labelled immoral regardless of resultant behavioral manifestations. The regular marihuana user will reduce the threats of these sanctions by spending increasingly more of his or her time exclusively with a marihuana "in-group" whose values support and protect the smoker.

The precepts of the labelling perspective have been applied to various phenomena involving the breaking of social rules, such as aberrant sexual behavior (Hoffman, 1968), drunken driving (Marshall and Purdy, 1972), and heroin addiction (Schur, 1965). Labelling theory also has been applied to discrediting phenomena that do not directly transgress official rules of society but which reflect an individual's ascribed inability to act in accord with vague and amorphous notions of "normalcy."

For example, Mercer (1965) has shown how mental retardation is a label that can be applied not only to physiologically defined states of intellectual incapacity, but to statistically marginal populations. Members of subcultures are identified as retarded most often by culturally biased IQ tests. Freidson (1970: 205–223) argues that the profession of medicine maintains a monopoly on creating "illness" as a social attribute based upon criteria distinct from biological pathology. Indeed, the labelling of normal and pathological mental states by psychiatrists according to the medical term has been labelling theory's most fruitful area of study and criticism.

The Labelling Perspective and Mental Illness

As a broad category of unusual behavior, mental illness has become a valuable testing ground for the explanatory power of labelling theory. The process of formally or informally denoting a person as mentally ill immediately imputes a discrediting stigma and affects the self-image and future life plan of the person so labelled.

Functional mental disorders—those that interfere with normal behavior and perceptions—have been extensively examined by physicians, psychologists, psychiatrists, and other professionals for many years. However, all this interest has resulted in little agreement on the precise definition of mental illness or its causes and treatment. There have been well over 5,000 research reports written on schizophrenia alone since 1920, but there has been little progress in understanding this problem (Scheff, 1966: 7). Medical science has failed to deal effectively with the issue. Jackson (1960: 3–4) isolated a probable reason for this failure in light of the dramatic advances made in other areas of health care:

> At present, schizophrenia is one of our major medical problems. This is not only because of its incidence (estimated at from one to three percent of the population) and its chronicity (keeping one quarter of the hospital beds in the country occupied), or because of the fact that its major incidence is during the most productive periods of life, roughly between 15 and 44. It is also because medicine has made progress against many other major disorders, thus allowing schizophrenia to loom large by contrast.

Szasz (1960) insightfully argued that the reason for the confusion stems from the definition of aberrant behavior as a medical problem or disease of the individual. In fact, aberrant behavior represents a social problem, a *problem in living*. "Illness" has been traditionally used to describe unusual behavior because the medical profession has regarded such behavior as the result of a neurological defect, that is, it has assumed visible behavior has physical origins. Szasz has remarked that a true physiological abnormality of the brain would actually be displayed physiologically in conditions like blindness or paralysis, and not in social behavior. The symptoms of mental illness, on the contrary, are unusual beliefs and views of reality, phenomena that cannot be reasonably reduced to physiological causes. Moreover, the beliefs stated by a person labelled mentally ill are not nearly as definitive as physiological symptoms. They are judged normal or deviant by someone who must use his or her own belief system as a standard of comparison. Consequently, the diagnosis of mental illness is a socially determined one:

> We speak of mental symptoms . . . when we refer to a patient's *communication about himself, others and the world about him.* He might state that he is Napoleon or that he is being persecuted by the Communists. These would be considered mental symptoms only if the observer believed that the patient was not Napoleon or that he was not being persecuted by the Communists. This makes it apparent that the statement that "X is a mental symptom" involves rendering a judgment. This judgment entails, moreover, a covert comparison or matching of the patient's ideas, concepts, or beliefs with those of the observer and the society in which they live. The notion of mental symptom is therefore inextricably tied to the *social* (including ethical) *context* in which it is made in much the same way as the notion of bodily symptom is tied to an anatomical and genetic context (Szasz, 1960: 114).

Instead of couching mental problems in misleading medical terms, Szasz proposes that mental problems be viewed in terms of a game-playing model of human behavior. This analytical framework explains various behavioral disorders such as hysteria and schizophrenia as the intentional impersonation of sick persons by those who incur problems of living. The perceived symptoms are conscious or subconscious strategies used by individuals to obtain help from others in dealing with the stresses of everyday life.

Lemert (1962) applied the labelling principle of societal reaction to paranoia. Traditional psychiatric thought views paranoia as the reaction of an individual who has not learned how to conduct himself competently in social interaction with others. He symbolically constructs a pseudo-community of others whom he perceives as posing a threat. This imaginary fear of others leads him into conflict with and isolation from his real community of others.[8] Lemert contends that although the paranoid person does react to his real community in odd and unexpected ways, the community also reacts to him, often in terms even the sociologist would regard as conspiratorial. This conspiracy compounds the confusion in the mind of the paranoid person, whose imagined conspiracy has become a real one. The crucial aspect of Lemert's research is similar to Szasz's in that the *social construction of mental illness* is given theoretical preference over the traditional medical model:

> By thus shifting the clinical spotlight away from the individual to a relationship and a process, we make an explicit break with the conception of paranoia as a disease, a state, a condition, or a syndrome of symptoms. Furthermore, we find it unnecessary to postulate trauma of early childhood or arrested psychosexual development to account for the main features of paranoia—although we grant that these and other factors may condition its expression (Lemert, 1962: 3).

In addition to explaining the social nature clinically defined abnormal behavior, labelling theory has also been applied to the study of mental illness within a broader historical context. Foucault (1965) traces the origins of the mental asylum back to seventeenth-century France to isolate the social and political factors in its development. In 1656, Louis XIII established the *Hôpital Général* in Paris in order to institutionalize the care of the mad. At that time to be defined as mad and admitted to an asylum simply required that a person be abandoned, poor, destitute, of low moral standing (e.g., a prostitute), blind, crippled, or uncontrollably wild. The asylum served to protect the larger society from the "threat" these undesirables posed to the moral order of the state. This goal was accomplished by designing the asylum in such a way as to emulate the functions of the bourgeois family. The psychiatrist (father) taught the moral values of discipline and hard work to the patient (child). By strengthening the moral order within the asylum, it was hoped that the larger social order would subsequently be strengthened.[9]

Erikson (1966) observes the same function of deviance in indirectly strengthening the moral order of the Massachusetts Puritan community. Records indicate that the Puritan community underwent three distinct "epidemics" of deviance, the most notorious of which was the Salem witchcraft episode. Although these eruptions of deviance were historically unique, theories on deviance can be extrapolated from them. First, every community has unique styles of deviance that depend upon the values it most highly esteems. In the Puritan community, the religious values were held highest, so that any religious transgression, like witchcraft, was most feared. Second, the amount of deviance experienced by a community tends to be fairly constant over time. As the number of witchcraft cases in Puritan New England increased, for example, the prosecution of other crimes such as theft decreased, leaving the overall crime rate essentially the same. Third, each community punishes individual transgressors in a manner compatible with the overall moral order of the community. Puritan justice centered around the religious doctrine of predestination, which assumed that there were two classes of people on earth: those who were destined to enter everlasting life and those who were doomed forever to hell. Thus, a judge could in good conscience sentence a convicted witch to the harshest of punishments, for he or she would soon suffer immeasurable misery in hell anyway. We again see how the attribution of deviance depends on the interests of the powerful.[10]

Scheff (1966) provides the clearest and most systematically developed theory of mental illness from the labelling perspective. He delineates the ways a community classifies rule-breaking:

> . . . the culture of the group provides a vocabulary of terms for categorizing many norm violations: crime, perversion, drunkenness, and bad manners are familiar examples. Each of the terms is derived from the type of norm broken, and ultimately from the type of behavior involved. After exhausting these categories, however, there is always a residue of the most diverse kinds of violations for which the culture provides no explicit label (Scheff, 1966: 34).

Rule violations that lack explicit categorization are called "residual rule-breaking" by Scheff. Agents of social control, such as the police, physicians, and psychiatrists, are at a loss to make sense of the actions of a person who engages in residual rule-breaking, so he or she is labelled and placed in the catch-all category of mental illness. By examining mental illness in this light, "we can categorize most psychiatric symptoms as instances of residual rule-breaking or residual deviance" (Scheff, 1966: 33). The phenomenon of residual rule-breaking is widespread, performed by large segments of the total population, but only vulnerable people such as the poor or homeless are ordinarily labeled mentally ill.

Official labelling ordinarily begins when life's contingencies, such as family or occupational troubles, turns one's behavior into a public issue resulting in referral to psychiatric analysis. At this point, a person usually begins a long and extensive career as a mental patient, for "the official societal reaction (tends to) exaggerate both the amount of and degree of deviance" (Scheff, 1966: 154). The patient finds it quite difficult to dispose of his label, even during confinement and treatment, for "the status of the mental patient is more often an ascribed status, with conditions for status entry and exit external to the patient, than an achieved status with the conditions for status entry and exit dependent upon the patient's own behavior" (Scheff, 1966: 129). In fact, the decision to release a patient may depend more upon strictly social factors (e.g., the patient's social status, the availability of hospital beds, and the willingness of the community to reinstate the patient) than on psychiatric grounds.

The Labelling Perspective:
An Analysis of the Issues

Since its inception in the early 1960s, labelling theory has raised crucial issues about the study of deviant behavior. The resulting debates have included most sociologists, from macro-sociologists who contend that labelling theory ignores the ways social structures may cause deviance, to the phenomenological and existential sociologists who feel that the construction and use of moral meanings is even more problematic and situational than the labelling theorists claim.

In the following section, we will discuss rule creation and enforcement; the etiology of deviant acts; the concept of a "label"; and the concept of a "deviant career" (or secondary deviance).

Rule Creation and Enforcement

A common criticism of labelling theory by macro-sociologists, especially Marxists, is that it is used primarily to examine rule-making and enforcing at the lowest bureaucratic levels and ignores the structural relations in society that allow the ruling class to exercise power (see N. Davis, 1975: 169; Manders, 1975: 53–66; Taylor et al., 1975: 166–171).

Instead of viewing political power as monolithic in society, the critics allege, the labelling theorists adhere to a strictly pluralistic political viewpoint. This emphasis is a result of their insistence on analyzing deviance as it occurs on a face-to-face level and ignoring the "bigger pictures." A classic example of this pluralistic notion is Becker's concept of *moral entrepreneurship* (1963:147–163). According to Becker, there are two sets of moral entrepreneurs in our society: crusading reformers who create or destroy laws, and rule enforcers who apply the laws once they become statutes. While the rule creators may well believe that their mission has moral and humanitarian ends, the rule enforcer "may not be interested in the content of the rule itself, but only in the fact that the existence of the rule provides him with a job, a profession, and a raison d'être" (Becker, 1963: 156). Becker applies his model to the process that led to the institution of the Marihuana Tax Act of 1937. According to Becker, the primary force behind the passage of this legislation was the Treasury Department's Bureau of Narcotics. The officials' motive for taking a strong position on marihuana is attributed to moral concerns that fall within the jurisdiction of the Bureau's responsibilities:

> While it is, of course, difficult to know what the motives of Bureau officials were, we need assume no more than that they perceived an area of wrongdoing that properly belonged in their jurisdiction and moved to put it there. The personal interest they satisfied in pressing for marihuana legislation was one common to many offi-

cials: the interest in successfully accomplishing the task one has been assigned and in acquiring the best tools with which to accomplish it (Becker, 1963: 138).

The Bureau cooperated with state legislators, the media, the legitimate hemp growers, and other relevant groups who had a vested interest in legislation controlling marihuana. This group interaction led to the creation of a new, official category of deviance: marihuana use.[11]

Becker's argument has been criticized for not including the larger implications of such bureaucratic undertakings. The Marxist contention is that a government bureaucracy, as an arm of the ruling class, must strive to expand as well as maintain its power. Dickson (1968: 145), for example, also researched the Marihuana Tax Act and found it to be the result of amoral internal strain within the structure of the Narcotics Bureau:

> Similar to the earlier expansion of narcotics legislation, the Marihuana Tax Act was the response of a bureaucracy to environmental pressure—that the Narcotics Bureau, faced with a non-supportive environment and a decreasing budgetary appropriation that threatened its survival, generated a crusade against marihuana use which resulted in the passage of the act and the alteration of a societal value.

In a more general sense, labelling theory is accused of attributing real political power to low-level bureaucrats who are simply the most visible instruments of ruling-class power. Thus, labelling theory ignores "the larger processes which form the governing framework for the smaller processes and transactions" (Taylor et al., 1975: 170). According to the argument, the ruling class uses governmental bureaucracies to create laws against common crimes in order to secure the necessary civil order in capitalist society. As Quinney (1974: 7) argues:

> Contrary to pluralistic assumptions, law is determined by those few . . . who dominate the political process. Although law is supposed to protect all citizens, it starts as a tool of the dominant class and ends by maintaining the dominance of that class. Law serves the powerful over the weak; it promotes the war of the powerful against the powerless. Moreover, law is used by the state . . . to promote and protect itself. Yet, we are all bound by that law, and we are indoctrinated with the myth that it is our law.

Labelling theorists answer this by arguing that the "power elite" argument, however impressive rhetorically, does not refute the essential position of the labelling perspective. The implementation of political power must be observable at the interactional level, unless one believes in some kind of "invisible hand" phenomenon. While it is true that labelling theorists have concentrated on observing rule usage on the most accessible levels of everyday life, their framework could also be useful if applied to the legislative and corporate levels. In other words, the process of rule use is certainly more complex than the early labelling theorists assumed, but it is not basically different from the micro to macro levels of society. More sophisticated methods and strategies are required to study the powerful than are needed to study the powerless. Researchers have recently begun to study rule use among the powerful by investigative field methods (Douglas, 1976), similar to the techniques used by journalists to "uncover" truths. These methods help break down the massive organizational fronts that prevent outsiders from learning how power is actually used and abused on the corporate level (see Johnson and Douglas, 1978).

The Marxist theory of a monolithic power elite is challenged by the growing awareness among the sociologists of everyday life that rule creation and rule use in our conflictful society reflect the complexity of power relations in contemporary life. Social rules are not simply the creations of situated interest groups, legislatures, or corporate leaders acting in conspiracy. All of these various groups share some degree of responsibility for the institution of new categories of deviance.[12] The growing role of government bureaucracy must be added to this matrix of rule creators. For example, government agencies dealing with environmental or energy issues create many categories of deviance by means of bureaucratic regulations. These non-legislative rules serve the purposes of neither Becker's moral entrepreneurs nor of the corporate elites, but in fact often label *them* as deviants. For example, heavy fines are imposed upon large corporations for their inability to meet rigid air- and water-quality control regulations.

The Etiology of Deviant Acts

A cogent argument has been made that labelling theory is not actually a theory at all because it fails to explain the genesis of deviant acts (Akers, 1968; Gibbs, 1966; and Taylor et al., 1975). In fact, Becker disregards the theoretical need for isolating specific causes for deviant acts because the motivation to deviate is fairly well distributed throughout the population:

> There is no reason to assume that only those who finally commit a deviant act actually have the impulse to do so. It is much more likely that most people experience deviant impulses frequently (Becker, 1963: 26).

With few exceptions, labelling theorists withhold the term "deviant" from characterizing any inherent quality of an act, and reserve it for designating the discrediting social response attributed to certain acts. Critics of this position contend that causes of deviant acts are not only discoverable, but must be discovered in order to truly understand deviance. In response to Scheff's treatise on mental illness, for example, Gove (1975: 35) takes the traditional position of psychiatry that "persons who are reacted to as being mentally ill are in fact mentally ill, and they manifest the attributes that mark them as such." He argues that the clinical conditions existing when Scheff did his research have been improved so that the fear and superstition that previously surrounded mental illness have been replaced by sophisticated diagnostic and therapeutic methods. Mental illness is no longer considered a stigma. Furthermore:

> There is very little evidence of victimization. The evidence shows that a substantial majority have a serious disorder quite apart from any secondary deviance that may be associated with the mentally ill role (Gove, 1975: 67).

Gove argues that as medical science takes mental illness more seriously strictly psychological causes are being discovered that eliminate many of the immoral overtones traditionally associated with abnormal behavior.

Gibbs (1972) argues that labelling theory, at least as espoused by Becker, clouds the issue of whether an act is deviant only when it is publicly recognized. In analyzing Becker's typology of deviance (*see* Table 4–1), Gibbs remarks that Becker cannot speak of secret deviance when defining deviance strictly in terms of audience reaction. Instead, Gibbs proposes that the sociologist's sights should be set on any rule-breaking activity, whether observed or sanctioned or not, for societal reaction is only one factor in the total phenomenon of deviance.

Writing from the ethnomethodological perspective (see chapter 5), Pollner (1974) criticizes labelling theorists for linking theory too closely with common sense. Labelling theory is built upon the assumption that the basic elements of sociological theory are to be found in the categories by which nonsociologists interpret their world. Its objective is to see these categories as a member sees them. To do this, the labelling theorist participates in the member's world and sometimes even comes to adopt the member's perspective. The kind of theory that emerges is most often a somewhat abstract version of commonsensical explanations of social reality. The ultimate result of this tendency, according to Pollner, is to transform sociology into a folk discipline. The problem he anticipates is not simply the sociologist's unwitting acceptance of lay values and prejudices, but the incorporation into theory of common sense. For example, the concepts Becker uses in labelling theory—such terms as "secret deviance," "conforming," and "falsely accused"—are but formal synonyms for common sense expressions like "bum rap." Even the term "deviance" is closely bound to member concern for order and belonging.

Looking at sociology as a whole, its topical division into studies of organizations, race relations, collective behavior, and, of course, deviance, is an outgrowth of modern social values and concerns. The result is not a science but the apotheosis of common sense. Pollner's alternative is to devote less attention to the substance of member categories, and more attention to the process of categorization. Topical studies of social problems would become the practical side of a social science whose first task is to formulate a general theory of common sense social relations.

Labelling is not a theory in the sense that it does not fit the formal requirements of a theory; it is not a logically related set of propositions that totally explain the phenomenon under question. It could more correctly be referred to as the *labelling perspective,* for it is a way of approaching the study of deviance more than a way of explaining it. Nevertheless, this play with words does not minimize the insights produced in research by labelling theorists.

The problem of etiology, however, is one of the labelling perspective's greatest shortcomings. It is crucial for the sociologist to analyze the cause of social phenomena as they are understood and used by the layperson. Warren and Johnson (1972: 79–80), for example, clearly demonstrate in phenomenological terms how etiology is an important concern for the sociologist of deviance because it is important to the rule breaker. Moreover, all people are more or less preoccupied with the notion of causality and regularly use it to make sense of their everyday lives. Warren and Johnson showed how homosexuals reconstruct their own past, much like a criminologist would, in order to explain their present condition. Homosexuals are able to normalize their aberrant sexual preferences by showing to themselves how their condition is somehow beyond their immediate control. The homosexual may in fact "positively reinforce and legitimate the reality of the present... by rendering his present condition (and/or actions) compatible with causes from the (now) irrevocable past" (Warren and Johnson, 1972: 79).

The ethnomethodological critique of the labelling perspective's commonsensical ways of thinking and talking about deviance is reasonable (as is Warren and Johnson's critique), since some of the work in labelling reads as little more than journalistic accounts of bizarre behavior. However, Pollner's argument that deviance is simply a lay designation that should be ignored by the sociologist, and that the social experiences that fall under this rubric should be analyzed like any other behavior, is much too extreme. Deviance is not just another social form; the process of stigmatization is often a highly emotional procedure in which a person's actions and self are not merely defined but are discredited. In other words, the social designation "murderer" is categorically different from "mother" or "carpenter" and has unique consequences on the life of the person so designated. The deep feelings underlying the phenomenon of deviance should be explored more and not disregarded as irrelevant for the sociologist (see Kotarba, 1979).

The Concept of the Label

Labelling theorists have been accused of not clearly defining and operationalizing the concept of label. Little distinction has been made, for example, between labels as mechanisms of social control and labels as aspects of identity (Gove, 1975: 14). The meaning of the label and its effect upon the actor who is labelled depends upon several factors not foreseen by the early proponents of labelling theory.

Orcutt (1973: 260–261) has shown how a societal reaction to deviance can either be inclusive or exclusive. Inclusive societal reactions are intended to help the rule breaker solve his or her problem while allowing him or her to remain a viable member of the group. An exclusive societal reaction is intended to reject the rule breaker from the group and make him or her an outsider. The exclusive reaction is hostile and results in greater change in the self than the inclusive reaction.

The concept of a label has been presented most often as if the accused has little power in dealing with its effects. The actor's real power in negotiating the effects and meaning of the label has been discussed most cogently in two studies. Davis (1964) describes the process of *deviance disavowal* by which a visibly handicapped person overcomes the discomfort produced when interacting with a normal person. When the interaction begins, both parties behave as if nothing were unusual, as if the handicapped person were normal; this forms the basis for more genuine contact. In moving beyond his fictional version, the handicapped person will present images of his self that allow the normal person to identify with him in terms other than those associated directly with his handicap. The handicapped person accomplishes this by engaging in conversation he can handle competently. Hopefully, the handicapped person will eventually be able to present a self that is morally correct, in spite of the physical circumstances that surround his identity.

Trice and Roman (1970) have examined the techniques used by members of Alcoholics Anonymous to manage their stigma. Membership in AA, if successful, results in members being able to rid themselves of a morally degrading status ascribed to them as alcoholics in favor of an amoral designation that indicates a physical predisposition to alcohol that is beyond their control. Alcoholics can then shift to the repentent role of a person who has willfully conquered his problem. AA has allowed alcoholics to regain moral stature in the community by teaching them how to claim normalcy in their motives toward drinking.

The Concept of a Deviant Career

The labelling proponents' contention that the cause of career deviance is different from the cause of the original act has been challenged. Rock (1973: 23–24) argues that the idea of the moral career, presented by labelling theorists, conceives of the social processing of deviants as a predetermined and necessary path of social stages. There is little room left for voluntarism or uncertainty, and the future life chances of the accused are seen as governed by "inevitable and irreversible social forms. . . . the deviant becomes a mechanical and simplified automaton who is ruled by forces over which he has little control" (Rock, 1973: 23; see also Taylor, et al., 1975: 153). Put differently, the labelling proponents have not clearly demonstrated the social or psychological difference between motivation in the original act and motivation in subsequent acts. They assume that the original motive to deviate ceases to exist, and that all deviance after labelling has occurred is caused by the discrediting reaction of others:

> The most salient theoretical difficulty is in the conception of initial rule-breaking and the nature of the sources which bring it into being. There is a premise in the writing of the labelling theorists that whatever the causes of the initial rule-breaking, they assume minimal importance or entirely cease operation after initial rule-breaking . . . Without such a premise, one might attribute career deviance and its consequences not to societal reaction but to the continued effects of social structural strains, psychological stress, or disease states which produce initial rule-breaking (Mankoff, 1971: 211).

The power of the label in shaping either the self-image or life chances of the labelled varies across situations and categories of deviance. The label of mental illness, for example, usually has profound effects on a person's self, whereas a label relating to a physical illness usually has a transitory effect. Kotarba's (1977) research on patients with chronic pain demonstrates how they learn to adapt to pain in their everyday lives while continuously searching for a cure. Their motivation for pursuing such unorthodox and devious health care modalities as chiropractic, acupuncture, and hypnosis is not the result of being labelled as a hypochrondiac by significant others or by members of the medical profession; it is the result of the initial motivation for seeing a doctor—pain. The core motive at all steps of the career is the search for relief from the physical sensation of pain, not any intermediate social definitions of the self or of the patient's physical condition.

The concept of a deviant career in labelling theory can be a useful device for understanding how a labelled deviant adapts to and manages relevant social audiences. The emphasis on the public aspect of deviance precludes considering secret rule-breaking. A complete understanding of deviance requires an examination of the means used by rule breakers to avoid labelling. The *subversion of labelling* (Kotarba, 1978) occurs when an individual (or members of a deviant subculture) actively takes steps to minimize the probability of being caught by a rule enforcer. Regular and heavy tavern drinkers, for example, often exchange information on ways of avoiding arrest for driving while intoxicated. They mention heavily patrolled roads that should be avoided, methods for bribing an arresting officer, and names of lawyers with clout in the courts. In certain tavern settings where off-duty police congregate, the regular clientele establish friendships with the police for the sole purpose of using them as resources in the event of being stopped while drunk and driving. These friendships are then used as in-group membership devices that place the arresting officer in the morally awkward position of having to arrest a person who shares important identity traits with him (e.g., both may be aware that they are city workers, or Irishmen, or drinking buddies in the same bar). Often the traffic officer resists making an arrest under such circumstances.

Labelling Theory and the Future Study of Deviant Behavior

In response to the many negative reactions to the early formulations of labelling theory, its original proponents have modified their views. In the revised edition of *Outsiders*, Becker (1970) agrees that the labelling perspective is really not a theory, but insists that it was never intended to explain all facets of deviance, especially not its etiology. The original goal was simply to expand the scope of the study of deviance to include the activities of all parties concerned: the rule makers, enforcers, and breakers. Becker now rejects the use of the term "rule-breaking" altogether and substitutes the word "commission." He intends this change in terminology to lead to focusing on the accusation and definition of deviance, as well as to mitigate problems in labelling terminology. Becker also responds to his Marxist critics by reiterating the "leftist" leanings of the labelling proponents and by calling for more research into power relations as factors in the creation of deviance.

Among the original labelling theorists, Lemert (1974) goes furthest in repudiating the value of labelling theory. He has disassociated himself from the perspective for several reasons. First, he believes labelling theory places so much emphasis on the underdog that it compromises the researcher's scientific integrity. Second, labelling theorists use "dramatic metaphors" that lead to an analysis of interaction implying that the "other" (such as the "agent of social control") is a set of unbending rules. These metaphors ignore the likely possibility that dissension is common within the ranks of the dominant group. Instead of concentrating on the development of a social-psychological model such as labelling theory, Lemert now opts for a group interaction model. As in game theory, this model focuses upon "the shifting significance of ends and means and their costs in the emergence of new patterns of social control" (Lemert, 1974: 459) that can be analyzed scientifically. In other words, Lemert sees the creation of deviance as a process of interactional negotiation in which certain "old" social rules are no longer worth enforcing, as is occurring with marihuana use today. In a sense, one could say that Lemert's new position is similar to Pollner's, in that he calls for a more objective and scientific interpretation of deviance.

Scheff (1974) reviews the recent literature on mental illness and finds nothing to refute his original theory. He feels that continuing research from many perspectives has supported his model. The medical-psychiatric model of mental illness still relies on data collected in medical settings, which is therefore biased in its formulation and intent. Although diagnosis and treatment have been improved, designating mental illness is still dependent upon judgments made of behavior with uncertain meanings.[13]

What verdict, then, can be passed on the labelling perspective? By and large, labelling theory has had a good effect on sociology. First, it has sensitized sociologists to features of deviance, to what is deviant, who is deviant, and who considers an act deviant. These aspects of deviance were previously ignored or taken for granted by sociologists (see Goode, 1975: 581–582). Second, labelling theory focused upon the creation of deviance at the level of interaction. By returning to the field-research tradition of the "Green Bible," students of labelling theory have been able to vividly describe how deviance occurs in everyday life; they have reaffirmed the humanism missing from structural-functionalism. Third, labelling theory has brought the issue of power to the fore. Although they have missed the full implications of differences in social power, labelling theorists have at least countered the value-consensus position of the structural-functionalists.

The greatest contribution of the labelling theorists has been as an intermediary between micro and macro research and conceptualization. Because of its conceptual limitations, labelling theory serves sociology best through its vivid ethnographic descriptions of phenomena that form the necessary foundations of any theory of deviance. In other words, the labelling and symbolic interactionist orientation allows the researcher to begin at the everyday level of deviance and, after conceptualizing his other research, to return to the everyday level so that his or her findings can be read and made sense of by both colleagues and laypersons.

In dealing with micro and macro issues, we must avoid oversimplified theories which, like previous theories of deviance, do not explain. We must explore as many facets of morality construction and conceptualization as we can. Several writers in the field of deviant behavior are already directing their efforts in that direction. Rock (1973 and 1974) argues that process and structure are both relevant to deviant behavior, at least insofar as the actors involved maintain and react to ideas of social structure in their everyday lives. These notions of social or moral structure can be systematically studied through the process of eidectic (i.e., phenomenological) reduction (see chapter 5). Manning (1975) argues that the addition of an historical dimension to the labelling perspective would serve two functions. First, historical analysis would supplant the labelling proponents' insistence on interest group rule-creation by demonstrating how certain social movements and trends originate from a combination of factors or "causes." Second, historical analysis would demonstrate how the use of meanings in everyday life changes over time. Finally, Douglas (1978) connects deviance and social change in light of the emotional/affective elements of human behavior. Rules reflect the conservative bias of culture and society that is threatened when changes in feelings and perceived situations occur within large segments of the population, especially when they occur within what are known as deviant subcultures. Creative deviance is the process by which these affective changes are reflected in routinized rule-breaking that spreads throughout the population and eventually becomes codified itself, culminating in what is known as social change.

We can see, then, that the labelling perspective, in spite of its many shortcomings, has opened the door to many new and exciting approaches to deviant behavior. Our current responsibility is to engage in productive research without shutting this door:

> On inspection, the policeman and delinquent, prison officer and prisoner, bailiff and debtor, judge and defendent, are inhabitants of a world which is marked by pluralism *and* absolutism, consensus *and* dissensus, conflict *and* unity. It is the disentanglement of these features, the mapping out of their connections, and the understanding of their effects that is the critical research task, not the simple application of a few over-arching concepts (Rock, 1974: 148).

Notes

1. See Douglas (1971) for a valuable discussion of the various sociological views on order and disorder, especially as they relate to perceptions of deviance in contemporary American society.

2. Although Merton further developed Durkheim's notion of anomie, he in effect reversed its meaning. Durkheim felt that the breakdown of normative controls in a society led to anomie or normlessness. Merton, on the other hand,

feels that anomie results from the correct internalization of values and norms whose satisfaction is structurally inhibited (see Taylor et al., 1973: 91–96).

3. Merton lists four possible modes of adaptation for people who either cannot or will not conform. These are *innovation,* when illegitimate means (e.g., crime) are used to attain cultural goals; *ritualism,* when the lofty goals of success are lowered and legitimate means are used to acquire moderate goals; *retreatism,* when both the institutionalized means and goals of society are rejected; and *rebellion,* when the person wishes to replace the established system and means and goals. Innovation is by far the most common adaptation, due to the high value placed upon the goal of success in our society. This is the course usually taken by members of the lower class who cannot bear the strain of their social position (according to Merton's theory).

4. The problems inherent in using official statistics as a data base in sociological research are well documented in Kitsuse and Cicourel (1963), Matza (1964); and Douglas (1967).

5. Matza (1964 and 1969), who is often included among the labelling theorists, proposes what is probably the most descriptive form of deviance analysis. His major theme is *naturalism,* the constant attempt to remain true to the phenomenon. His writings purport to relay a vivid picture of deviant behavior that the deviant himself would recognize.

6. See Faris (1967) and chapter 2 of this book for other comments on the early and formative years of the Department of Sociology at the University of Chicago.

7. Altheide, et al. (1978) present a concise summary of writings on secret deviance as it occurs routinely in employee theft at all levels of business and industry.

8. Cameron (1943) relates the traditional psychiatric view of the paranoid pseudo-community.

9. Rosen (1963) views the historical and political development of the mental asylum in a similar way.

10. Katz (1972) argues that the designation of witchcraft throughout history has not been the reaction to any specific rule violation, but is the imputation of a demeaning label to offenders who elicit great irrational fear among community members.

11. Rosenthal (1968) utilized this model to account for the institution of informal rules within the classroom setting. Gusfield (1963) applied the notion of interest groups to the development of the W.C.T.U. that eventually led to Prohibition. Prohibition was originally proposed by traditional, rural, Protestant, and abstaining groups who viewed the influx of Catholic and European immigrants (and their supposedly excessive use of alcohol) as a threat to traditional American values. Thus, alcohol became a symbolic issue that allowed the "old Americans" to reassert their own values and status.

12. Manning (1975 and 1977) has shown how simplistic notions of interest group power do not adequately explain complex social creations. For example, some writers perceive the origin of the civil police in England as the work of the ruling class in maintaining control over the masses. Manning, on the other hand, argues that many cultural and social factors that cut across class lines led to the formation of the police.

13. Anderson and Wilkinson (1974) are among many researchers who present strong empirical evidence in support of Scheff's position.

References

AKERS, RONALD L. "Problems in the Sociology of Deviance: Social Definitions and Behavior." *Social Forces,* 46: 455–65.

ALTHEIDE, DAVID et al. "Employee Theft." In Jack D. Douglas and John M. Johnson (eds.), *Business and Professional Deviance.* Philadelphia: J P. Lippincott, 1978.

ANDERSON, JOHN P. and G. S. Wilkinson. "Psychiatric Illness and Labelling Theory: An Analysis of Gove's Critique." Paper presented at the meetings of the A.S.A., Montreal, August 1974.

BECKER, HOWARD S. *Outsiders.* 2nd ed. New York: The Free Press, 1973.

CAMERON, NORMAN. "The Paranoid Pseudocommunity." *American Journal of Sociology,* 46 (1943).

CAVAN, RUTH S. *Suicide.* Chicago: University of Chicago Press, 1928.

COHEN, ALBERT K. *Delinquent Boys: The Culture of the Gang.* Glencoe, Ill.: The Free Press, 1955.

DAVIS, FRED. "Deviance Disavowal: The Management of Strained Interaction by the Visibly Handicapped." In Howard S. Becker (ed.), *Outsiders.* 2nd ed. New York: The Free Press, 1973.

DAVIS, NANETTE J. *Sociological Construction of Deviance.* Dubuque, Iowa: Wm. C. Brown Co., 1975.

DICKSON, DONALD T. "Bureaucracy and Morality: An Organizational Perspective on a Moral Crusade." *Social Problems,* 16 (1968).

DOUGLAS, JACK D. *The Social Meanings of Suicide.* Princeton, N.J.: Princeton University Press, 1967.

DOUGLAS, JACK D. *American Social Order.* New York: The Free Press, 1971.

DOUGLAS, JACK D. and JOHN M. JOHNSON, eds., *Existential Sociology.* New Sagarin (ed.), *Social Change and Deviance.* Beverly Hills, Calif.: Sage, 1977.

DOUGLAS, JACK D. and JOHN M. JOHNSON, eds., *Existential Sociology.* New York: Cambridge University Press, 1977.

DURKHEIM, EMILE. *Rules of the Sociological Method.* New York: The Free Press, 1964.

ERIKSON, KAI T. "Notes on the Sociology of Deviance." *Social Problems,* 9 (1962).

ERIKSON, KAI T. *Wayward Puritans.* New York: John Wiley & Sons, 1966.

FARIS, ROBERT E. L. *Chicago Sociology.* San Francisco: Chandler, 1967.

FOUCAULT, MICHEL. *Madness and Civilization.* New York: Random House, 1965.

FREIDSON, ELIOT. *Profession of Medicine: A Study of the Sociology of Applied Knowledge.* New York: Dodd, Mead and Co., 1970.

GIBBS, JACK P. "Conceptions of Deviant Behavior: The Old and the New." *Pacific Sociological Review*, 9 (Spring 1966).

GIBBS, JACK P. "Issues in Defining Deviant Behavior." In Robert A. Scott and Jack D. Douglas (eds.), *Theoretical Perspectives on Deviance*. New York: Basic Books, 1972.

GOFFMAN, ERVING. *Stigma: Notes on the Management of Spoiled Identity*. Harmondsworth, England: Penguin, 1968.

GOODE, ERICH. "On Behalf of Labelling Theory." *Social Problems*, 22 (1975).

GOULDNER, ALVIN W. "Anti-Minitaur: The Myth of the Value-Free Sociology." *Social Problems*, 9 (1962).

GOVE, WALTER R. *The Labelling of Deviance*. New York: John Wiley & Sons, 1975.

HAWKINS, RICHARD and GARY TIEDEMAN. *The Creation of Deviance*. Columbus, Ohio: Charles E. Merrill, 1975.

HOFFMAN, M. *The Gay World: Male Homosexuality and the Social Creation of Evil*. New York: Basic Books, 1968.

HUGHES, EVERETT C. "Dilemmas and Contradictions of Status." *American Journal of Sociology*, 50 (1945).

HUGHES, EVERETT C. "Introduction." In Richard Wright, *Black Metropolis: A Study of Negro Life in a Northern City*. New York: Harcourt Brace, 1945.

JACKSON, D. D. *The Etiology of Schizophrenia*. New York: Basic Books, 1960.

JOHNSON, JOHN M. and JACK D. DOUGLAS, eds., *Crime at the Top: Deviance in Business and the Professions*. Philadelphia: J. B. Lippincott, 1978.

KITSUSE, JOHN I. and AARON V. CICOUREL. "A Note on the Uses of Official Statistics." *Social Problems*, 11 (1963).

KOTARBA, JOSEPH A. "The Chronic Pain Experience." In Jack D. Douglas and John M. Johnson (eds.), *Existential Sociology*. New York: Cambridge University Press, 1977.

KOTARBA, JOSEPH A. "One More for the Road: The Subversion of Labelling within the Tavern Subculture." In Jack D. Douglas (ed.), *Observations of Deviance*, 2nd ed. New York: Random House, 1978.

KOTARBA, JOSEPH A. "Existential Sociology." In Scott G. McNall (ed.), *Theoretical Perspectives in Sociology*. Boston: Allyn and Bacon, 1979.

LEMERT, EDWIN M. "Paranoia and the Dynamics of Exclusion." *Sociometry*, 25 (1962).

LEMERT, EDWIN M. *Human Deviance, Social Problems, and Social Control*. New York: Prentice-Hall, 1967.

LEMERT, EDWIN M. "Beyond Mead: The Societal Reaction to Deviance." *Social Problems*, 21 (1974).

MANDERS, DEAN. "Labelling Theory and Social Reality: A Marxist Critique." *The Insurgent Sociologist*, 6 (1975).

MANKOFF, MILTON. "Societal Reaction and Career Deviance: A Critical Analysis." *The Sociological Quarterly*, 12 (1971).

MANNING, PETER K. "Deviance and Dogma." *British Journal of Criminology.* 15 (1975).

MANNING, PETER K. *Police Work: The Social Organization of Policing.* Cambridge, Mass.: The MIT Press, 1977.

MARSHALL, H. and R. PURDY. "Hidden Deviance and the Labelling Approach: The Case for Drinking and Driving." *Social Problems,* 19 (1972).

MATZA, DAVID. *Delinquency and Drift.* New York: John Wiley & Sons, 1964.

MCHUGH, PETER. "A Common-sense Conception of Deviance." In Jack D. Douglas (ed.), *Deviance and Respectability.* New York: Basic Books, 1970.

MERCER, JANE R. "Understanding Career Patterns of Persons Labelled as Mentally Retarded." *Social Problems,* 13 (1965).

MERTON, R. K. "Social Structure and Anomie." *American Sociological Review,* 3 (1938).

MERTON, R. K. "Anomie, Anomia and Social Interaction." In M. B. Clinard (ed.), *Anomie and Deviant Behavior.* New York: The Free Press, 1964.

ORCUTT, JAMES. "Societal Reaction and the Response to Deviation in Small Groups." *Social Forces,* 52 (1973).

PARK, ROBERT E. and E. W. Burgess. *Introduction to the Science of Sociology.* Chicago: University of Chicago Press, 1921.

POLLNER, MELVIN. "Sociological and Common-Sense Models of the Labelling Process." In Roy Turner (ed.), *Ethnomethodology.* Harmondsworth, England: Penguin Books, 1974.

QUINNEY, RICHARD. *Critique of Legal Order.* Boston, Little, Brown and Co., 1974.

Rock, Paul. "Phenomenalism and Essentialism in the Sociology of Deviancy." *Sociology,* 7 (1973).

ROCK, PAUL. "The Sociology of Deviancy and Conceptions of Moral Order." *British Journal of Criminology,* 14 (1974).

ROSEN, GEORGE. "Social Attitudes to Irrationality and Madness in 17th and 18th Century Europe." *Journal of the History of Medicine and Allied Sciences,* 18 (1963).

ROSENTHAL, ROBERT. *Pygmalion in the Classroom: Teacher Expectation and Pupil's Intellectual Development.* New York: Holt, Rinehart and Winston, 1968.

RUBINGTON, EARL and MARTIN WEINBERG. *The Study of Social Problems.* New York: Oxford University Press, 1971.

SCHEFF, THOMAS J. *Being Mentally Ill: A Sociological Theory.* Chicago: Aldine Publishing Co., 1966.

SCHEFF, THOMAS J. "The Labelling Theory of Mental Illness." *American Sociological Review,* 39 (1974).

SCHUR, EDWIN M. *Crimes without Victims: Deviant Behavior and Public Policy.* Englewood Cliffs, N.J.: Prentice-Hall, 1965.

SHAW, CLIFFORD R. and H. D. McKAY. *Juvenile Delinquency and Urban Areas.* Chicago: University of Chicago Press, 1931.

Sutherland, Edwin H. *Principles of Criminology*. Philadelphia: J. B. Lippincott, 1939.

Tannenbaum, Frank. *Crime and the Community*. New York: Columbia University Press, 1938.

Taylor, Ian et al. *The New Criminology*. London: Routledge Kegan Paul, 1973.

Trice, Harrison M. and Paul Roman. "Delabeling, Relabeling, and Alcoholics Anonymous." *Social Problems,* 17 (1970).

Warren, Carol A. B. and John M. Johnson. "A Critique of Labelling Theory from the Phenomenological Perspective." In Robert A. Scott and Jack D. Douglas (eds.), *Theoretical Perspectives on Deviance*. New York: Basic Books, 1972.

Wright, Richard. *Black Metropolis: A Study of Negro Life in a Northern City*. St. Clair Drake and Horace R. Cayton. New York: Harcourt, Brace, and Co., 1945. ("Introduction").

5

Phenomenological Sociology and Ethnomethodology

C. ROBERT FREEMAN

More than any other sociology of everyday life, phenomenological sociology is a study of ideas and thinking. In its most disciplined form, it seems less a study of everyday life than a study of cognition. In general, individuals attracted to phenomenological sociology have had a keen interest in general questions of theory and method. When they are antitheoretical, it is on the basis of a reasoned commitment to a highly abstract view of humans and cognition. Even in their studies of method they have been more concerned with presuppositions than with substance or outcomes. Phenomenological sociology is the most "lifeless" of the sociologies of everyday life.

One outcome of this cleaving to the abstract is the relative scarcity within phenomenological sociology of empirical research. What little research exists has been actually an exercise in theory or an unnecessary appendage. Although there are signs that this tendency is abating (see Jules-Rosette, 1978), phenomenological sociology is still predominantly a field for the thinking person who is against intellectuals.

Because of the paucity of research in this field, this essay will take a somewhat different form from the preceding discussions of the sociologies of everyday life. Rather than using research to illustrate theory, we will consider the advent, persistence, and change of certain ideas within phenomenological sociology. These ideas have their origins in philosophy—in the phenomenologies of Edmund Husserl and Alfred Schutz. Although phenomenological philosophy is often difficult to understand, it is very important because it is the core around which modern phenomenological sociology has developed.

Most broadly, *phenomenological sociology* refers to the work of a number of sociologists who share certain sympathies regarding phenomenological philosophy. Ther work, however, is not philosophical, nor have their sympathies for the philosophy always taken a constant expression. Indeed, the sociologists to be discussed are somewhat uneven in their regard for and implementation of phenomenology.

In this chapter we will review a number of attempts to incorporate phenomenology into sociology. The discussion will draw from both philosophy (Husserl, Schutz, and Luckmann) and sociology (Tiryakian, Douglas, and Blumensteil). It of course will not be exhaustive. We will consider the difference between phenomenological sociologists studying the conditions of social order (Tiryakian, Wagner, and Jehenson) and those studying the conditions of competent social interaction (Garfinkle, Zimmerman, Pollner, Weider, and Cicourel). This division is somewhat artificial and may obscure other differences. Nevertheless, the division is important because it originates in alternative interpretations of the work of Schutz.

Phenomenology and Common Sense

Phenomenological analysis has as its subject matter the world of conscious experience. When looked at in terms of its rudimentary elements, this world consists of the numerous and shifting inputs of perception. Since most perception is quickly and effortlessly organized into certain customary patterns, the world appears as a familiar one. It is not unusual for the familiarity of the world to become so compelling that the work that goes into achieving this familiarity is overlooked. The major thrust of phenomenology is to reverse this process by penetrating to the formative core of consciousness. To understand phenomenological philosophy —and much of phenomenological sociology—it is important to understand the implications of this peculiar interest in the constituents of the familiar world.

Perhaps the most basic implication, and the one most often misunderstood, lies in the need for phenomenological analysis to proceed from a stance alien to that of the common-sense individual. This individual, through experience and socialization, is so adept at seeing his or her world as ordered that the work which goes into seeing this order becomes automatic, a matter of unthinking common sense. Most people would fall into the category of the common-sense individual. The phenomenologist, on the other hand, emphasizes the complexity of even the most basic acts of perception. Husserl put the matter clearly in addressing how "the general thesis of the natural standpoint" (his phrase for designating the presuppositions of the perspective of common-sense) tends to organize apprehension of the environment. Describing the character of his own uncritical everyday awareness, Husserl said:

> I find continually present and standing over against me the one spatio-temporal fact-world to which I myself belong, as do all other men found in it and related in the same way to it. This "fact-world," as the word already tells us, I find to *be out there,* and also *take it just as it gives itself to me as something that exists out there.* All doubting and rejecting of the data of the natural world leaves standing the *general thesis of the natural standpoint.* "The" world is a fact-world always there; at the most it is at odd points other than I supposed, this or that under such names as "illusion," "hallucination," and the like, must be struck *out of it,* so to speak; but the "it" remains ever, in the sense of the general thesis, a world that has its being out there. (Husserl, 1962: 96; emphasis in the original)
>
> . . . this world is not there for me as a mere *world of facts and affairs,* but, with the same immediacy, as a *world of values, a world of goods,* a *practical world.* Without further effort on my part I find the things before me furnished not only with the qualities that befit their positive nature, but with value-characters such as beautiful or ugly, agreeable or disagreeable, pleasant or unpleasant, and so forth. Things in their immediacy stand there as objects to be used, the "table" with its "books," the "glass to drink from," the "vase," the "piano," and so forth. These values and practicalities, they too belong to *the constitution of the actually present objects as such,* irrespective of my turning or not turning to consider them or indeed any other objects. (Husserl, 1962: 93; emphasis in the original)

The natural standpoint or attitude is much like common sense; both are an outgrowth of our routine involvement in daily life. We see in the natural attitude only the highly structured contents of an ordered world, wherein much is accepted as evident prior to any reflection.

Of course, some types of reflection do occur within the natural attitude. Goffman (1959) has shown that a social actor may be deeply concerned about the merits of his or her performance, reflecting at length about the alternative strategies for presenting himself or herself. Lyman and Scott (1970) have further suggested that even the standards by which a performance is judged are uncertain. The modern actor cannot simply mold her performance in accord with certain clear principles; she must consider the varied and problematic tastes of her audience. Since these tastes are discerned only ambiguously, fleeting clues must be quickly interpreted and acted upon. This makes social life a risky venture requiring both the talents of a performer and the judgment of a skilled social analyst.

Reflection occurring within the natural attitude is not radical in the manner of phenomenological reflection, because it presupposes a world that is already constituted and familiar. For every aspect of everyday life in need of attention, there are yet many more that may be taken for granted. Even Lyman and Scott, who call their enterprise a "sociology of the absurd," do not see the individual as confronted by a meaningless world. Their view of a world without intrinsic meaning is balanced by an awareness of the extent to which this same world is experienced by those within it as meaningful. The use of the term "absurd" indicates not the absence of meaning, but its variability and uncertain availability.

The radical nature of phenomenological reflection has often been misunderstood. Often this is because phenomenological analysis lends itself to certain errors in interpretation. Phenomenology is often mistakenly confused with the study of common sense. Many problems in the interpretation of phenomenology derive from a failure to distinguish the phenomenologist's more narrow use of the term "common sense" from that of the educated layperson's use of the word. The educated layperson—who today often has some knowledge of the results of sociological investigation—recognizes that individuals living in different social contexts tend to regard the world differently. Consider beliefs about something as basic as bodily health. In Western culture, it is regarded as normal for one to go to a doctor if ill. Some cultures regard Western medicine with suspicion; even those who have assimilated such a culture may prefer to employ the services of local healers whose diagnoses and treatments are derived from a different theory of sickness. Many of the differences among people have their locus in the character of the social environment.

Given that certain beliefs do vary across cultures, is there not also something common in the manner in which individuals regard the world? A phenomenologist would suggest that certain basic patterns of mental organization characterize all people. The natural attitude, for example, appears to be a constant feature of the processes of interpretation. Regardless of the specific contents of a perspective, the world it reveals is not without some structure and consistency. This availability of an ordered world—so basic to mundane awareness that it escapes all scrutiny—is the subject matter of phenomenological investigation.

The radical nature of such investigation derives from its concern with the basic processes that underlie any version of common sense. This concern with the unnoticed constituents of everyday awareness may be illustrated by showing how a typical phenomenological analysis would address a familiar scene. Schutz used this strategy often, and the following remarks rely on his work (especially 1962; 1970; and Schutz and Luckmann, 1973). For simplicity, my own perceptual field will provide the subject matter.

The world does not appear to me with all its aspects possessing equal clarity. Looking closely at my perceptions, I find that my awareness contains a "kernel" that appears clear and self-evident, and a "horizon" or "fringe" that remains undetermined. My attention is now focused on the words that I am writing, but I am also vaguely aware of the texture of the pen and a dog barking in the background. These "items on my horizon" are apprehended with the tacit belief that my awareness of them can be heightened and made clear. If I should redirect my attention, what is within the fringe could become the kernel of my awareness.

Continuing my analysis, I find myself in a world that is largely taken for granted. This familiarity is the unexamined ground of everything given in my experience and the taken-for-granted frame in which the problems I encounter are placed. This familiarity partially derives from my previous experience. I have written at a desk often in the past and the sedimentation of these experiences greatly influences the expectations that flow from my present circumstances. I do not question the usefulness or purpose of the items on my desk, but instead allow my attention to be directed by the requirements of my practical involvements. Drafting this essay, my thoughts and behavior are dominated by the desire to work through the analysis; awareness of the pen I am holding is a peripheral concern. Only when the familiarity of the world is interrupted by the unexpected must I redirect my attention to the taken-for-granted. Perhaps the pen stops working. No longer do I continue writing, but the state of mind characteristic of this concern is supplanted by an awareness of the pen. What was once clear and distinct fades into imprecision; what was only vaguely apprehended now dominates my attention. The world does not appear in an even glow; it presents itself to me in zones of clarity and imprecision that shift with the changing locus of my practical concerns.

My analysis of my awareness, related above, describes the texture of the common-sense world and the structures that create and sustain its familiarity. It does not deal with the particulars of subjective interpretation, but with the architecture of human thought. Some have confused phenomenological analysis with a study of common sense probably because it describes the familiar. But the processes sought by the phenomenologist are as evident in "uncommon" sense as in "common" sense; it is just that the latter is more readily available.

The illustration of my awareness of writing at my desk dealt with the shift in perspective that occurs when the taken-for-granted features of awareness are reduced to the basic contents and processes from which they arose. Phenomenologists are concerned with the natural attitude—

its structure, durability, and pervasiveness. The natural attitude does not have the same significance for all phenomenologists. For Husserl, the founder of phenomenology, the natural attitude was an obstacle to absolute truth. His most strenuous efforts were devoted to ridding the researcher of the presuppositions that deny unbiased access to the *a priori* structures of subjective experience. Schutz, on the other hand, saw the natural attitude as the foundation of social experience. He sought to explicate the natural attitude in order to expose the basic structure of common-sense experience.

For the rest of this chapter, the term "common sense" will be used to refer to the basic constituents of familiarity. The "common-sense individual" will designate anyone who is viewing the world from the natural standpoint.

Phenomenological Philosophy

Edmund Husserl

Edmund Husserl (1859–1938) was the founder of phenomenology. His voluminous and difficult work has been of fundamental importance within phenomenology and has an influence far beyond philosophy to psychology, anthropology, history, linguistics, and sociology. The range of this influence may be partly attributed to Husserl's opinion that philosophy was capable of the rigor of science. In his essay "Philosophy as Rigorous Science" (1965), Husserl argued that philosophy could reveal truths that were at once fundamental and invariable. In this view, his work was a radical departure from the ideas that dominated the intellectual environment of the turn-of-the-century.

The radical nature of Husserl's work might perhaps be understood most clearly by first considering its objectives. The phenomenology of Husserl was an attempt to rebuild the foundations of the natural sciences. Husserl thought the weakness of these foundations had given rise to a crisis that promoted two opposite but equally dangerous views (Husserl, 1965). First, some scholars doubted the possibility of absolute truth. They held truth to be a matter of belief, relative to the cultural and historical positions of its adherents. They regarded science as a collection of opinions, neither universally shared nor capable of rigorous justification.

The second prevailing view naively affirmed the validity of the scientific method. The result was the affirmation of absolute truth, but the advancement of false procedures for its discovery. Husserl was particularly wary of those who offered the methods of the natural sciences as the model for all scientific inquiry. Although he had great respect for the natural sciences, Husserl rejected the assertion that they could disclose absolute truth. However powerful, the natural sciences were erected upon unexamined foundations: all accepted the existence of the spatio-temporal world and the servicibility of scientific procedures (Husserl, 1962; 19). Husserl felt that ultimately this would preclude rigorous claims about the nature and validity of scientific investigation.

Husserl was also concerned about the use of the natural sciences as a model for investigations into human thought and consciousness (Husserl, 1965; 152–153). He believed this would result in limiting scientific attention to only those phenomena available to direct observation. Consciousness by necessity would be either rejected as a fiction or transformed into something physical. Both ideas would lead to the substitution of the visible expressions of consciousness, such as overt behavior or physiological measurements, for the whole of the subjective process. Mind was transformed by fiat into another aspect of the natural, amenable to the same modes of exploration.

Husserl rejected the belief that consciousness could be studied as if it were an object. Consciousness is not an object, nor a product of an object. Its nature is not only a reflection of the outer world, but also a creation of its own activity. Husserl said that consciousness is neither objective nor subjective, but is at once both. Husserl expressed this dual nature of consciousness as intentionality. *Intentionality* refers to the fact that consciousness is always consciousness of something, that consciousness always points beyond itself—it intends—some object. One is never just conscious, but conscious of things or feelings or thoughts. At all times awareness has an object. The corollary of this is also true: there is no apprehension of the world that is not evident in consciousness, since consciousness is the experiential form in which the world appears.

Husserl's ambition to create an absolute science led him to seek a foundation in a realm whose availability was certain and unquestionable. He found such a realm in the depths of immediate awareness, that substratum of experience whose aspects are wholly contained within consciousness. Founded within this certain realm, phenomenology was to have avoided two basic errors. First, its reliance on solely the certain data of immediate experience meant that phenomenology did not presuppose the value of logic or deductive proof. Husserl considered it important that his investigations not presuppose the legitimacy of any particular explanatory form. Rather, he sought in his studies to use only the data of immediate experience.

And second, phenomenology avoided a commitment to the empirical world as the first and most basic source of certainty and truth. Husserl considered this important because any limitation of investigation of the empirical world would make phenomenology dependent on the limited range of items disclosed in nature.

But what else is available? Husserl's answer to this question pointed to the capacity of consciousness to extend the field of investigation by imagining variations of its factual experience. The fact that no unicorns exist, for example, does not prohibit the researcher from using this image to test the limits of consciousness. Moreover, investigation is not limited to an object in consciousness; the very grasping of the object can be made a topic of inquiry. For example, Husserl examined the differences in clarity and distinctness that occur when a perception is replaced by a memory of the perception. Investigation may thus include systematic description of pure intentional processes. With the addition of investigations into the different modes of consciousness (e.g., perception and imagination), Husserl provided the basis for what he regarded as an essential science of pure possibility.

Although it is not clear whether Husserl considered it possible for a science to be completely free of presuppositions (Farber, 1967), he did regard the ideal as approachable. The first step was to "disconnect" the natural standpoint, or the standpoint of the common-sense individual, from practical reflection. Since practical reflection diverts attention from the presuppositions of the natural standpoint, disconnecting practical reflection from the standpoint serves to make these presuppositions evident. But Husserl did not stop here. This step, which Husserl called the *epoché*, was only preliminary to a distillation of experience to its invariable core. Husserl relied on the formative character of consciousness: by imagining variations of his experience, Husserl sought to remove from an experience all that was incidental or contingent. This process—which he called the *reduction*—would presumably reveal what aspects of an experience could not be removed without making an experience fundamentally different. That which remained after the reduction—the *essence* of the experience—represented an invariable core, which could be incorporated into absolute science.

Husserl increasingly emphasized the need for a further reduction of experience, a reduction that would disclose the constitution of the world within the transcendental Ego.[1] This last step required that the empirical Ego, the Ego naturally immersed in the world, be reduced and the phenomenological Ego established as a disinterested onlooker (Husserl, 1970: 34–35). This point in Husserl's work was marked by increasing idealism. It posed in its most basic form the problem of *intersubjectivity*, or our knowledge of other beings. This last problem received attention from Husserl in his famous Fifth Meditation (Husserl, 1970: 89–151), wherein he attempted to derive intersubjectivity from within the transcendental sphere.

In sum, Husserl's work should be understood as an attempt to provide an adequate foundation for the natural sciences by tracing all scientific investigation to its origins in immediate experience. He sought to eliminate presuppositions, the greatest obstacle to clear understanding, by confining all claims to truth to that which is disclosed within the realm of consciousness. He regarded consciousness not merely as a product or receptor of some feature of reality, but as an active force in the constitution of that reality. He used this recognition of the formative character of consciousness as a basis for criticizing sciences that naively accepted their subject matter as well defined and ordered. In addition, Husserl used the idea of the formative nature of consciousness to supplant the sciences of nature with a science of pure possibility. By imagining variations of factual experience, he sought to investigate the limits of consciousness, independent of the limits of nature. In this way, he hoped to create a science of pure possibility. Finally, Husserl sought to investigate the constitution of the world from within the transcendental sphere.

Alfred Schutz

Social Implications of the Natural Attitude.   Husserl, who attempted to provide a foundation for the natural sciences, was not explicitly concerned with the social sciences.[2] The thrust of his work was to shift attention from the common-sense individual and his and her world to the essential structures of the transcendental Ego. Alfred Schutz (1899–1959) clearly demonstrated the fruitfulness of redirecting Husserl's program from transcendental investigation to a systematic description of the natural attitude. He sought to employ Husserl's insights into the nature of consciousness to explain the structures, basis, and dimensions of social knowledge.

Schutz's high regard for Husserl's work is evident throughout his writings. Although he departed from Husserl's transcendental approach, Schutz clearly accepted the value and even necessity of transcendental investigations.[3] But Schutz could not accept what he regarded as a subtle shift in Husserl's use of the term "constitution":

> At the beginning of phenomenology, constitution meant clarification of the sense-structure of conscious life, inquiry into sediments in respect of their history, tracing back all *cogitata* to intentional operations of the on-going conscious life. These discoveries of phenomenology are of lasting value; their validity has, up to now, been unaffected by any critique, and they are of the greatest importance for the foundation of the positive sciences, especially of the social world. For it remains true that whatever is exhibited under the reduction retains its validity after return to the natural attitude of the life-world. But unobtrusively, and almost unaware, it seems to me, the idea of constitution has changed from a clarification of sense-structure, from an explication of the sense of being, into the foundation of the structure of being. It has changed from explication into creation . . . . (Schutz, 1966: 83).

Schutz is saying that Husserl's use of the term "constitution" implies that the world is simply an artifact of the formative character of consciousness. The view, a version of idealism, locates the source of all things in the individual human mind. Schutz observed that any such idealistic view is foreign to the thinking of the common-sense individual, who has little trouble accepting the existence and intelligibility of the world. This led Schutz to conclude that the foundation for understanding the world as it is experienced by the common-sense individual is the natural standpoint.

Schutz's commitment to the world of the common-sense individual led to a crucial departure from Husserl's work. As we said previously, Husserl tried to prove the possibility of knowledge of other minds (intersubjectivity) from within the transcendental sphere. But Schutz, who was content to stay within the common-sense world, observed that intersubjectivity seldom becomes an issue for the common-sense individual: "But the solution of this most difficult problem [intersubjectivity] of philosophical interpretation is one of the first things taken for granted in our common-sense thinking and practically solved without difficulty in each of our everyday actions" (Schutz, 1962: 57). The common-sense individual never questions whether it is possible to understand others; he simply does so. This of course is not to say that he never errs in his judgments of others. Often he does. But he sees his errors as routine misunderstandings, unconnected to abstract philosophy.

The pervasiveness of intersubjectivity is evident in even the most commonplace of experiences. For example, this chapter I am writing is a solitary enterprise, but it is by no means a private one. I recognize the objects before me as books and take for granted that in consulting them my understanding of Schutz can be promoted. A passage may occasionally seem somewhat obscure, but I attribute this to the complexity of Schutz's work, not to the absence of intelligibility. In the same vein, I also assume that the chapter I am writing will be found intelligible by others. Perhaps my readers also will find certain passages obscure. Indeed, it is important that I recognize this and devote much effort to ensuring the intelligibility of my work. I write with a particular audience in mind and take for granted that my own and their stocks of knowledge coincide and depart in certain predictable ways. Since the reader is unlikely to be a student of phenomenology, the essay must provide him with a sufficient background to make the more difficult points understandable. And finally, if the work still remains obscure, I assume, and assume my reader will assume, that the problem lies not in any insurmountable divergence in perspective, but in a flaw correctable through our collaborative efforts to communicate.

How does intersubjectivity originate and persevere? Schutz suggests two possible reasons. First, one can treat intersubjectivity as a practical achievement of the routine mental habits of the common-sense individual. In its general outline, this approach is a type of phenomenological investigation. The second approach accepts intersubjectivity and accounts for it by pointing to the social origins of individual perspective. Since this approach embodies a commitment to ideas and assumptions that are not verifiable within the stream of immediate consciousness, it is not strictly phenomenological.

Schutz's ideas about intersubjectivity were originally offered as two different aspects of the socialization of knowledge:

1. The reciprocity of perspectives or the structural socialization of knowledge.
2. The social origin of knowledge or the genetic socialization of knowledge. (Schutz, 1962: 11)

The reciprocity of perspectives, or the structural socialization of knowledge, is the point most closely related to phenomenology. It makes explicit an observation brought out earlier: the common-sense individual assumes, (and assumes that others do also) that if he and someone else were to exchange positions (both in space and perspective), each would see the world as the other had. The issue is not whether a reciprocity exists, but whether it is *believed* to exist. And if such belief is present, it must by definition be evident in consciousness, the basic field of phenomenological investigation.

The social origin of knowledge, or the genetic socialization of knowledge, refers to the effects of the socio-historical context on the development of an individual's knowledge and perspective. Since knowledge is socially derived, to be part of society is to share in a heritage of accumulated learning (Schutz, 1962). Through social interaction with parents, friends, and teachers, one develops the perspective that allows one to "see" the world as culture prescribes. This connection between the individual's social existence and intersubjectivity is intimate and fundamental. "As long as man is born of woman, intersubjectivity and the we–relationship will be the foundation for all other categories of human existence" (Schutz, 1966: 82). However, none of the evidence necessary for confirming the connection between social existence and intersubjectivity has a locus in immediate experience, the realm of phenomenological interest.

The first view of reciprocal perspectives, in confining attention to the organization and structure of conscious experience, adopts the techniques and subject matter of phenomenological investigation. The second view, the social origin of knowledge, places the individual in a larger and external order. Schutz made no connection between these two views and phenomenology. However, Schutz's position on intersubjectivity has been an important source for the diversity of programs within phenomenological sociology.

Meaning and Action. The influence of Husserl on Schutz was substantial despite Schutz's subsequent departure from the specific program advocated in Husserl's work. Much the same can be said about the influence on Schutz of the German sociologist Max Weber (1864–1920).

Schutz regarded Weber's work, especially the first chapters of *Economy and Society* (1968), as the groundwork for a refined view of human action.

Schutz was attracted to Weber by the latter's insistence on tracing all claims about social phenomena to the behavior of actual people. Weber, however, rejected the popular expression of this position, known as "behaviorism." Behaviorism was an attempt to confine scientific explanation to that which can be directly observed. Behaviorism limited the social sciences to the connection established between an aspect of the visible environment (called the stimulus) and an aspect of the resulting behavior (called the response). In its most extreme form, behaviorism rejected the idea that the locus of this connection was the mind of the human actor.

Both Weber and Schutz regarded behaviorism as too narrow a view of science. Although a few of the least complex of the physical sciences might prosper within such limitations, the social sciences could not. Compare the resources necessary for studying the game of billiards with those necessary for studying human interaction. When in billiards a rolling ball hits a stationary ball, the resulting path of the stationary ball can be determined by calculating the sum of the energy transferred. This calculation relies on information easily observable (e.g., the speed and direction of the first ball) and on our knowledge of the laws governing physical reality. Understanding the course of human behavior is more complicated. While the laws of physics set parameters on social behavior, they by no means determine its course. Much that is relevant for understanding social behavior is unavailable for direct observation. For example, the response evoked when one person strikes another depends in large part on how the meaning of the blow was interpreted. (Was it done in jest or anger? Could it have been accidental? What would be the likely outcome of a physical confrontation?) But the specific reasons for making interpretations can only be inferred from other features of the interaction. And this of course is no less true for the observing scientist than it is for the common-sense individual.

Weber argued that in order to understand behavior, one must grasp its meaning in the subjective intentions of individuals. This position—which has come to be known as "interpretive sociology"—not only grants that subjective intentions exist, but acknowledges their role in the unfolding of some types of human behavior. Weber made a distinction between types of behavior in terms of the presence or absence of an underlying intention or meaning. If meaning were present, then Weber called the behavior "action." And if meaning were absent, he said the behavior was merely "reactive."

Although Schutz generally agreed with Weber's aim to clarify the role of meaning in human behavior, he regarded the resulting distinction among types of behavior as unsystematic and ambiguous. Schutz pointed out that behavior could be meaningful in any number of ways. Much behavior is meaningful in the sense that its course is consciously directed for the realization of certain desired ends. The meaning of behavior derives from its intentions. But what of habitual behavior, which makes no attempt to formulate its meaning as it occurs? Does not subsequent reflection often find meaning in even this? Perhaps the actor recalls the deliberations that in the past led him or her to originally enact the now habitual activity. Habitual behavior, then, becomes meaningful retrospectively; once an intentional action, it has become an unreflective adaptation to a recurrent situation.

But is intention a requirement for meaningful behavior? May not meaning be attributed to a slip of the tongue, an unnatural gesture, or other such isolated and unplanned happenings? Perhaps it is precisely the unplanned aspects of behavior that are the best indexes of meaning (Goffman, 1959: 7). But if the most unreflective and uncontrollable activities are meaningful, how useful or precise is the concept of "meaning"?

Weber did not address these difficulties. In basing his interpretive sociology on the study of the meaning of behavior, Weber assumed that he had reached the most basic and rudimentary level of analysis. In stating his objections to Weber's work, Schutz said:

> [Weber] breaks off his analysis of the social world when he arrives at what he assumes to be the basic and irreducible elements of social phenomena [meaning]. But he is wrong in this assumption. His concept of the meaningful act of the individual—the key idea of interpretive sociology—by no means defines a primitive, as he thinks it does. It is, on the contrary, a mere label for a highly complex and ramified area that calls for much further study. (Schutz, 1967: 7–8)

Schutz regarded meaning as itself a summary term for more basic processes. To study these processes, he brought together the work of Husserl, Bergson (1913), and Weber into a synthesis penetrating to the origin of meaning in the intentional consciousness of the social actor. Schutz' difficult and sensitive remarks on this topic (esp. 1967: 45–96) should be read carefully; I shall try to present only the basic thrust of his painstaking analysis.

To make clear the nature of "meaning" Schutz relied on a close description of conscious experience. Following Bergson (1913), he observed that much of experience is apprehended as a stream of duration (the *durée*) within which nothing is discrete or well defined. Moments in the *durée* are part of a constant and unbroken transition. This transition is interrupted only in the reflective glance of consciousness, which in focusing on aspects of the stream produces segments (intentional unities) that are regarded as discrete. Schutz emphasized that the reflective glance of consciousness can only focus on a past (and thus already completed) experience, since experience in its immediate presence is part of an unbroken flow. For Schutz, meaning resided in intentionality, which transforms an experience into something distinct and discrete; in short, into "an experience." Schutz applied this analysis of meaning to human behavior:

> Behavior, then, consists of a series of experiences which are distinguished from all other experiences by a primordial intentionality of spontaneous activity which remains the same in all intentional modifications. Now it becomes clear what we meant when we said that behavior is merely experiences looked at in a certain light, that is, referred back to the activity which originally produced them. The "meaning" of experiences is nothing more, then, than that frame of interpretation which sees them as behavior. (Schutz, 1967: 57)

Schutz's analysis was to show that meaning must always refer to the intentional activities of the human subject. Weber tended to confuse the subjective experience of the person to be studied with that of the scientific observer, a circumstance that renders the subject matter of interpretive sociology ambiguous. Weber's definition of motive shows his confusion: "A motive is a complex of subjective meaning which seems to the actor himself *or to the observer* an adequate ground for the conduct in question" (Weber, 1968: 11, *emphasis added*).

Another source for confusing the motives of actor and observer was Weber's distinction between observational and motivational understanding. Weber used the term *observational understanding* to refer to the observer's ability to grasp the meaning of an activity solely through observation. To exemplify this, he pointed to the ease with which we immediately understand the meaning of such simple activities as chopping wood, turning a door knob, or aiming a gun (Weber, 1968: 8). Weber used "motivational understanding" to refer to a more penetrating grasp of an activity; in this case the observer is able to place the activity in an intelligible and inclusive context of meaning. For example, the heightening of understanding that occurs if we know the motive of a woodcutter's actions; that is, whether he chopped wood for salary, recreation, or for some other reason. The implication of Weber's remarks is that only motivational understanding demands the observer's close concern with the meaning of an activity for an actor.

Schutz regarded the distinction between observational and motivational understanding as a product of Weber's failure to separate two different types of motives.

> When Weber uses the term "motive" he means sometimes (a) the "in-order-to" of the action—in other words, the orientations of the action to a future event—but at other times (b) the "because" of the action, that is, its relation to a past lived experience. (Schutz, 1967: 87)

The "in-order-to motive" is the end result, the project, the actor wishes to accomplish. If the actor is a thief, for example, his project may be to steal something valuable. Schutz was careful to point out that often there was a hierarchy of in-order-to motives; thus, the thief stole in-order-to finance his education, which was in turn desired in-order-to realize his ambition of becoming an architect. The "because-motive" relates the actor's project to events in the past that led the actor to adopt the project. In our example, the actor might have become a thief "because" of poor family environment or "because" of membership in a group committed to deviant values. Schutz's point with respect to Weber is this: the unity of the project is determined by the intentions of the human actor. Therefore, observational understanding cannot dispense with considerations of motive, but must identify the subjective project (i.e., the in-order-to motive) guiding the actor's behavior.

Schutz redefined "action" by limiting the application of the term to behavior carried out in accordance with a preconceived plan. *Action* is the expression of a subjective project, and its meaning is the goal that the project is intended to realize. For example, the meaning of my neighbor's walk to the corner is established by her goal; in this case, to go to the store. This project was called by Schutz the "act." He distinguished the "act" from the numerous activities (e.g., locking the apartment, walking to the corner, paying the cashier) that together comprise the project; these were called by Schutz "action." Although the actor's project is oriented to the future, it is subjectively prefigured as a completed act. This idea follows Schutz's observation that reflection—which is the source of meaning—can operate upon only that which in some sense is already in the past. If a completed act is a project with known intermediate goals, then the resulting action is regarded as rational (Schutz, 1967: 61). By giving both action and rationality a subjective locus, Schutz made the perspective of the actor the principal topic of investigation.

Origins of a
Phenomenological Methodology
for the Social Sciences

Schutz did not claim to be a social scientist. Instead, he viewed his work as comprising a phenomenology of the natural attitude (Schutz, 1967: 44). Schutz tried in this to use phenomenology to elucidate the basic structures of common-sense experience. His work (of which we have examined only a fragment) sought the starting point of the social sciences in the durability of the mundane world. Regardless of his focus, Schutz addressed basic questions regarding the foundations of any social science.

Occasionally Schutz ventured to give a description of a suitable methodology for the social sciences (1962: 3–47; 1964: 64–68; 1967: 215–250). He pointed to the necessity for an interface between the interpretations and theories of the common-sense individual and those of the social scientist. More specifically, Schutz regarded the task of the social sciences as that of creating an objective context of meaning out of subjective meaning contexts (Schutz, 1967: 241). By an "objective context of meaning" Schutz meant a set of related statements that could be understood apart from the special perspective of the person making the statements. The meaning context may be considered anonymous since the features that bind it to a particular mind are ignored in favor of its most general properties. Complete objectivity occurs when the meaning context is invariant with respect to every consciousness giving it meaning (Schutz, 1967: 37).

Schutz emphasized that the creation of an objective context of meaning is not unique to the activities of the scientist. The common-sense individual may also organize his experience into types of great anonymity. For example, knowledge of a casual acquaintance is apt to be far more general and abstract than knowledge of a close friend. Indeed, many persons are known only in terms of highly abstract constructions that specify the types of activities they perform. One may know that one's letter will be handled in accord with certain general procedures even without knowing anything about the postal carrier. By routinely objectifying experience through the construction of types, the common-sense person approximates what Schutz regarded as the task of the scientist.

Although similarities exist between the constructs of common sense and science, there are also differences. First, when taken as a system, scientific constructs must be compatible with the principles of formal logic (Schutz, 1962: 43; 1967: 223). This of course requires a degree of clarity and consistency seldom found in the thought objects of common sense. Second, scientific constructs differ from their counterparts in common sense insofar as they do not refer back to face-to-face experience (Schutz, 1967: 223). Because the scientist must construct types far surpassing in rigor and clarity actual common-sense behavior, he constructs models that are unlikely to have counterparts in the real (common-sense) world. Indeed, Schutz would have the scientist dispense with any claim of reproducing the common-sense perspective. The models constructed are not meant to be lifelike, but to portray with perfect clarity those features and behavior of the actor of interest to the scientist. This results in the construction of homunculi, or puppets, not of models of actual or concrete social actors (Schutz, 1962: 40–42).

Schutz regarded the construction of such homunculi as an objective technique for dealing with subjective meaning. The homunculi were formulated in accordance with three postulates (Schutz, 1962: 43–44):

1. The postulate of logical consistency
2. The postulate of subjective interpretation
3. The postulate of adequacy

The *postulate of logical consistency* requires that the constructs designed by the scientist possess a high level of clarity and distinctness and be compatible with the principles of formal logic. The *postulate of subjective interpretation* requires that any model of human action specify what contents must be attributed to the actor's mind for an action to possess an understandable relation to a mental process. And finally, the postulate of adequacy requires that:

> Each term in a scientific model of human action must be constructed in such a way that a human act performed within the life-world by an individual actor in the way indicated by the typical construct would be understandable for the actor himself as well as for his fellow-men in terms of common-sense interpretation of everyday life. (Schutz, 1962: 44)

Thus the first postulate establishes the objective validity of the constructs of scientific thought, while the second postulate ensures that the constructs will refer to the subjective realm of intention and meaning. And, since neither of these postulates can ensure that the subjective attributes of the homunculus bear a relation to those of the common-sense individual, the third postulate is meant to warrant the consistency of the constructs of social science with the constructs of common sense (Schutz, 1962: 44).

The postulate of adequacy reveals Schutz's contribution to the methodology of the social sciences. In requiring the consistency of common sense and scientific constructs, Schutz avoids confusing the actor and observer. Unfortunately, Schutz's contribution is solely theoretical. Having demonstrated the central position of the actor, Schutz gave no attention to the numerous practical difficulties of grasping the actor's perspective. He did not even discuss how the adequacy of a scientific construct is to be tested. Is it even possible for a scientific model to be explicit, rational, and logical while remaining consistent with the experience of the common-sense individual? These difficult and important questions were not addressed in Schutz's work.

Schutz's ability to avoid such questions rested in part on his failure to separate theory formulation from theory construction (Ten Houten and Kaplan, 1973). In his concern for the form in which a theory is presented (theory formulation), Schutz tended to neglect the activities by which theory is produced (theory construction). The reader is thus told what a theory should look like (e.g., it should be objective, logically consistent, etc), but not how theory originates in the experience of the scientist. Indeed, the term "scientist" is itself a construction in Schutz's work.

In describing the scientist, Schutz presented a person who is disinterested, divorced from his biographical situation, and completely attuned to the problems, techniques, and knowledge of his discipline (Schutz, 1962: 36–40). But how could such a scientist grasp the subjective intentions of the common-sense perspective? Would not the very differences that make a person a scientist undermine the convergence in perspective necessary for understanding? Schutz presented the scientist only at work on a model, never at work in the world. His implication is that subjective understanding can be scientific *only* if reached in isolation from the social processes by which such understanding is attained.

Phenomenological Sociology

Phenomenology and Sociology

As conceived by Husserl and Schutz, phenomenology was a method for investigating the contours of consciousness. By contrast, sociology is generally considered an empirical discipline whose subject matter lies in the observable regularities of the behavior of people. Phenomenology and sociology thus differ in both method and subject matter, which makes it necessary to carefully consider the compatibility of the two approaches.

The differences between phenomenology and sociology are many and important. Phenomenologists, we have seen, rely on a reflexive ability to penetrate to the core, or essence, of their own experience as it takes form in consciousness. Their research proceeds on the certain ground of intentional consciousness. Through the techniques of reduction and the capacity for imaginative variation, the phenomenologist is able to find the rudimentary structures and processes of experience. Sociologists, on the other hand, take as their subject matter the activities of others. Since a sociologist cannot assume that he and the other share a perspective, he cannot rely solely on his subjective experience of the other's environment. This openness with respect to the idiosyncracies of the other forces the sociologist to consider evidence that is indirect and ambiguous. Unlike the phenomenologist, the sociologist must confront a social world whose variations demand empirical, not only reflective, study.

Given these important differences between phenomenology and sociology, how can they be synthesized into a stance that preserves the interests of each? The first part of this section shall consider a number of the more important attempts to address this question. From philosophy, Husserl (1970a), Schutz (1962; 1967), and Luckmann (1973) will be discussed; and from sociology, Tiryakian (1973), Douglas (1970a; 1970b) and Blumenstiel (1973). It must be pointed out that their responses do not form a logically closed and exhaustive sample. This selection is simply an attempt to cover the remarks of Husserl and Schutz, and a few figures whose work is indicative of the more diffuse aspects of the movement in its modern phase. The final sections shall extend the review to include representatives from what appears to be two distinct approaches growing out of the work of Schutz.

Husserl's development of the notion of a science of essences suggests one possible connection between phenomenology and the social sciences. (This discussion draws on Heap and Roth, 1973: 359–361.) Husserl argued (1962: 56–57) that every empirical science presupposes a corresponding eidetic science in the realm of pure possibility. Underlying empirical sociology, then, is an eidetic sociology whose purpose is to disclose the invariant core and basic relationships of the concepts employed. Notions such as "society," "culture," and "family" would be strictly delimited in terms of their essential features, and grounded in the appropriate regional ontology. In turn, empirical sociology would be given a truly scientific foundation.

Not all phenomenologists have accepted the feasibility of such an eidetic science. Schutz has expressed doubt that the concepts of empirical science presuppose an eidetic basis. Given that all concepts are typifications derived from experience, how can the concepts of empirical science possess an essence separate from the activities of type construction (Schutz, 1966: 114–115)? [4] If they do not, then eidetic sociology would disclose only the specific and contingent patterns of schemes for conceptualizing social existence.

Schutz suggested a somewhat different relationship between phenomenology and the social sciences. He located the significance of phenomenology for sociology in its potential contribution to the study of methods in the social sciences.

> It must be clearly stated that the relation of phenomenology to the social sciences cannot be demonstrated by analyzing concrete problems of sociology or economics, such as social adjustment or theory of international trade, with phenomenological methods. It is my conviction, however, that future studies of the methods of the social sciences and their fundamental notions will of necessity lead to issues belonging to the domain of phenomenological research. (Schutz, 1962: 116)

Schutz suggested that the methods of the social sciences are built upon phenomena that are themselves taken-for-granted. The possibility of mutual understanding is assumed, and the major concepts of interpretive sociology—meaning, motive, ends, and acts—refer to structures of consciousness that the methods of empirical social science cannot address. Schutz noted that this makes it impossible to assess these methods because the assumptions that underlie them are left unexamined. He concluded by suggesting that the best avenue for addressing such topics was phenomenology.[5] Schutz did not, however, use the relevance of phenomenology for sociology as a reason for forming a phenomenological sociology. Although complementary, phenomenology and sociology remained distinctive approaches to understanding the social world.

Thomas Luckmann, a student and collaborator of Schutz, has also suggested (1973) that the specific contribution of phenomenology to the social sciences is methodological. He argues that phenomenology provides the basis for a program of formalization and theory of measurement appropriate for the structures of everyday life (Luckmann, 1973: 166):

> . . . the aims are to generate some principles for the construction of a metalanguage into which the observational languages of the various social sciences could be translated with a controlled decrease of historical specificity and without loss of the intrinsic significance of observational statements. (Luckmann, 1973: 169)

Luckmann went on to suggest that the structures of the life-world are themselves the elements of the metalanguage. That is, when taken together, these structures may be treated as a sign system with a capacity for representing the empirical analyses of concrete historical structures in a precise and universal language. For the structures of the life-world to be able to stand as a metalanguage, they must be able to express enough data about the context in which they exist to preserve a sense of the specific. Although the structures may have this potential, Luckmann made no attempt to demonstrate its existence.[6] And given his failure to cite persuasive evidence, it must be clearly understood that Luckmann's claims go beyond those of Schutz: one may grant (as Schutz) the structures of the lifeworld have methodological implications for the social sciences and yet deny they may serve as a metalanguage.

Tiryakian has proposed a conception of phenomenological sociology in which Husserl's notion of the *epoché* is used as a technique for getting at the ideas, sentiments, and images that comprise what he calls the individual's "assumptive frame of reference," or AFR (1973: 199). Unlike the conceptions of the natural attitude of Schutz, the AFR denotes the specific and variable perspectives of different groups of people. Tiryakian emphasizes the variability of meaning, not the precise nature of its origin in consciousness. Although Tiryakian linked the AFR to a version of the *a priori,* he failed to distinguish what parts of the AFR may vary among people and what parts are invariant. This results in some confusion since Tiryakian's research presumably addresses the substantive particulars of sociocultural change with phenomenological methods. This would seem to confound the variable with the invariant in experience by the application of techniques of self examination (*epoché,* reduction) to subjective phenomena, which presumably differ among people. Since the researcher can reduce only his own experience, there is no access to the idiosyncracies of another's perspective.

One solution to the disjunction between the researcher and the experiential locus he describes is to condition the success of the *epoché* on the researcher's accurate grasp of his subjects' experience. This solution, which is only implied by Tiryakian, is evident in the work of Jack Douglas (1970*a*, 1970*b*, and 1971) Douglas joins a version of the *epoché*, which he calls the "theoretic stance," with the method of participant-observation. Since participant-observation gives the researcher close contact with the world as it is experienced by his or her subjects, it serves as the basis for the claim that the researcher has actually grasped the life-world he or she is studying. The version of the *epoché* or reduction employed by Douglas is used as a technique to overcome a central problem of participant-observation: a close familiarity with the experience of one's subjects renders the experience difficult to recognize and report. The theoretic stance is a distancing technique by which the researcher makes what has become familiar through participant-observation alien enough to ensure its visibility.

The sense of phenomenology that emerges from this position is most starkly stated by Blumenstiel, who regards phenomenology as "the trick of making things whose meanings are clear meaningless and then discovering what they mean" (Blumenstiel, 1973: 189). Blumenstiel's work is an excellent example of how a phenomenological approach may be claimed without ever being used. In his essay on "good times," he concludes by saying:

> Although phenomenological analysis is the method used in [these] studies, the presentations of actual good times will frequently not include the details of that analysis. Rather than detailing all of the particulars of what sometimes seem rather picayune points, they are put together in more general form for purposes of presentation. (Blumenstiel, 1973: 189)

Such a casual invocation of phenomenology is odd since the essay appeared in a recent anthology on phenomenological sociology and was recommended by the editor as an example of the empirical application of phenomenology. Blumenstiel presents an account of "good times" which in its minute and unqualified detail, suggests the researcher's omniscience of his subjects' most intimate intentions and strategies. He discusses, for example, courtship as a "good time" from a game perspective. The reader is not informed of the source of the materials, the significance of the *epoché* or reduction in their clarification, or the relationship between the researcher's report and the subject's experience. The latter is surprising given the potential incongruity between the game perspective and the member's own interpretation of his activities. Douglas, and to a lesser extent Tiryakian, are, in their commitment to participant observation, at least aware of the difficulty of getting at member perspectives. Blumenstiel either does not experience this problem or regards it as less important than artfully reporting his findings.

The relationship between phenomenology and sociology thus has been formulated variously, with different degrees of rigor. Some authors have broadened the scope of phenomenological analysis to include their own research interests or visions for sociology. This has tended to introduce a certain amount of imprecise use of the term "phenomenology." Ironically, much of this imprecision has resulted from the ongoing dissemination and acceptance of the work of Schutz. Schutz's reputation as a phenomenologist has led some to regard the full extent of his work as falling within this tradition. Others, perhaps more in accord with the views of Schutz himself, have attributed to phenomenology a more limited role. The contrasting perspectives and sociologies that have resulted from this may be briefly delimited in considering the two major lines of interpretation of Schutz's writings on intersubjectivity.

The first interpretation develops from Schutz's treatment of intersubjectivity as an aspect of an individual's social nature and from his writings on the social origins of knowledge and the emergence of shared typifications through socialization. This view of Schutz provides a basis for a perspective in which society is regarded as an organization of sentiments, values, and ideas both constraining the individual and being sustained by him. The second interpretation develops from Schutz's treatment of intersubjectivity as a belief upheld by the reciprocity of perspectives and other aspects of the natural attitude. This view promotes a perspective in which society is regarded as originating in the sense of social structure members sustain through their interpretive procedures.

Each of the two interpretations has provided a nucleus for what its adherents call "phenomenological sociology." It is doubtful, however, whether the first view preserves the meaning of phenomenology as it was understood by Schutz. Intersubjectivity and conceptions of social order go beyond what is evident in phenomenal experience. The rudimentary condition for intersubjectivity—that two individuals share an understanding—cannot be verified within the experience of the lone human subject.

The following pages will consider the versions of phenomenological sociology that have developed around the interpretations of Schutz's work. Since the first view, is an elaboration of the work of Berger and Luckmann (1967), their position provides a convenient starting point for addressing more recent discussions of macro-phenomenology. (Jehenson, 1973; Psathes, 1973; Tiryakian, 1973; Wagner, 1973). The second view, has found its most cogent expression in the works of sociologists writing under the rubric of "ethnomethodology." Although the authors that will be considered do not generally employ the term "phenomenological sociology," their work elaborates what has been presented here as the more classical phenomenological interpretation of Schutz. For simplicity, the first view shall be discussed under the heading "Phenomenology and Social Structure" and the second under "Phenomenology and Social Competence."

Phenomenology and Social Structure

Berger and Luckmann

The Social Construction of Reality by Berger and Luckmann (1967) is a provocative and lucid attempt to incorporate within the sociology of knowledge a concern for common-sense interpretations of everyday life. Following Schutz, Berger and Luckmann recommend that the sociology of knowledge look at what people "know" as "reality" in their everyday non- or pre-theoretical lives (Berger and Luckmann, 1967: 15). Because reality is socially constructed, the sociology of knowledge should deal at least in part with the processes by which any body of knowledge comes to be socially established as reality (Berger and Luckmann, 1967: 3). In contributing to this latter aspect of the sociology of knowledge, Berger and Luckmann draw on the work of Schutz. Although their discussion of Schutz is quite sensitive, few of the details of Schutz's work are incorporated into Berger and Luckmann's core sociological argument. Indeed, Berger and Luckmann regard their discussion on "The Foundations of Knowledge in Everyday Life" (1967: 19–46), in which they use the work of Schutz extensively, as a "philosophical prolegomena" that may be skipped by readers interested in only the sociological argument. For Berger and Luckmann, phenomenology holds a significant but peripheral position: it is helpful in clarifying the foundations of knowledge in everyday life, but it cannot substitute for sociological analysis.

How can subjective meanings become objective facts? Berger and Luckmann suggest that the answer lies in an ongoing dialectical process. The first stage in this process is externalization, or the expression of one's nature in activity. Human activity is thus the basic material from which all social forms arise. The second stage is objectivation, during which human activity takes expression in a form that confronts the actor as objective, that is, as divorced from himself.

Berger and Luckmann discuss objectivation in terms of the dual processes of habitualization and institutionalization. *Habitualization* refers to the development of consistent strategies for confronting recurrent situations. In the course of life, a human being develops a great many habitualized responses. When two actors reciprocally generalize one another's habitualized actions, there occurs what Berger and Luckmann call "institutionalization" (Berger and Luckmann, 1967: 54). Since institutions arise out of shared generalizations, called typifications, their reality is solidified through social consensus. An individual therefore cannot ignore the institutions in his or her social environment; to do so would be to risk the sanction of others.

The final stage in the dialectic is internalization. *Internalization* refers to the processes by which the objective world is incorporated into consciousness in the course of socialization (Berger and Luckmann, 1967: 61). Berger and Luckmann's discussion draws on the conceptual lexicon of George Herbert Mead (1934), with whom they share the belief that socialization is a life-long process in which the individual continually adapts to a changing environment.

Berger and Luckmann suggest that each phase in the dialectical process corresponds to a basic characterization of the social world: society is a human product; society is an objective reality; and the individual is a social product (Berger and Luckmann, 1967: 61). If any one of these characterizations is emphasized to the exclusion of the others, the actual nature of social reality will be distorted.

The implications of Berger and Luckmann's position for sociological research is left rather vague. To call a process "dialectical" does not establish the precise nature of the relationships among different moments within the dialectic. Berger and Luckmann offer neither a program for research nor a criticism of existing programs. Their remarks are easily assimilated to a wide variety of perspectives. They do not deny, for example, that "purely structural analyses of social phenomena are fully adequate for wide areas of sociology" (1967: 186). They add, however, that the integration of such analyses into the body of sociological theory requires more than "casual obeisance" to the "human factor behind the structural data." (1967: 186). What this requires in terms of concrete research is left unstated.

Macro-Phenomenology

Berger and Luckmann draw on phenomenology in two ways. First, they use it to establish their assertion that the reality of the world as experienced by the common-sense individual is a result of learned patterns of common-sense interpretation. This is the foundation for their claim that reality is socially constructed. Second, Berger and Luckmann use phenomenology to provide a view of subjective experience as an evolving organization of typifications. In suggesting that typifications are embedded in concrete patterns of social interaction, Berger and Luckmann link the subjective experience to social structure.

In using the concept of typification in this fashion, Berger and Luckmann go beyond what is available in phenomenal experience. The immanent (or subjective) experience of a single individual cannot provide the evidence necessary for determining whether a particular typification is shared among different individuals, and this is a prerequisite for it to become an aspect of social structure. Berger and Luckmann are thus correct in distinguishing their perspective on society from phenomenology. Their work, however, demonstrates that phenomenology is at least compatible with some versions of structural sociology. Their demonstration has led some to employ the term "phenomenological sociology" to denote sociologies that, although not strictly phenomenological, are informed by the work of Husserl and Schutz. A result has been the recent interest in "macro-phenomenology."

Macro-phenomenology may be characterized as an attempt to clarify the concrete relationship between specific contents of consciousness and the larger socio-historical milieu. The added consideration of the social environment presumably gives phenomenology its "macro" dimension.[7]

> There is a "macro" dimension to existential phenomenology in relation to sociology, a dimension more developed in European than in American sociology. The embodied consciousness of subjectivity, or selfhood, exists in a sociohistorical milieu, which is a structure of our experience, a constituent part of the horizon of our perception. The self's experience of the social world, or more broadly of the ambient world (*Umwelt*), is not the experience of an isolated monad. The moods, feelings, and cognitive experience of subjectivity are also reflections of the *collective* representations, moods, and aspirations of a given historical moment or epoch shared by a group of contemporaries. (Tiryakian, 1973: 211, emphasis in original)

The way in which the social environment is incorporated into the work of various macro-phenomenologists is not always the same. Tiryakian (1973: 214–221), for example, looks for a "constellation of experiences and meanings—in other words, intersubjective essences—underlying the various empirical settings" (1973: 215).

Wagner (1973), on the other hand, is more concerned with the effect of changes in the social environment on an individual's ways of making the world sensible. Intimate relationships, occupational fortunes, and the sociocultural environment all have potential to disrupt and alter an individual's schemes for normalizing his or her environment. Particular changes in the structure of the social environment are related to corresponding changes in an individual's outlook.

While Wagner shows how changes in the environment may provide impetus for an individual to reorganize habits of interpretation, Jehenson (1973) implies that certain habits of interpretation are functional for certain environments. He cites Weick's (1969) notion that an act of interpretation may itself constitute an adaptive mechanism. He illustrates this using materials from the study of formal organizations.

In a hierarchial system, in particular, the consequences of a course-of-action resulting from the empathic interpretation would be extremely prejudicial to the functioning of authority relationships . . . In order to elude this impasse, organization members may have recourse to another type of interpretation, one that takes place at the *diagnostic level*. By imputing to the partner an attitude of which he is not supposedly unaware, one evades the self-destructive response called forth at the face value of the partner's gesture." (Jehenson, 1973: 237)

Jehenson gives an example of how a psychiatrist is able to avoid the complaints of subordinates by interpreting them as symptomatic of the subordinates' needs for a "powerful papa" (1973: 233). In this fashion, attention is shifted from the content of a communication to its origin in an irrational motivation. The shift permits the interpreter to avoid any lengthy consideration of the specific complaints, since they are merely the manifestation of an underlying and irrational disposition. The relationship between the interpretation and environment is thus functional. Indeed, the interpretation itself specifies the environment to which the interpreter then adapts.

The sociohistorical environment must ultimately be considered external to any particular consciousness. If this were not the case, it would be impossible to document the specific contribution of the environment to intentional consciousness. This fact alone renders "macro-phenomenology" different from phenomenology in its philosophical sense. No strictly phenomenological account could regard any domain as distinct from its apprehension in consciousness. But if research is to address the theoretical concerns of conventional sociology, which incorporate and build upon lay conceptions of social reality, it must do precisely this. Macro-phenomenology should thus be regarded as a sociological application of certain ideas derived from phenomenology, not as a version of phenomenological philosophy.

Phenomenology and Social Competence

The macro-phenomenologists share an interest in the relationship between the individual and his social environment. The individual is conceived of as a thinker, a seeker of meaning, who, although partially free must confront an obdurate world. With but a small change in emphasis and vocabulary, macro-phenomenology could easily be taken for a child of Blumer (*see* chapter 2). Like the symbolic interactionists, macro-phenomenologists grant a measure of independence to the social environment with respect to its embodiment in consciousness; they accept, if only in part, the natural standpoint of the common-sense individual.

The next group of thinkers we shall consider look to an even more radical break from conventional sociology. These are the ethnomethodologists [8] who object not only to viewing society and culture as rigid, but even to the more circumspect and tentative interpretations of the symbolic interactionists. More than the typical interactionist, they are interested in the "how-to" of understanding. While a symbolic interactionist will often go into a setting and ask "What is going on here?" the ethnomethodologist is interested in how anyone understands what is going on anywhere. He or she examines processes that are elemental insofar as they inform all attributions of meaning or sensibility. The principal focus of ethnomethodologists is the process by which members create, sustain, and communicate a world view. Although symbolic interactionists recognize the importance of perspective and interpretation, they tend to ignore their processual aspects by quickly fixing them in "the definition of the situation" (see Cicourel, 1972a). Even the concept of emergence, with its emphasis on the dynamic and unpredictable, often becomes little more than a catchword for looking at a sequence of interpretations rather than the dynamic of interpretation.

Ethnomethodologists use several distinct vocabularies to present their objections to the tendency to view social interaction as the exchange of fixed and stable meanings.[9] The vocabulary most widely used addresses the limitations of conventional sociology in terms of an alleged confusion of the *topic* of investigation with the *resources* through which the investigation proceeds (see Saks, 1963: 10–11; Bittner, 1965: 240; Garfinkle, 1967: 31; Zimmerman and Pollner, 1970: 81; Zimmerman and Wieder, 1970: 288). For example, using the term "instinct" to explain behavior can mistake the formulation of a concept for the establishment of a cause. Since instinct is only a name applied to certain observations, it has not motive power of its own; it can only be identified in terms of the behaviors it explains. Instinct becomes a resource in its own investigation.

In similar fashion, ethnomethodologists argue that the concepts and explanatory forms of conventional sociology tend to confound topic and resource. Or as Bittner says: ". . . the sociologist finds himself in the position of having borrowed a concept from those he seeks to study in order to describe what he observes about them" (1965: 240). While many object to the direct, unelaborated, often simply tautological, substitution of an "explanatory" concept for a specific body of description, ethnomethodologists object to *any use of any formulation whose derivation employs any part of any version of the topic addressed.* This may be restated in more concrete form: if a sociologist chooses to study common sense, she may not use her own common-sense knowledge as a resource.

The emergence of sociology will take a different course (when it emerges) from that of the other sciences because sociology, to emerge, must free itself not from philosophy but from the common-sense perspective. . . . The discovery of the common-sense world is important as the discovery of a problem only, and not as the discovery of a sociological resource." (Saks, 1963: 10–11)

What constitutes a topic (and thus what is proscribed as a resource) is conceived of in very general terms. The ethnomethodologist expects to eliminate from use any element belonging to common sense. It is as if a moralist who wishes to prohibit incest chose to do so by prohibiting all sex. A species cannot long exist under such strictures; can sociology?

It is true that virtually nothing in sociology currently conforms to these strictures. All of the favored concepts in sociology—values, social rules, beliefs, needs, and attitudes—invoke stable elements of culture or personality as the underlying cause of behavior. Used as such, these concepts presume the existence and availability of an order of phenomena whose content and relevance transcends any given situation. In short, they presume these phenomena are trans-situational.

In this view, common sense is regarded as those processes of interpretation that permit individuals (including sociologists) to see order and consistency in their experience. Without recourse to common sense, the world would appear as a sequence of discrete and unconnected situations: no one moment would bear a demonstrable relationship to any other. The task of the ethnomethodologist is to return to the vision—present before ordering by common sense—in order to reveal how ordering occurs.

But how can this be done? Zimmerman and Pollner suggest (1970) replacing our normal perspective on everyday life with a new way of seeing. They begin by offering a new vocabulary, which they suggest is uncontaminated by the presumption of order implicit in the English language.[10] To this end they propose the new term "occasioned corpus" as a way of denoting the content of a perspective without the presumption that its constituent elements [11] persist from one moment to the next.

By the use of the term *occasioned corpus,* we wish to emphasize that the features of socially organized activities are particular, contingent accomplishments of the production and recognition work of the parties to the activity. We underscore the occasioned character of the corpus in contrast to a corpus of member's knowledge, skill and belief standing prior to and independent of actual occasions in which such knowledge, skill, and belief are displayed and recognized. (Zimmerman and Pollner, 1970: 94)

What is lost and what is gained in this new and clumsy way of speaking?

By this proposal a given setting's features are not referable for their production and recognition to "cultural resources" transcending a particular occasion. The analyst cannot have recourse to such explanatory devices as a shared complex of values, norms, roles, motives, and the like, standing independent of and prior to a given occasion. On these considerations we are led to specify the occasioned corpus as a corpus with no regular elements. In consequence of this specification (in conjunction with the other specifications of the occasioned corpus) we are able to retain as *phenomenon,* but exclude as *resource,* members invocation of such notions as the common culture as a means of detecting and arguing the orderly features of a given setting. (Zimmerman and Pollner, 1970: 3–7, emphasis in original)

Consider again how radically Zimmerman and Pollner depart from conventional sociology. Most sociologists acknowledge the need for caution in imputing values and intentions to social actors. Few believe that an actor's "definition of the situation" may be reliably inferred from core values of a given social system. Mere caution, however, does not satisfy the strictures of ethnomethodology. Ethnomethodologists conceive of the world as not only problematic, but as *beyond problematic.* By this we mean that ethnomethodologists reject any concept whose referent is alleged to be a shared mental content, no matter how much care went into its formulation.

Whether "problematic," "negotiated," or "processual," whether couched in the language of norms, as in the case of structural functionalists, or shared emergent meanings, as in the case of interactionists, the end result is the same: stable social action is the product of the actor's orientation to and compliance with shared, stable (if only within a particular interaction) norms or meanings. . . . To assume that these subjective but intersubjectively shared constructions perform such functions is to make them available as a resource for social-scientific analysis and explanation of regularities in social life. (Zimmerman and Wieder, 1970: 288)

The typical actor would fare poorly as an ethnomethodologist: his interpretations are laden with presumptions as to their intelligibility or sharedness. Do ethnomethodologists propose simply to ignore what others take for granted? No, but they insist that the sociologist's interest in such matters must not merely reflect members' interests. The intelligibility or sharedness of a construct may appear obvious to the individual of common sense, but the ethnomethodologist must demonstrate how the appearance of intelligibility or sharedness is a specific achievement of the members' methods of interpretation and display.

The specific object of ethnomethodological interest has been formulated variously. Garfinkle speaks of "procedures" (1967: 1), "methods" (1967: 30) and "practices" (1967: 33); Zimmerman and Pollner speak of "a family of practices and their properties" (1970: 98) and also of "procedures" (1970: 99); and Cicourel speaks of "basic rules" (1972: 244), "induction (interpretive) procedures" (1972: 244), "interpretive rules" (1972: 250) and "interpretive procedures" (1970: 154). These have been described in a single essay (Cicourel, 1970) as "invariant" (p. 146), with an "analytic status . . . paralleling . . . linguistic universals" (p. 166), and as "always operative" (p. 140), but "acquired" (p. 139) in a socialization process that "alters" (p. 154) them. Cicourel goes on to say that these procedures "advise" (p. 146), "provide continuous instructions" (p. 152), and "prepare the environment for substantive or practical considerations" (p. 144).

Ethnomethodologists have succeeded in avoiding standardizations in their terminology. But then few disciplines are easily grasped only by looking at their major concepts. For most one must look at how these concepts take form in the course of actual research. To this end we will look more closely at work by Garfinkle, Mehan and Wood, and Cicourel.

If one man could be said to have invented ethnomethodology, he would be Harold Garfinkle. In the early 1960s he created the intellectual and social foundation from which ethnomethodology emerged. Unfortunately, his seminal work is only poorly integrated and its shifting message escapes the theoretical edifice he builds to contain it.[12] As a consequence, his readers tend to experience by turns revelation and narcolepsy. His principal work, *Studies in Ethnomethodology* (1967), is an uneven collection of essays written at different stages in his working out of ethnomethodology. It begins with perhaps the richest and most difficult statement in all ethnomethodology: ". . . the activities whereby members produce and manage settings of organized everyday affairs are identical with members' procedures for making those settings 'account-able' " (1967: 1).

In the light of Garfinkle's subsequent research, this statement may be interpreted in several distinct ways. First, an *account* is a vehicle through which members create both a setting and their understanding of that setting. Garfinkle expresses this meaning when he says that "talk is a constituent feature of the same setting it is used to talk about" (Hill and Crittenden, 1968: 9).[13] His point—basic to not only ethnomethodology but also to phenomenology (see Heap and Roth, 1973: 367) —is that an object may not be separated from the mode of inquiry that makes it available.[14] An account can also be considered a managed effort on the part of members to phrase their activities in terms that will be accepted within a given social and interactional context. Garfinkle gives a good illustration of this in his research of jurors (1967: 104–115). A juror will often decide a given case before he reconstructs an account of how he decided. The latter may or may not be a good description of the former. Or, as Garfinkle indicates in a study of an outpatient clinic, accounts may "consist of a persuasive version of the socially organized character of the clinic's operation, regardless of what the actual order is, perhaps independently of what the actual order is, and even without the investigator having detected the actual order" (1967: 23).

On the one hand, accounts help to arrive at a social understanding: on the other, they help to ensure social acceptability. To the extent that members understand their own activities in the same terms that give social acceptance, the two versions overlap. But people also lie, mislead, or otherwise dupe an audience by giving accounts that misstate their private understanding of the same matters the accounts publicly describe. Such false accounts are often called "fronts." They are a common, even accepted, feature of most settings. Moreover, members also distinguish among accounts on other grounds: some accounts are said to be more complete, more accurate, or otherwise "better" than other accounts. How does Garfinkle treat such distinctions?

> Ethnomethodological studies of formal structures . . . are directed to the study of such phenomena . . . while abstaining from all judgments of their adequacy, value, importance, necessity, practicality, success, or consequentiality. We refer to this procedural policy as "ethnomethodological indifference." (Garfinkle and Saks, 1970: 345)

What is the effect of this policy? By withholding concern with the "adequacy . . ." of members' accounts, Garfinkle collapses the two interpretations of accounts into one. Indeed, he will even counterpose the two interpretations in consecutive sentences: "In indefinitely many ways member's inquiries are constituent features of the settings they analyze. In the same ways, these inquiries are made recognizable to members as adequate-for-all-practical purposes" (1967: 9).

Nevertheless, the two interpretations do not always cohere in Garfinkle's research. His well-known study of Agnes, a young male who possessed many of the physical attributes of an adult woman, is a good example (1967: 116–185; 285–288). He ("Agnes") in fact wished to be a woman and had requested a sex-change operation. At length the doctors consented to this operation and Agnes became a "woman." Only later was it learned that Agnes had engineered this consent by concealing her long use of hormones to induce the original physical ambiguities. The doctors and Garfinkle were misled into ratifying an assumed identity. Garfinkle, however, had indicated in a passage written long before the deceptions became known that he was uncertain whether Agnes were answering his questions truthfully.

> When I read over the transcripts and listened again to the taped interviews while preparing this paper, I was appalled by the number of occasions on which I was unable to decide whether she was answering my questions or whether she had learned from my questions, and more importantly from subtle cues both prior to and after the questions, which answers would do. (1967: 147)

Garfinkle, like most of us, is aware of more as a person than he is as a sociologist. In showing how public and private knowledge may differ, Garfinkle acknowledges that one may understand in a manner quite different from that used to gain social acceptance.

Accounts are important for Garfinkle in still another way, one unaffected by members' willingness to lie or dissemble. No matter what questions may be raised regarding the truthfulness of an account, there remains the possibility that, at bottom, the act of formulating an account requires the same basic abilities as originally grasping that which is recounted. How one lies, in terms of the abilities one must draw on to lie, differs little from how one understands. An account, because it is public, is far more accessible to sociological examination than are the internal processes that produce understanding.[15] The study of accounts thus circumvents the tendency in phenomenology to confine analysis to one's own thought-processes.

Although Garfinkle makes a good point, the implicit nihilism of his position encourages other ethnomethodologists to abandon all notion of truth and falsity. Blum and McHugh (1970), for example, have argued that theorizing is nothing less than world construction—and that from among these worlds there is little to choose. Mehan and Wood (1975) are especially adamant in this respect. They argue that if one way of attributing truth is as good as any other, then no doctrine, not even Western science, holds any special claim to validity. Science in their view is on the level of witchcraft, tarot cards, and astrology, none of which is deserving of privileged status.

Mehan and Wood make their case by pointing to presumed similarities between Western science and Azande folklore. The Azande believe that the future may be foretold by feeding a chicken the bark of a certain poisonous tree. An oracle is then believed to communicate to the Azande through the chicken by either letting the chicken live or die. Each outcome has a predetermined meaning. Mehan and Wood reason that the Azande must confront many contradictions to their faith since the oracle, when asked a question twice, will sometimes kill the chicken and sometimes let it live. Nevertheless, the Azande never question their faith. When a contradiction occurs, they attribute it to some human failing, such as a mistake in the preparation of the bark or some breach in ritual. Mehan and Wood suggest that a scientist preserves belief in science in very much the same way. Scientists, for example, have long observed that ice floats on water. Mehan and Wood offer, however, that this is true only within the universe of discourse provided by Western science, and in the context of the vague caveat "all other things being equal." Since this caveat does not specify what may or may not serve as an exception to the general principle, it allows the scientist to preserve his belief by inventing exceptions *ad hoc*. "For example, yes, ice floats on water, but not a single ice cube with a weight on top of it. Or, yes, it is 'universally true' that ice floats on water, but only if there is 'enough' water" [16] (Mehan and Wood, 1975: 94).

Mehan and Wood's point has some validity, but they do not give enough weight to the fact that a scientist knows in advance what ice will do if it must support a given amount of weight. The scientist has no need to guess what ice will do if placed in a given amount of water. The statement "ice floats on water" may not specify every particular, but Western science does not leave undecided the outcome of such routine tests. The scientist has no need for the sort of retrospective elaborations that characterize the Azande's experiments, except in areas where science has yet to advance.

Mehan and Wood also raise questions about the foundations of science, which they believe are in formal logic. Since science often involves putting an object into a class, and since this requires a measure of constancy in both the object and in the definition of the class, science ultimately is founded upon such forms of logic as the law of identity and the law of the excluded middle. To refresh the reader's memory, the *law of identity* states that an object must be itself, or that "A" is "A." The *law of the excluded middle* states that an object can only be "A" or "not A," not both simultaneously. Or, as Mehan and Wood say, once an object has been defined as having certain properties, it retains these properties because an object cannot be two things at once according to the law of the excluded middle." (1975: 65).

Mehan and Wood go on to argue that individuals do not speak and act in conformity to these requirements of formal logic. "Having children means one thing to a virgin, another to the same woman during pregnancy, yet another when she is giving birth—still another when she is talking to an interviewer, and so forth. The law of the excluded middle requires constancy. Sociological explanations adopt meanings from everyday life and impose that constancy. This destroys the experiential essence of everyday life, its constant ebb and flow" (pp. 65–6).

Mehan and Wood's argument, however, betrays a serious misunderstanding of formal logic. Logic requires, for example, an oak tree to be an oak tree; it does not require that it remain so. If a person were to chop down the oak tree and turn it into newsprint, formal logic would only require that newsprint be newsprint. Formal logic is silent regarding an object's likelihood or capacity for change; it only says that *at one moment* an object must be itself and cannot simultaneously be not itself. There also is a difference between bad science and bad logic, or for that matter, between bad thinking and bad logic. Mehan and Wood show how much more easily logic is misunderstood than violated.

Despite the critical posture toward conventional science and sociology, Mehan and Wood insist that ethnomethodology also has problems.

Its early versions especially were weakened by so strong a commitment to the individual and his perceptions that it was rendered almost solipsistic. If the conventional sociologist was more interested in social structure and the facts of social reality, the ethnomethodologist was preoccupied with "structuring activities" to the point where he risked losing touch with the real world. This led Mehan and Wood to suggest that ethnomethodology and sociology existed in a dialectical relationship with one another, each one looking at society in a way that complemented the other. Borrowing from Berger and Luckmann, they placed interpretation and understanding in a spiral and thereby offered an objective world that at its core is a human creation. The approach is faultless, at least at the programmatic level. Unfortunately, Mehan and Wood do not go on to distinguish the separate contributions to a given reality of social structure and human structuring activities. Their position offers a conceptual solution to what is an empirical problem.

A more detailed working out of ethnomethodology may be found in the work of Aaron Cicourel (see especially 1970, 1972a, 1972b). Perhaps more than any other ethnomethodologist, Cicourel has tried to find the source of the familiar world in a set of universal interpretive procedures. These procedures presumably permit a social actor to recognize and produce behavior in accord with the normative conventions of a given society. Unlike some ethnomethodologists (e.g., Zimmerman and Weider, 1970: 288) who disparage the role of rules and norms, Cicourel does not believe that specific interpretations are an outcome of interpretive procedures alone. These procedures are wed to a social and cultural context that helps direct how the outcome of interpretive procedures is expressed. Although the cultural and normative setting is important, it delineates only very general possibilities of ordering; interpretive procedures order the environment at the most basic levels.

Cicourel has presented (1970, 1972a) some instances of what he believes are interpretive procedures, one of which is the "reciprocity of perspectives." Following Schutz, Cicourel describes this procedure as consisting of a member's assumption that he and others in a setting would have the same experiences should they but trade places, and that they can disregard any personal differences in assigning meaning in favor of believing in a common world. Cicourel also identifies what he calls the "et cetera assumption" whereby members routinely "fill in" one another's utterances to make them understandable in terms of what they assume "everybody knows." Both the "reciprocity of perspectives" and the "et cetera assumption" have the effect of allowing members to presume a social consensus despite talk that is fragmentary and vague.

Cicourel goes on to distinguish a third interpretive procedure, which he calls "normal forms." By this he means that people have certain idealized forms of acceptable talk and appearance which they use in sorting out what they experience. Cicourel's interest is in both the content of these normal forms and the work people put into seeing normal forms in their environment. Normal forms are thus instances of both form and process.

Although Cicourel's work is promising, even a brief look at his interpretive procedures exposes certain problems in their conception. First, they are a motley group without a common source, object, or means of expression. Indeed, they are not even at the same level of abstraction: the "reciprocity of perspectives" is general and broadly applicable, while "normal forms" are presumably quite concrete. Second, the relevance of interpretive procedures for empirical research is not described. In his studies on Argentine fertility and juvenile justice (1968, 1974a), Cicourel engaged in an analysis that relied very little on the substance of his theoretical position. And finally, Cicourel's piecemeal conceptualization of interpretive procedures leaves it unclear what the outcome of their study will be. How many interpretive procedures are there? What may we learn from them? To what extent can a researcher ignore their role in his formulation of a setting? These and other questions remain to be answered.

Mehan and Wood acknowledge that "though interpretive procedures can be used [to "fill in" the essential incompleteness of normative rules] it would be inconsistent to conclude that they are immune from the feature of incompleteness found in normative rules" (1975: 114). Cicourel, who otherwise presents a very tough-minded view of science, occasionally seems troubled by his own vulnerability to the charges he levels at conventional sociology:

> The ethnomethodologist employs glosses while operating within the mundaneity principle at different levels, and these glosses forever remain a member's account of practices said to make up the properties of mundane reasoning. Because these glosses recommend that a sense of "stepping back" is possible . . . the ethnomethodologist is also vulnerable to the charge of having adopted a privileged position. (1974b, 123)

Despite such problems, Cicourel has begun in his work to specify a model of the actor. He uses the interpretive procedures in this as elements comprising what he calls social competance. Very much like Schutz, whom Cicourel acknowledges freely, Cicourel emphasizes the value in making explicit one's view of the actor. But unlike Schutz, who would have the researcher construct a model carefully bound to his specific research interests, Cicourel attempts to construct a model of common-sense man as he actually negotiates his everyday life. If Cicourel is correct in believing interpretive procedures to be the principal source for members' sense of social structure, his work, along with that of other ethnomethodologists, may point to a valuable synthesis of phenomenological philosophy and sociology.

Conclusion

The previous discussion is not a complete inventory of what goes by the name "phenomenological sociology." As is evident, the term is used rather loosely among sociologists, often encompassing research informed by quite different views on human consciousness and methods for studying it.

We distinguished two strains of phenomenological sociology in this chapter. One strain describes shared but contingent patterns of subjective experience in the language (worked out by Husserl and Schutz). Terms such as "typification," and "recipe" tend to shift somewhat from describing universal features of intentional consciousness to specific contents of a social member's perspective. The research of phenomenological sociology does not differ greatly from that produced within more conventional approaches such as symbolic interactionism; it is, however, more fully grounded in direct observations of human behavior. Since this tends to ensure that research maintains a solid basis in the everyday world, the difference is important. Nonetheless, the approaches described in this chapter are not phenomenological if that term is confined to its narrow philosophical meaning.

The second strain of research is more closely related to the founding concerns of phenomenological philosophy. Basic questions of method, theory, and human action comprise its subject matter. As in phenomenology, attention is confined to the stream of immanent experience in which the familiar world emerges as the dominant background and arena for a person's daily activities. The familiarity of the world is attributed to the use of certain fundamental and universal interpretive procedures that act together to organize disparate observations into customary patterns. The interest in these procedures has led to recent attempts to construct a model of the common-sense individual. In the emerging model of phenomenological sociology, the actor's sense of social structure is a product of a competence whose explication is considered basic to social science.

Like most new approaches, phenomenological sociology suffers from the enthusiasms and insecurities of youth. Because of a lack of enough research, it is uncertain whether the fine points of its theoretical reflection have any empirical substance. And as one might expect, the movement itself is beset by disputes over how the emerging perspective is to be defined.

There has been very little critical give-and-take among those who call themselves phenomenological sociologists. Most theorists within the movement have developed their work without any explicit consideration of competing versions of phenomenological sociology. The field—to the extent that it can be called that—remains fragmented, with no outstanding spokesperson, no widely accepted program, and no shared vision for sociology.

Notes

1. The notion of a transcendental Ego is a difficult and sometimes confusing aspect of Husserl's work. The term "transcendental" does not in Husserl's usage mean the same as "transcendent," which usually implies the occupancy of a superior and unknowable position. On the contrary, "transcendental" refers to that which underlies or makes possible the occupancy of any position. The "transcendental Ego," then, designates the basic conditions for the appearance of the world. It has a subjective connotation because this appearance can only take place in consciousness. Nonetheless, it is not the same as the "empirical Ego" (what a person usually means when he says "I"), which is itself rooted in transcendental ground. Since Husserl's version of transcendental phenomenology is more popular as a point of departure than as a program, it will not receive an extended discussion.

2. This is not entirely true. In his final work (1970a), Husserl discussed the everyday world and the relevance of phenomenology in its study. Although the substance of his remarks have generally been ignored in favor of his earlier work, certain aspects of his position will be addressed later in this chapter.

3. Schutz accepted, for example, that analyses made in the reduced sphere were valid for the realm of the natural attitude. (Schutz, 1962; 149) Moreover, Schutz accepted that for purposes such as clarifying the constitution of meaning or the temporal features of typification, a transcendental phenomenology is indispensible. (Schutz, 1967; 97–138)

4. Schutz puts the issue clearly in perspective in the following remark:

> Is it possible, by means of free variations in phantasy, to grasp the *eidos* of a concrete species or genus, unless these variations are limited by the frame of the type in terms of which we have experienced, in the natural attitude, the object from which the process of ideation starts as a familiar one, as such and such an object within the life-world? Can these free variations in phantasy reveal anything else but the limits established by such typification? If these questions have to be answered in the negative, then there is indeed merely a difference of degree between type and *eidos*. Ideation can reveal nothing that was not preconstituted by the type. (Schutz, 1966: 115).

5. Although Schutz did not enumerate the specific implications of phenomenological analysis for social science, Phillipson has attempted (1972: 131–146) to draw out of Schutz's remarks the relevance of phenomenology for such basic issues in social science methodology as concept formation, standards of validity and reliability, and the relationship of these to the empirical world.

6. Luckmann's programmatic statements also left many issues undeveloped. He did not, for example, specify the procedures by which statements within the different historical vernaculars are to be translated into the metalanguage derived from the structures of the lifeworld. He subjected this translation to only two conditions: one simply reasserted the necessity for the language to consist of genuinely universal structures and the other established a criterion of subjective adequacy. The criterion—a restatement of Schutz's postulate of adequacy —is formulated as follows:

The "translations" of the statements (but not necessarily of their theoretical explanations) from the historical languages into the metalanguage or, more appropriately, the protolanguage, would have to be plausible in principle if not in immediate fact to the speakers-actors who produced the statements. (Luckmann, 1973: 181)

What it means to be "plausible in principle if not in immediate fact" is left unspecified. Luckmann's remarks suffer from the same problem as Schutz's postulate of adequacy; that is, an unaddressed tension between the formal properties of the translation and the necessity that the translation remain plausible to the common-sense individual. And as Schutz, Luckmann did not address the need for an interrogation of the speaker-actor with respect to the plausibility of a particular translation to presuppose a theory of interaction.

7. The mechanics of the transition from Schutz through Berger and Luckmann and then to a view acknowledging a version of "objective reality" is evident in the following remark by Wagner:

Phenomenological sociology is relatively most advanced in areas of structural inquiries. Schutz' contributions in this respect, are basic . . . Peter Berger and Thomas Luckmann's inquiry into *The Social Construction of Reality* transcends Schutz' work in several ways. It preserves and accentuates the fluidity of Schutz' starting point and is concerned with the dialectic interweaving of subjective and objective factors in the formation of cognitive structures in which the "objective reality" of "society" is confronted with the "subjective reality" of the individual's acquisition of his knowledge about society. (1973: 69)

8. Ethnomethodology is a term coined by Harold Garfinkle. "You want to know where I actually got the term? I was working with the Yale cross-cultural files. I happened to be looking down the list without the intent of finding such a term. I was looking through their taglines, if you will permit that usage, and I came to a section: ethnobotany, ethnophysiology, ethnophysics. . . . That is the way 'ethnomethodology' was used to begin with. "Ethno" seemed to refer, somehow or other, to the availability to a member of common-sense knowledge of his society as common-sense knowledge of "whatever."

9. In addition to the important distinction between topic and resource, ethnomethodologists also state their position using the concepts of "indexicality" and "basic" (vs. "surface" or normative) rules of interpretation. Indexicality (see Bar Hillel, 1954; Garfinkle, 1967: 4–7; Cicourel, 1970: 150–151) refers to the fact that any vocabulary is a constituent feature of the experience it describes. In other words, meaning and context are mutually dependent. Cicourel's distinction between "basic" and "surface" rules is another important source for formulating ethnomethodology.

10. At many points ethnomethodologists speak in terms that may only be described as convoluted. Ironically, and perhaps with some justification, a few ethnomethodologists regard a new (or fully described) "language" as a precondition for precise description. Saks (1963: 2) goes furthest in this direction by requiring every term in the researcher's "descriptive apparatus" to be itself fully

described. Others (Garfinkle, 1967) would presumably regard this as but another fruitless attempt to substitute objective for "indexical" (*See #9*, above) expressions.

11. "By the term "elements" we mean those features of a setting that members rely on, attend to, and use as the basis for action, inference, and analysis on any given occasion" (Zimmerman and Pollner, 1970: 96)

12. Filmer (1972: 206–210), for example, has drawn from Garfinkle's work "four definitions, plus at least one exegesis of ethnomethodology." Although Filmer does not present these definitions as competitive, he indicates they differ.

13. Garfinkle may also be expressing the idea that one never truly understands something until he can put it into words.

14. The interpretation of accounts as the formulation of sensibility is very similar to Schutz's interpretation of meaning. Schutz argued that meaning does not reside in events, but in the reflective glance that transforms an initially unbroken flow of events into something distinct and discrete (e.g., into an experience). In brief, meaning is simply that mental attitude which formulates events into experience.

15. Garfinkle's ideas in this respect are not completely accepted by all ethnomethodologists. Cicourel (1972b) has argued that verbal accounts only imperfectly reflect the experiential nexus they purportedly describe since much of this experience is non-verbal and, by implication, derivative of different interpretive procedures. Cicourel, however, does not reject Garfinkle's empiricism, only its limitation to that which is rendered verbally.

16. A more widely shared misunderstanding among ethnomethodologists is that science must in some way be free of presumptions, and thereby capable of literal measurement. Their arguments is that given the irremedial nature of indexicality, the scientist must ultimately fail in his attempt at precise description. This failure is judged harshly. Saks (Sociological Description, 1963 12–14) argued that since no description can ever be complete, any description may be elaborated without end, and therefore any description may be regarded as far from complete, or as close to complete, as any other. This argument, like that of Mehan and Wood, tends to reduce science to the level of any other consistent belief system.

References

BERGER, PETER and THOMAS LUCKMANN. *The Social Construction of Reality*. Garden City, N.Y.: Doubleday and Co., 1966.

BERGSON, HENRI. *Time and Free Will*. New York: Macmillan, 1913.

BITTNER, EGON. "The Concept of Organization." *Social Research* 32.

BLUM, ALAN and PETER McHUGH, "The Social Ascription of Motive." *American Sociological Review* 36, 1971.

BLUMENSTIEL, ALEXANDER D. "The Sociology of Good Times." In George Psathas (ed.), *Phenomenological Sociology*. New York: John Wiley & Sons, 1973.

CICOUREL, AARON V. *Method and Measurement in Sociology.* New York: The Free Press, 1964.

CICOUREL, AARON V. *The Social Organization of Juvenile Justice.* New York: John Wiley & Sons, 1968.

CICOUREL, AARON V. "The Acquisition of Social Structure: Toward a Developmental Sociology of Language and Meaning." In Jack D. Douglas (ed.), *Understanding Everyday Life.* Chicago: Aldine Publishing Co., 1970.

CICOUREL, AARON V. "Basic and Normative Rule in the Negotiation of Status and Role." In David Sudnow (ed.), *Studies in Social Interaction.* New York: The Free Press, 1972.

CICOUREL, AARON V. *Theory and Method in a Study of Argentine Fertility.* New York: John Wiley & Sons, 1974a.

CICOUREL, AARON V. *Cognitive Sociology: Language and Meaning in Social Interaction.* New York: The Free Press, 1974b.

DOUGLAS, JACK D. "Understanding Everyday Life," In Jack D. Douglas *The Relevance of Sociology.* New York: Appleton-Century-Crofts, 1970a.

DOUGLAS, JACK D. "Understanding Everyday Life," In Jack D. Douglas (ed.), *Understanding Everyday Life.* Chicago: Aldine Publishing Co., 1970b.

DOUGLAS, JACK D. *American Social Order.* New York: The Free Press, 1971.

FARBER, MARVIN. "The Ideal of a Presuppositionless Philosophy." In Joseph J. Kockelmans (ed.), *Phenomenology.* Garden City, N.Y.: Doubleday and Co., 1967.

FILMER, PAUL. "On Harold Garfinkle's Ethnomethodology." In Paul Filmer, Michael Phillipson, David Silverman, and David Walsh. *New Directions in Sociological Theory.* Cambridge, Mass.: MIT Press, 1973.

GARFINKLE, HAROLD. *Studies in Ethnomethodology.* Englewood Cliffs, N.J.: Prentice-Hall, 1967.

GOFFMAN, ERVING. *The Presentation of Self in Everyday Life.* Garden City, N.Y.: Doubleday and Co., 1959.

HEAP, JAMES L. and PHILLIP A. ROTH. "On Phenomenological Sociology." *American Sociological Review* 38, June.

HILL, R. C. and K. S. CRITTENDEN. "The Purdue Symposium on Ethnomethodology." Monograph No. 1, Institute for the Study of Social Change, Purdue University, 1968.

HILL, RICHARD J. and KATHLEEN STONES. Proceedings of the Purdue Symposium on Ethnomethodology, Purdue Research Foundation, 1968.

HUSSERL, EDMUND. *Ideal: General Introduction to Pure Phenomenology.* New York: Collier Books, 1962.

HUSSERL, EDMUND. "Philosophy as Rigorous Science" and "Philosophy and the Crisis of European Man." In Quentin Lauer (trans.) *Phenomenology and the Crisis of Philosophy.* New York: Harper & Row, 1965.

HUSSERL, EDMUND. *The Crisis of European Sciences and Transcendental Phenomenology.* Evanston, Ill.: Northwestern University Press, 1970a.

HUSSERL, EDMUND. *Cartesian Meditations.* The Hague: Martinus Nijhoff, 1970b.

JEHENSON, ROGER. "A Phenomenological Approach to the Study of the

Formal Organization." In George Psathas (ed.), *Phenomenological Sociology.* New York: John Wiley & Sons, 1973.

LYMAN, STANFORD M. and MARVIN B. SCOTT. *A Sociology of the Absurd.* New York: Appleton-Century-Crofts, 1970.

LUCKMANN, THOMAS. "Philosophy, Science, and Everyday Life." In Maurice Natanson (ed.), *Phenomenology and the Social Sciences,* vol. I. Evanston, Ill.: Northwestern University Press, 1973.

MARTINDALE, DON. *The Nature and Types of Sociological Theory.* Boston: Houghton Mifflin Co., 1960.

MEAD, GEORGE HERBERT. *Mind, Self and Society: From the Standpoint of a Social Behaviorist.* (Edited by Charles W. Morris.) Chicago: University of Chicago Press, 1934.

MEHAN, HUGH and HOUSTON WOOD. *The Reality of Ethnomethodology.* New York: John Wiley and Sons, 1975.

NATANSON, MAURICE. "Phenomenology and the Social Sciences." In Maurice Natanson (ed.), *Phenomenology and the Social Sciences,* vol. I. Evanston, Ill.: Northwestern University Press, 1973.

PHILLIPSON, MICHAEL. "Phenomenological Philosophy and Sociology." In Paul Filmer, Michael Phillipson, David Silverman, and David Walsh. *New Directions in Sociological Theory.* Cambridge, Mass.: MIT Press, 1973.

POLLNER. "On the Foundations of Mundane Reason." Unpublished PhD dissertation. University of California, Santa Barbara.

SAKS, HAROLD. "Sociological Description." *Berkeley Journal of Sociology,* 8, 1963.

SCHUTZ, ALFRED. *Collected Papers I. The Problem of Social Reality.* The Hague: Martinus Nijhoff, 1962.

SCHUTZ, ALFRED. *Collected Papers II. Studies in Social Theory.* The Hague: Martinus Nijhoff, 1964.

SCHUTZ, ALFRED. *Collected Papers III. Studies in Phenomenological Philosophy.* The Hague: Martinus Nijhoff, 1966.

SCHUTZ, ALFRED. *The Phenomenology of the Social World.* Evanston, Ill.: Northwestern University Press, 1967.

SCHUTZ, ALFRED. *Reflections on the Problem of Relevance.* New Haven, Conn.: Yale University Press, 1970.

SCHUTZ, ALFRED and THOMAS LUCKMANN. *Structures of the Lifeworld.* Evanston, Ill.: Northwestern University Press, 1973.

SPIEGELBERG, H. *The Phenomenological Movement,* vols. 1 and 2. The Hague: Martinus Nijhoff, 1969.

TENHOUTON, WARREN and CHARLES KAPLAN. *Science and Its Mirror Image.* New York: Harper & Row, 1973.

TIRYAKIAN, EDWARD A. "Sociology and Existential Phenomenology." In Maurice Natanson (ed.), *Phenomenology and the Social Sciences,* vol. I. Evanston, Ill.: Northwestern University Press, 1973.

WAGNER, HELMUT R. "The Scope of Phenomenological Sociology: Considerations and Suggestions." In George Psathas (ed.), *Phenomenological Sociology.* New York: John Wiley & Sons, 1973.

WEBER, MAX. *Economy and Society.* New York: Westminister Press, 1968.

WEICK, KARL E. *The Social Psychology of Organizing.* Reading, Mass.: Addison-Wesley, 1969.

WIEDER, D. LAWRENCE. "Meaning by Rule." In Jack D. Douglas, (ed.), *Understanding Everyday Life.* Chicago: Aldine Publishing Co., 1970.

ZIMMERMAN, DON H. "The Practicalities of Rule Use." In Jack D. Douglas (ed.), *Understanding Everyday Life.* Chicago: Aldine Publishing Co., 1970.

ZIMMERMAN, DON H. and D. LAWRENCE WIEDER. "Ethnomethodology and the Problem of Order: Comment on Denzin." In Jack D. Douglas (ed.), *Understanding Everyday Life.* Chicago: Aldine Publishing Co., 1970.

ZIMMERMAN, DON H. and MELVIN POLLNER. "The Everyday World as a Phenomenon." In Jack D. Douglas (ed.), *Understanding Everyday Life.* Chicago: Aldine Publishing Co., 1970.

6

Toward a Complex Universe:
Existential Sociology

Andrea Fontana

Existentialism is not a philosophy but a label for several widely
different revolts against traditional philosophy. Most of the living
"existentialists" have repudiated this label and a bewildered outsider might well conclude that the only thing they have in common
is a marked aversion for each other. To add to confusion, many
writers of the past have frequently been hailed as members of this
movement, and it is extremely doubtful whether they would have
appreciated the company to which they were consigned. In view
of this, it may be argued that the label "existentialism" ought to be
abandoned altogether.[1]

It may seem rather paradoxical to suggest that the label "existentialism"
be abandoned at the beginning of a chapter on existential sociology. But
this rebellious attitude toward categorizations of any kind represents
the spirit of existentialism. Existentialists see all human beings as concrete individuals of blood-and-bones creating their ways through a
world in which meanings are highly problematic and situated. Existentialists refuse to believe that people are mere cognitive forms, mere
symbolic pawns in a world they cannot control. Therefore, any label,
including "existentialism," is often met with hostility by existential

thinkers, because it presents a threat to their individuality by categorizing and classifying away the concreteness and uniqueness of their work.

Even if agreement could be reached on what constitutes existential thought, an attempt to follow the development and the various paths of existentialism throughout the centuries would be a monumental task well beyond the scope of this work. Existential thought finds its sources in a multitude of forms ranging from paintings to novels, from dramas to poems, from philosophical treaties to sociological analyses.[2] Since modern existential sociology relies to some degree on the thoughts of previous existentialists, especially philosophers, a brief journey through the largely unstructured world of existentialism is necessary.

When the statement is made that existential sociologies rely upon the works of philosophers one must be careful not to take that too literally, as some have done.[3] Just as no one literally applies the "eidetic reduction" to the everyday world, no one applies verbatim Sartre's or Merleau-Ponty's precepts to sociological analysis. Existential philosophers did not provide a set of methodological practices with which to measure the world, and most existential sociologies do not deal explicitly with methodological practices.[4] Existentialists welcome any approach that will allow them to uncover the rational front presented by social performers and to reach down into the deep turmoil of human existence. Existential sociology is concerned above all with the experiential realm of everyday life; it argues that the topic of inquiry of sociological analysis is human beings in all their natural settings—in the everyday world in which they live.

Some sociologies have already advocated this general approach under different rubrics: field work (the Chicago School and its followers);[5] a return to things in themselves (naturalism);[6] and going back to the phenomena (phenomenology).[7] Existential sociology differs from these previous sociologies in its consideration of the immense complexity, problematicness and situatedness of life. No rational theory can fully capture the puzzling wonders of human life. Existential sociology argues that human beings themselves cannot grasp the vast flux of human processes. In our wonderment, we are forced to treat events as situational, since we are unable to understand or provide a systematized explanation of occurrences.

Existential sociology turns its attention to these everyday feelings and situationally created meanings, in the realization that:

> The eventual true explanation of them [of human processes] will almost certainly be vastly complex, and at present our only certainty must be uncertainty.[8]

The inclusion of situatedness and feelings alongside rationality attempts to solve an age-old problem: the separation of the realms of rationality (scholarship and science) and the realms of feeling (arts).[9] Although existential sociology does not often address this issue directly, it implicitly attempts to synthesize the two different paradigms.[10]

The Early Existentialists

Ancient Greek culture provides us with some early forms of existentialism. The Greek god Dionysus was the primordial figure of existentialism.[11] He was the god of tragic festivals, which were one of the highest expressions of Greek culture. But he also was the god of wine and wine festivals, thus representing the loss of rationality and the attainment of rhapsodic inspiration through inebriation. Dionysus represented a mythical, symbolic attempt to combine the highest rational form of his civilization, the tragic festivals, with the inner feelings of human beings, unbridled by any rational restrictions. Dionysus combined rational expressions and situated feelings, thus reflecting the complexity of human expressions characteristic of existentialism. The unbridled expression of feelings of Dionysus led to an image of the god as an animal. The Greek represented Dionysus as a bull and symbolically slaughtered him, thus, in a way, making him the first victim of existentialism.

This ancient conflict between feelings and rational expressions was soon resolved in favor of rationalism. Causal explanations began to justify all human conduct. Socrates exemplified the victory of rational, calculative thinking in the quest for providing an understanding of human beings within the cosmos. On the losing side was an early existential thinker, the ebullient Sophist from Chalcedon, Trasymachus, who resisted Socrates' rational explanations and was continually ridiculed for it.[12]

The debate that began in ancient Greece over the ways in which humans expressed themselves continues, but it would go far beyond the scope of this chapter to follow in detail existential thinkers up throughout history. For centuries the idea that the human condition is terribly problematic and can only be understood in reference to the irrational, emotional-situational endeavors of human beings was suppressed from the public arenas of life by centuries of dogmatic beliefs. Those who dared show the fragility of socially created paradigms found a grim fate awaiting them, including at times burning at the stake.

Niccolò Machiavelli (1469–1527) clearly understood the problematic, situational, feeling-based nature of human interaction and dared to state his beliefs publicly. In *The Prince* he attempted to provide a guide for human conduct in problematic times.[13] He found no reward for his trouble, either in his lifetime or in succeeding generations, which grossly misunderstood his work and turned a humanistic document into a monstrous example of unscrupulous perversity.[14]

The Italian humanist Giordano Bruno (1548–1600)[15] spoke out against the narrowly egocentric Ptolomeiac conception of the universe and showed how the new Copernican notions removed earth from the center of the universe. Bruno spoke of the infinity of the universe but the vast implications of that idea for the understanding of humanity terrified the orderly world of Bruno's contemporaries. He was burned alive at the stake as a heretic. Bruno's compatriot Galileo Galilei (1564–1642) [16] had gazed at the stars and seen the complex wonders of the universe of which, he realized, we are but an infinitesimal part. Once more the ruling order saw its dogmas endangered by these revelations. Rather than acknowledge the uncertainty of human destiny, order and certitude were restored by torturing Galileo into recanting his brilliant observations and insights.

In succeeding centuries, the struggle over the human condition assumed different names: objectivism versus subjectivism, romanticism versus rationalism, positivism versus existentialism. Scientific views of the world gained the upper hand, especially with the scientific breakthrough of the nineteenth century. The German materialist Karl Vogt stated that: ". . . the brain secretes thought, just as the liver secretes bile." [17]

A few years earlier in France, Adolphe Quetelet had claimed that "moral statistics" could explain the patterns of crime independently of human beings' free will. Herbert Spencer applied his evolutionary principles to biology, psychology, and sociology, receiving great public acclaim. The great success of the natural sciences rolled on. Sociology grew out of this positivistic movement as an attempt to measure and quantify the world in a rational way.

But some individuals refused to accept dogmas which, in attempting to provide an order in the world, oversimplified it. In Denmark Søren Kierkegaard (1813–1855) attacked the attempt to depersonalize human beings. He assailed the notion that existence can be derived from reason, as in the philosophy of Hegel, and launched his attack against the religion of unreflective churchgoers, who take for granted that they are Christians, and make no effort to really become Christians.

Kierkegaard argued that *existence is prior to essence*. Human beings cannot be reduced to scientific objects because they exist prior to the abstracting process of deriving essences or symbolic forms (*cf.* Husserl, chapter 5). Truth can only be grasped through commitment, not through uninvolved, detached objectivity. Logical deductive reasoning will not lead us to truth, since there is no "first premise" from which to begin the deductive process.[18] We ourselves as concrete, involved, freely acting individuals *choose* our starting point.

While Kierkegaard was profoundly religious, Nietzsche (1844–1900) began his philosophy from the premise that God is dead. Human beings must learn how to live by themselves and on their own terms now that their gods are gone. Nietzschean beings launched themselves in a world empty of meaning because of the loss of God, fighting the shadows of despair with the will to power. He too emphasized existence over essence. Nietzsche thought individuals could think and feel for themselves, beyond the constraints of a purely logical or moral world that reduced human beings to impersonal, unquestioning symbolic categories or automata acting out the dictates of absolute morality.

Philosophers were not the only ones to rebel against an overly rational or moralistic model of human beings. Literature was another fertile field in which the existential seeds were sown. Dostoyevsky (1821–1887) was perhaps one of the best exponents of literary existentialism. This sensitive Russian writer portrayed the plight of human beings who were brought face to face with existence by desperate living conditions—by the frozen Siberian tundra in which the irrational, demoniac side of human nature emerged, or by the everyday bureaucratic world in which human beings were squelched by rational, precise, and pedantic boundaries. Dostoyevsky screamed out at the world that closed in on him coldly and mercilessly from all sides. This world prevented him from being what he wanted to be—a human being with warmth, feelings, and sensations, rather than a cold piece of machinery or a distant, unreachable crystal palace:

> You believe in a palace of crystal that can never be destroyed—a palace at which one will not be able to put one's tongue or make a long nose on the sly. And perhaps that is just why I am afraid of this edifice, that it is of crystal and can never be destroyed and that one cannot put one's tongue out at it even on the sly.[19]

Tolstoi (1828–1910) was another Russian writer who tackled the meaning of existence and looked beneath the castle of cards that humanity had built around itself. Tolstoi's message was not as strident as Dostoyevski's, but possessed a majestic self-realization of one's purpose, or lack of purpose, in life. For instance, in *The Death of Ivan Illych* [20] Ivan was suddenly faced with the realization that his compassed, rational, bureaucratic life was but an empty shell. Faced with the approach of his own death from cancer, Ivan realized that what had seemed to be the important concerns in his life—family, career, money and prestige—had been but empty cocoons compared with the beautiful butterfly of existence itself.

Another powerful cry for concrete selfhood came from Henrik Ibsen (1828–1906), as exemplified by the play *Brand*.[21] In *Brand* one is confronted with the irreducible strength of an uncompromising parson who flinches at nothing, is afraid of nothing, and forgives nothing in his attempt to carry the burden of his own existence. The parson does not unload the weight of the anguished relation between human beings and life upon the shoulders of God, but carries on relentlessly supported only by a Nietzschean will to live.

In the wake of the vacillating, uncertain post–World War II period, literary existentialism became a cult, especially in France, sustained by the works of Jean-Paul Sartre, Albert Camus, and Simone de Beauvoir.[22] The widespread spectre of death suddenly brought human beings face to face with the meaning of their existence, and human beings became aware that they were more than mechanical automatons, that life was more than an organized set of stable rules. Human beings began to search their souls for the meaning of life. This, however, did not last long. As the spectre of war faded away, Western Europe began to prosper. The petty political squabbles over the fruits of prosperity replaced the anguished search for the meaning of human existence. Some existentialism made its way to the United States, mainly in literary works, and especially those of Jean-Paul Sartre. In the spirit of American practicality and the frantic pace of the industrial boom, these introspective literary works were often seen as nihilistic.

But existentialism was and is much more than a rejection of values and beliefs. It is an attempt to see human beings as concrete beings-in-the-world, or, in other words, as individuals both creating and being created by the world they made no choice to be in. The existentialist's strong outcries against conventional values are attempts to tear aside the peaceful, orderly, unquestioning dogmas under which humankind hides and to expose human beings to the vortex of a complex universe in which no absolute answers exist. This quest for the meaning of existence took various paths. One of these paths carried some scholars to the phenomenology of Husserl.

The Relation between Phenomenology and Existentialism

Husserl's attempt to create a rigorous foundation for a scientific enterprise took a very different path from that of another great philosopher, Wilhelm Dilthey. Husserl, who saw Dilthey's notions as being completely unscientific, put forth his phenomenology as an attempt to remedy what he considered the flaws of Dilthey's work. Husserl's work has been examined already in this text (*see* chapter 5), so let us turn to Dilthey.

Dilthey (1833–1911) argued that the process whereby the study of human beings is accomplished is radically different from that of looking at the quantifiable, scientific, natural world. The difference is that in attempting to understand human beings, one must always introduce previous knowledge of what it means to be a human being. What follows, for Dilthey, is that one should not rely upon the theory and methodology of the natural sciences, but that life itself should be the starting point of inquiry [23] when human beings are concerned.

What logic should be available for such an enterprise? Certainly not that of causal categories, says Dilthey, since this logic lies outside of human beings and does not represent the way the human experience is understood by living human beings. Life is understood in terms of meaning, so meaning should be the starting point of one's inquiry. By "meaning" Dilthey did not mean abstract categorizations, but meaning in one's everyday, lived, concrete experience. By lived experience Dilthey means experience during the *act,* rather than in the reflexive act of consciousness. Experience, then, cannot experience itself, but has meaning in its doing. Hence, experience is not an interpretive process apart from the act itself but is at one with the act:

> The way in which "lived experience" presents itself to me is completely different from the way in which images stand before me. The consciousness of the experience and its constitution are the same: there is no separation between what is there-for-me and what in experience is there for me. In other words, the experience does not stand like an object over against its experiencer, but rather its very existence for me is undifferentiated from the *whatness* which is presented for me in it.[24]

Thus there is no difference, for Dilthey, between the object that one experiences and the experiencing itself; the two are one and the same. People can only apprehend the world through their experiences within it.

Understanding (*verstehen*) is the most important element in Dilthey's philosophy. It represents more than a cognitive exercise. It comprises the totality of one's perceptive, cognitive, and affective apparatus in the comprehending of another individual. Understanding, along with meaning, is paramount in human beings' everyday life. It is part of a circle, since there is no starting point from which to understand. Instead, life takes on meaning only from a particular, situated, concrete viewpoint, since it is only from this viewpoint that one can experience and understand the world.

Dilthey used *hermeneutic* (interpretive) *procedures* for looking at the world. Hermeneutic refers to the study of understanding, as its etymology indicates:

> The Greek word *hermeios* referred to the priest at the Delphic oracle. This word and the more common verb *hermeneuein* and noun *hermēneia* point back to the wing-footed messenger-god Hermes, from whose name the words are apparently derived (or vice versa?). Significantly, Hermes is associated with the function of transmuting what is beyond human understanding into a form that human intelligence can grasp. The various forms of the word suggest the process of bringing a thing or situation from unintelligibility to understanding. The Greeks credited Hermes with the discovery of language and writing—the tools which human understanding employs to grasp meaning and to convey it to others.[25]

Dilthey argued that presupposition-less knowledge, such as Husserl was seeking, is impossible. He felt that meaning takes place only within a frame of reference. Meaning was seen as historical by Dilthey and his interest was the interpretive study of human history.

Martin Heidegger (1889–1976) began where Dilthey left off:

> Fundamentally the following analysis of temporality and historicity is solely concerned with preparing the way for the assimilation of the researches of W. Dilthey which the present generation has yet to achieve.[26]

Of course, Heidegger was influenced by many other sources than Dilthey, and there is a great deal of ambiguity about the inspirational sources of Heidegger. Connections with Nietzsche and Kierkegaard are often made, and pre-Socratic philosophers undoubtably influenced Heidegger's work. But for our purpose we shall limit ourselves to examining the influence of Dilthey and Husserl on Heidegger.

Heidegger can in a way be seen as the precursor of existential sociology in that he draws upon the scientific methodology of Husserl's phenomenology and the historical understanding of Dilthey's hermeneutics to gain understanding of being-in-the-world. Husserl's phenomenology sought to elucidate the consciousness of transcendental subjectivity. But Heidegger interprets phenomenology by returning to the ideas contained in the Greek roots of the word; *phainomenon* and *logos* refer to the manifesting of the phenomenon itself as it is, rather than to a meaning acquired through categorization of, or reflection upon, the phenomenon.[27] By attempting to "bracket the everyday world," Husserl takes away what for Heidegger constitutes the very topic of inquiry—the everyday world.

By considering understanding as a practical endeavor occurring in the unfolding of a phenomenon in the everyday world, Heidegger leaves both Husserl and Dilthey behind. Husserl's understanding lay outside of historical flow and Dilthey's understanding was a theoretical notion leading only to a historical understanding. Heidegger's hermeneutics are not abstract ways of apprehending the meaning of humanity, but an attempt to understand and interpret *human beings in their historical present, as they are in-the-world*. For Heidegger, a human being is not a static entity, but a dynamic one who can only be understood by relying on the historical (or previous) knowledge of that being and on the contextual situation at the moment in which the understanding occurs. The understanding of human beings is immersed in its historical flow and occurs in the world at only one moment in time.

Heidegger yanked human beings down from the lofty theoretical clouds of previous philosophical concepts and restored them to the world of everyday life in which they live. However, the Heideggerian human being (*Dasein*) still lacks many human traits, for he is too abstract and his humanity is often lost in the difficult prose of the German philosopher. It is in French existentialism that human beings were conceived of as free to reveal their full beings as carnal, feeling, living creatures.

Jean-Paul Sartre (born 1905) is often seen as the primary exponent of existentialism. Like Heidegger, Sartre was influenced by the phenomenology of Husserl. But he rejected Husserl's transcendental ego because he believed that the ego cannot exist apart from the acts in which it engages itself—that the ego takes shape in the doing of acts in the world itself. Sartre distinguishes two types of being. Being-in-itself (*en-soi*) refers to the things themselves as they are. Being-for-itself (*pour-soi*) resembles Heidegger's *Dasein*; it is an evolving self that can never be stopped and become in-itself, but which changes historically and contextually.[28]

Sartre's existentialism is extremely dramatic, and his most powerful medium is his novels in which the characters are literally overcome by the nausea of the petty squalor of the everyday, routinized existence:

> It came like a sickness, not abruptly or insistently but slowly and insidiously; I felt a little uneasy, that's all. Once there, it refused to go away; it stayed quietly and I was able to persuade myself that nothing was wrong, that it was a false alarm. Now it is spreading.[29]

Having reached the point of nausea over their existence, some individuals choose a course of action and commit themselves to a cause. The decision to commit oneself to a tangible enterprise represents the existential choice of living as one chooses, having finally abandoned a pre-cast, routinized existence. For instance, Mathieu in Sartre's *Troubled Sleep* decides to fight the Germans and abandons himself almost orgiastically to this newly found cause:

> He fired, and the commandments flew through the air—Thou shalt love thy neighbor as theyself—bang! right in that mug—Thou shalt not kill—bang! right in that bastard's face. He fired on Man, on Virtue, on Freedom, on the World: Freedom is terror. A fire raged in the town hall, raged in his head.[30]

Mathieu has finally broken through the rigidity of a life in which values are not our own but are determined for us in an absolute manner by others. Many other individuals, according to Sartre, never choose to embark on an existential course of action and opt to live an easy, comfortable life in which decisions are made for them. Never choosing to reject, they remain almost unconscious beings. For Sartre this is "bad faith" and those who engage in it live a life of self-delusion and are nothing but *salauds:*

> I look around the room. What a farce! All the people are sitting there, looking serious and eating. No, they are not eating; they are fortifying themselves for the task that lies ahead. Each of them has

his own little personal bias which prevents him from being aware of his existence; every single one of them believes himself indispensable to someone or something.[31]

Sartre's triology, *Roads to Freedom*,[32] is an especially existential work. The protagonists of the novels commit themselves to the hard realities that face them in the everyday world. Sartre's characters are close to Heidegger's *Dasein*; they both shape and are shaped by the world. Unfortunately Sartre was soon to become so entangled in a political commitment that his writings lost significance for existentialism and became political statements instead.[33]

Maurice Merleau-Ponty (1908–1961) proved to be a more comprehensive, if less dramatic, spokesman for existentialism than his compatriot and one-time friend, Jean-Paul Sartre. Merleau-Ponty was very concerned with phenomenology as a methodology for understanding being. He clearly followed the lead of Husserl, although by no means uncritically. He did not seem to think that there existed much difference between the work of Husserl and that of Heidegger. (Heidegger in turn was not familiar with Merleau-Ponty's work.[34])

Merleau-Ponty saw phenomenology primarily as a descriptive enterprise that facilitates the examination of the relation between the subject and his world. He fused together the subject-object dichotomy still present in the work of Husserl and Sartre. Merleau-Ponty saw perception as the most important element of being, rather than consciousness (Husserl's key element). For Merleau-Ponty, consciousness was an integral part of being-within-the world (*être-au-monde*) that could not be separated from being-within-the-world:

> The most important lesson which the reduction teaches us is the impossibility of a complete reduction.[35]

Merleau-Ponty introduced another necessary element to the study of human being—the human body. Heidegger's work lacked this crucial element, as Heidegger was more interested than Merleau-Ponty in philosophical truths. Heidegger's examples tended to be abstract ones. For example, he reasoned that we can only understand what a hammer is at the crucial moment in which the hammer is broken, otherwise we are only able to measure it, weigh it, and categorize it. Merleau-Ponty held the same concept but his examples reflected his approach to an embodied human being:

> The question is not so much whether human life does or does not rest on sexuality as of knowing what is to be understood by sexuality.[36]

The focus is clearly on meaning as lived, not on symbolic categorizations, or logical abstractions.

Merleau-Ponty escaped the abstractions of Husserl, Sartre, and even Heidegger by emphasizing the *primacy of the perception of incarnate beings.* He abandoned the abstract consciousness of Husserl, the separation of being and the world of Sartre, and the intellectual abstraction of Heidegger's *Dasein.* Merleau-Ponty spoke of being-*within*-the-world (*être-au-monde*) rather than being-*in*-the-world (*Dasein*). With Merleau-Ponty, human beings have become beings-of-flesh-and-bones. They no longer are the shapers of the world, but are both shapers and shaped by the surrounding world. Human existence is a naturally situated existence, an everyday-life existence.

Merleau-Ponty considered the contextual setting of human beings a necessary element for understanding, because human beings are part of the situation and the situation is part of them. As the surroundings change, so do human beings. For Merleau-Ponty the individual describing himself in phenomenological terms is himself grounded in a situation and grounded in a particular history. Thus, his own describing becomes subject to phenomenological inquiry. The existentialist must study both other human beings and his own ways of knowing them. Ontology (the theory of being) and epistemology (the theory of knowledge) are necessarily interdependent.

Merleau-Ponty's phenomenology is a descriptive enterprise of being-within-the-world, in which being is incarnate, situationally grounded, historically grounded, and irremediably reflexive. As such, it is a forerunner of modern-day existential sociology. Of course, Merleau-Ponty speaks about understanding and meaning at the ontological level, but this understanding, as he himself said, is a necessary beginning to the understanding of the social world.

Phenomenological-Existential Philosophy and Sociology

Phenomenology and existentialism have crossed each other's paths often in our discussion of Heidegger, Sartre, and Merleau-Ponty. This intertwining of the two is due largely to the combined influences of Husserl's phenomenology and of Dilthey's hermeneutics. This overlap, however, has caused a great deal of confusion among many would-be existential sociologists, who often use the terms existentialism and phenomenology interchangeably or fail to point out the differences between the two.

Herbert Spiegelberg remedies this confusion by providing a clear distinction between the philosophies of phenomenology and existentialism.[37] Although Spiegelberg refers primarily to Husserl's and Sartre's philosophies, the differences pointed out in his study provide a good understanding of the basic differences between the two approaches. The differences are: (1) Phenomenology seeks to be a "rigorous science" in the more absolutist sense, while existentialism does not seek to discover any absolute structures. (2) Phenomenology focuses on consciousness and brackets the everyday world, while existentialism studies existence within-the-everyday-world. (3) Phenomenology relies on the method of describing the phenomena, while existentialism has no single necessary methodology. (4) Phenomenological reduction is replaced in existentialism by the hermeneutic understanding of a much larger spectrum of phenomena. (5) Phenomenology's aim is to arrive at universal statements about human consciousness, while existentialism points the way to a particular way of life. (6) Phenomenology is abstract and uninvolved, while existentialism is grounded on the concrete and involved.

The reader should bear in mind that Spiegelberg is discussing philosophies, not sociologies, and that there are some differences between the two. Namely, existential sociologies do seek to discover systematic structure, although without denying the necessarily problematic features of everyday life or of knowledge itself. Furthermore, existential sociologies, while not supporting a particular methodological stance, have relied on personal participation and participant-observation. These techniques seem to be better suited to allow the sociological researcher to penetrate behind "fronts", to grasp concrete experience as it is lived in its situated totality.

Heidegger and Merleau-Ponty have tried to bridge the two positions of existentialism and phenomenology, although their attempts have been usually scoffed at by "purists" such as Husserl as bastardizations of phenomenology. Existential sociologies are in the same boat with Heidegger and Merleau-Ponty, trying to navigate the rapids between the two disciplines.

Chapter 5 examined some sociologists who were influenced by the teachings of Husserl and Schutz. The remainder of this chapter will look at some sociologists whose work has been influenced by the teaching of Heidegger and Merleau-Ponty. Before proceeding, it should be made clear that when one speaks of existential sociologies, one is really referring to *existentially informed sociologies*.[38]

Existential philosophy looks at the ontological level of being, while sociology is less concerned with ultimate truths and more concerned with the details of everyday life. Sociology's concerns are not philosophical ones. Nevertheless, the understanding of existential philosophy is a necessary premise to the sociological study of human beings. The ontological concerns of philosophy can inform sociological studies in the realm of everyday life. Thus sociology can be directed to consider human beings as incarnate individuals. It can learn that situational features always influence human interaction. It can be led to understand that meaning is historically bound. It can be shown that sociologists themselves are not immune from contextuality and historicity and that sociology must be a reflexive discipline to be a truthful discipline.

Becoming the Phenomenon:
Primitive Existentialism

Scientific models of explanation continue to pervade the sciences in the twentieth century. Positivistic sociological inquiries based their explanation of human processes on theories that presented human beings as either cognitive beings making their decisions on purely rational bases [39] or as mere cogs in a societal monolith that ruled their lives.[40] But the models necessarily failed to capture the full import of human behavior because they failed to account for the very stuff of life. Human beings are not cognitive automatons who carefully map out their lives but incarnate beings who often act in anger, love, haste, and fear.

Even scientists in the highest academic spheres are not cold models of calculative reasoning. They come across their scientific discoveries through much trial and error, doing by fiat, guesswork, much anxiety, and inspiration. But they hide the situational nature of their discoveries and the doubts of their enterprise behind the cold mask of the public front of scientific rationality. Few scientists have allowed us into their back regions, although James Watson was quite candid about how he and his colleague Francis Crick discovered the structure of D.N.A.[41] Watson portrayed their search for the structure as a race in the dark based on hunches, hearsay guesses, and hints—not on rational, deductive reasoning. The wandering in the dark finally led them to the right answer, the double helix, but even then doubts prevailed:

> The question then became whether the A-T and G-C base pairs would easily fit the back cone configuration devised during the previous two weeks. At first glance this looked like a good bet, since I had left free in the center a large vacant area for the bases. However, we both knew that we would not be home until a complete model was built in which all the stereochemical contacts were satisfactory . . . Thus I felt slightly queasy when at lunch Francis winged into the Eagle to tell everyone within hearing distance that we had found the secret of life.[42]

Many sociologists felt that their discipline had hidden itself behind the mask of scientism and had consequently lost touch with the very subject of its inquiries—human beings in their natural, everyday setting. Many sociologists argued for a "return to the phenomena." But some of the advocates of "returning to the phenomena" grew overenthusiastic. In the old days of field work, sociologists used to warn researchers going out in the field against the dangers of "going native," that is of becoming so immersed in the setting that they would lose a sociological perspective. But some of the new advocates claimed that unless one *becomes* the phenomenon one cannot speak of understanding. Because of this radical claim that all ideas of science and method should be swept away from sociology, these sociologists can be referred to as primitive existentialists.

Primitive existentialists see all knowledge as ultimately stemming from the personal experience of being-in-the-world. The human being and his or her surrounding world become one, and immediate, concrete experiencing is the ultimate form of knowledge possible. This conception of knowledge is primitive. (This approach to knowledge is also found among Zen masters or mystical writers such as Ouspenski.[43]) If human beings immerse themselves in the world to the point of losing themselves in it, how can any knowledge be retrieved? Having become one with the world, their understanding no longer resembles sociological analysis, but rather becomes the bond of a quasi-religious sect.

The term *primitive existentialism* derives from a book by Robert Morrison bearing the same name.[44] Morrison himself is not engaged in sociological analysis. However, he is adamantly opposed to sociology:

> Every religion spawns a Calvin . . . The name under which this Calvin labored was Emile Durkheim and the Social Calvinism he professed is modern Sociology.[45]

According to Morrison, Durkheim and his fellow sociologists have imprisoned human beings within society and have thus taken away their ontological freedom. Morrison wants nothing to do with the "morbid" brand of existentialism advocating nothingness or anguish; he is very optimistic about the existential possibilities of humanities. He sides with Merleau-Ponty against Husserl's pure consciousness: [46] For Morrison, reflection is "a creative operation which itself participates in the facticity of that experience.[47] Morrison's work revolves around a biblical analysis that reiterates the supreme importance of human beings and their individuality in the world. His work ends with an ode to Cain and his superiority over Abel, since Cain was responsible to no one but himself and defied others and God to seek his own being in the world alone.

Another individual who can be seen as a primitive existentialist is Alan Blum. Blum himself makes no claim to be an existentialist but his ideas place him squarely within this tradition. Blum focuses on theorizing as the way to know oneself:

> Through theorizing the theorist searches for his self, and his achievement in theorizing is the recovery of this self.[48]

In theorizing, one explicates notions previously known to the self, which one now formulates as a new possibility of looking at the world. Blum transforms theory. In the classic sociological sense, a theory explains a phenomenon; For Blum, a theory becomes detached from the phenomenon from which it originated and assumes a life of its own. Theory becomes a method or procedure for viewing the world in various forms:

From my perspective, any other conception of theorizing is degenerate, concrete and practical, since it locates its own justification in terms of the service it renders, its contributions to other concrete selves, its effects upon the audience; to formulate one's self as an achievement of theorizing is to render one's common-sense audience irrelevant; it is to destroy the audience for one's theory.[49]

Theory for theory's sake is Blum's dictum. He thinks theories based on deductive reasoning change events to meet their own requirements, thus transforming the original meaning of the events. Deductive theorizing forces a performance, since it uses the sociologist's competence to modify the phenomena into a theoretical construct. Blum's intent is to look at the competence of the sociologist and disregard his performance:

What we want are the theorist's methods for the creation of his idea, for it is in his production of the idea that his activity acquires its analytic status as an instance of theorizing.[50]

In Blum's conception of theory, the theorist comes to understand himself by looking at how he articulates his theories, which are the sources of his knowledge. Blum takes Heidegger's conception of phenomonology, *logos* plus *phainomenon*,[51] and chops off *phainomenon,* disdaining to consider that the fulcrum of being may be in such a pedestrian locus as everyday life events.

Blum, his colleague McHugh, and others continue to follow the same approach in their most recent work.[52] No doubt they would reject the label of primitive existentialists, but they are primitive in the sense that they center exclusively upon the researcher and forget the phenomena. Their approach is a lofty one, as their researchers are ethereal theorists rather than incarnate beings:

A topic is chosen. One analyst writes a first saying about the topic. This analysis is then shared with one or more collaborators. These collaborators write a second analysis detailing the grounds that made the first analysis possible. One complete analysis requires at least these two steps. Any second analysis can be followed by a third revealing the grounds of the second. A third analysis can be followed by a fourth, ad infinitum.[53]

Thus, the reflexive insights of sociologists upon their work are not conceived of as methods to uncover the contextual and historical biases of the researchers. Instead of providing a necessary aid in understanding the problematic features of interpreting social settings, reflexivity becomes its own goal. Reflexivity becomes a thing in itself apart from that which it describes. The "sociologist" contemplates his or her own mind at work theorizing and the concrete world disappears.

Primitive existentialists are far from being a homogeneous group.

They suggest different approaches to the understanding of everyday life. However, they share the basic belief that social action cannot be lifted out of context and described.* While the radical nature of this statement severely limits its applicability to sociology, it points the discipline in the right direction. Both the researcher and the researched share the world in which they live and are therefore both part of the study. The sociologist cannot assume a privileged position outside of the study; he or she is irremediably bound in it. This boundedness is exactly what enables the researcher to understand the events. He becomes so immersed in them that he can gain an "insider" perspective on the action. The researcher thus comes to see the frail structures that we, as social members, put up daily to explain our life to ourselves and to others.

Phenomenological-Existential Sociology

Phenomenological existentialists attempt to improve upon or at times totally replace the unreflexive sociological modes that for so long have dominated the American scene. This group considers more than just rational behavior in the determination of human processes. They rely on the existential approach and, in seeking trans-situational features, consider elements such as the situated and problematic nature of social interaction and the importance of feelings.

Along with existential notions, this group of sociologists is heuristically informed by the phenomenology of Husserl. Thus, they are very much concerned with maintaining the integrity of the phenomena they study. They try to reduce the biases stemming from the temporal and spatial perspective of the researcher. Often these scholars are considered phenomenologists (*see* chapter 5). We shall limit our considerations to those few who clearly integrate existentialism and phenomenology in their work.

Edward Tiryakian [54] was one of the first to try to develop this particular approach. He reconsiders the work of many sociologists such as Mannheim, Weber, Simmel, W. I. Thomas, Sorokin, Durkheim, and Talcott Parsons with an existential-phenomenological perspective. Tiryakian finds a common trend in the work of these scholars, a trend he calls subjective realism:

> . . . at the heart of the major intellectual sources of the sociological tradition is an underlying consensus which may be called "subjective realism," . . . this view of the individual and society has a marked affinity with existential phenomenology. Subjective

---

* Blum, in this respect, goes to the other extreme, by "lifting" theory out of context.

realism approaches social reality as it is phenomenally experienced by actors . . .[55]

Tiryakian attempts to integrate mainstream sociology with the emergent existential-phenomenological tradition by showing that they are both concerned with subjective realism. According to Tiryakian, the quantitative objective techniques of traditional sociology can be enriched, rather than replaced, by the new existential and phenomenological insights on society.

Tiryakian is unique in his attempt to unify all sociologists under a common banner. Some of his points are well taken, especially his tie-in of clearly humanistic sociologists such as Weber to the existential-phenomenological tradition. After all, Weber owes much to Dilthey's notion of understanding (see earlier discussion in this chapter). However, Tiryakian's argument is weakened by trying to pull together such widely diverse notions as Durkheim's "social facts as things" and Heidegger's *Dasein* (being-in-the-world). Much of existential and phenomenological sociology developed as a reaction to the overrationalization and depersonalization of human beings by traditional sociology. Tiryakian is certainly right in seeing some agreement, but wrong in not seeing the major differences.

Peter Manning is fully aware of the differences between the various positivistic sociologies and existentialism. He does not attempt to reunite classical sociologies and existential-phenomenological sociologies. Instead, he attempts to group together all of the new sociologies that have arisen as a reaction against the causal, *a priori* theories of classical sociology.[56] He points out that existential sociology concerns itself with:

. . . viewing social organization as constantly being made apparent, destroyed, repaired or reconstructed situationally, and to exploring contradictions and conflicts within alternative systems of meaning and the conditions that give rise and support them.[57]

Manning is reaffirming the basic tenet of phenomenological and existential sociologies: Meaning is the topic of sociological inquiry and it is problematic and situational. Furthermore, human beings are central to the creation of meaning:

Existentialism above all was an attempt to place man at the center of philosophy, man as an agent and creator of both meaning and action . . .[58]

Manning cites six concepts that are important to sociological analysis and that clearly transcend the rational categories of classical sociologies: sentiments, body, self, situation, levelling of society, and structure. The elements point to the fact that social performers are always embodied in the world and relate to it from a certain place and at a given time. Thus, existential phenomenology is a discipline attuned both to the perspective of the group studied and to the position and biases of the researcher. According to Manning, this reflexivity in the end is the strength of the existential-phenomenological approach.

Stanford Lyman and Marvin Scott see existential phenomenology as an inspiration for their sociology, which they call *a sociology of the absurd*.[59] From phenomenology they draw "intentionality, consciousness, and subjective meaning." [60] Lyman and Scott see the world as being essentially meaningless. Social performers carry the weight of providing it with meaning. Often this is not done because social performers take for granted everyday reality and continue to act in normal ways, without ever questioning the meaning of their actions. But when the world provides the social performers with an *epoché,* with a new situation in which normal behavior and meaning no longer apply, then social performers are forced to choose a new course of action and to create their own meaning. Existential phenomenology for Lyman and Scott is more than an analytical tool. It is a guide to life in a historical time (ours) that is highly pluralistic and therefore lacks orderly, normal meanings for every situation.

Lyman and Scott come very close to the core of existential sociology by describing the everyday life of individuals in the social settings which they both shape and are shaped from. But their model differs from later existential sociology in two ways. It tends to draw more from Heidegger's being-in-the-world than from Merleau-Ponty's being-within-the-world, therefore placing less stress on the body itself. Also, Lyman and Scott invite researchers to step back from the taken-for-granted everyday reality in a quasi-Husserlian epoché, whereas existential sociologists try first to immerse themselves in the everyday reality in order to uncover its taken-for-grantedness and its deceitful appearances. Only later do they try to "stand back from" concrete reality and analyze it.

Existential Sociology

As soon as I saw the elephant I knew with perfect certainty that I ought not to shoot him . . . I decided that I would watch him for a little while to make sure that he did not turn savage again, and then go home . . .

But at that moment I glanced round at the crowd that had followed me. It was an immense crowd . . . They were watching me . . . They did not like me, but with the magical rifle in my hands I was momentarily worth watching. And suddenly I realized that I should have to shoot the elephant after all. The people expected it of me and I had got to do it; I could feel their two thousand wills pressing me forward, irresistibly.[61]

George Orwell shows the core of existential life in his short story "Shooting an Elephant." Although the British man with the rifle is cooly in control of the situation and has rationally decided to follow a certain course of actions, things suddenly change. The irrational forces of life—the situational mood of the crowd, the feeling of expectancy rising from it, the British pride in front of the natives, and a mixture of a thousand feelings—all sway the British man who changes his course of action and shoots the elephant.

Life is situated and problematic. Moment to moment things occur that one had not foreseen. Suddenly tempers arise or deep feelings gush out. We are faced with the puzzling mystery of living and we solve it as we go along. This is the core idea of existential sociology: to study life in its daily situatedness and problematic features, to see how feelings affect our actions; to understand how we master the doubts that constantly arise and that must be constantly solved if life is to go on.

In order to arrive at these understandings, existential sociology begins from the daily experiences of the members of society. The sociologist carefully attempts to maintain the integrity of the phenomena and to understand the social scene. This is done by participating in the scene, since becoming involved in the phenomena to be studied is generally the only effective way to penetrate the fronts that often hide the actions of human beings. Consider the following episode, witnessed by Joseph Kotarba in his study of corporal punishment in schools.[62] This episode clearly illustrates the difference between fronts of rational idealisms about dealing with problem children and the reality brought about by emotional involvement in the real-life situation:

> When I was an administrator at Middle School, one of my novice teachers was young, female, bright and overly optimistic regarding her ability to maintain classroom order through "constructive interpersonal relationships." One afternoon early in the school year, she buzzed my office through the intercom. I immediately rushed up to her classroom, since I had been expecting trouble for several weeks. Her classes were always loud and unruly, and her attempts to reason with the children and even shout them down were to no avail. When I arrived at her class, she was standing outside the door sobbing. After I quieted down the class I tried to normalize the situation and console the teacher, for she was obviously more upset than the child she hit. In near hysteria, she blurted out the following:
>
> I hate him! Ever since school began, he's done everything he could to get on my nerves. I tried talking to him, understanding him, everything. . . . I don't care if they fire me; I don't care what the kids think. He was asking for it. I'm not gonna take that shit anymore from any kid, I don't care how underprivileged he is.[63]

The immersion in the social scene by existential sociologists is done in order to reach a trans-situational understanding of human processes;

it is not the same as losing oneself in the phenomena, as primitive existentialists do. Existential sociology does not claim any exclusive right over its methods or goals. It is purposefully open-ended, since it must mold itself each and every time to the everchanging nature of its topic of inquiry—human beings in their natural setting. There are obvious overlaps with other humanistic disciplines, but there are also some important differences, noted below.

Existential Sociology is Different from Existential Philosophy. Existential philosophy seeks to lift the veils that obfuscate the vision of life of human beings to offer a way of life in which human beings actively participate in shaping their lives. Existential sociology is interested in more than returning human beings to an important part in the script of life. It seeks to empirically study everyday experiences in order to be able to theorize about the general features of human interaction.

Existential Sociology is Different from Phenomenological Sociology. Phenomenological sociology (ethnomethodology, cognitive sociology, sociolinguistics, etc.) is interested in bracketing everyday reality to describe the routinized features that enable social members to carry on their daily life. Existential sociology is interested in the routinized and general features of interaction, but it is also interested in the social structures in themselves. Phenomenological sociology's exclusive concern with routinized features causes it to become too detached from everyday concerns. For example, a phenomenological study of doctors would focus exclusively on the routinized ways in which doctors compile medical histories with no concern for the total, concrete interactional scenes between doctors, patients, and nurses and the concrete effects of their lack of concern on the life of the patient.

Existential Sociology is Different from Naturalism. Naturalism is interested in a return to the phenomena just as existential sociology is. But naturalism retains many of the faults of classical sociology. It shows little concern with the feelings of human beings. It fails to be reflexive about the role of the researcher in interaction. And, naturalism often forgets its own dictum of "telling it like it is" and seriously distorts the phenomena.[64] Existential sociology pays attention to the full gamut of human expressions, not only to the rational elements of human beings. Furthermore, it points out the role of the researcher in retaining as much of the integrity of the phenomena as possible.

Existential Sociology is Different from Journalism. Since existential sociology admits that knowledge is only possible from a particular standpoint, which is determined by the observer in a particular context at a particular historical time, it is often accused of being nothing more than high-level reporting. Existential sociology shares with journalism its concern for the daily matters affecting human beings. It also shares with journalism the concern for a style of reporting that will be emphatically understood by the readers. But existential sociology is also concerned with social theories about the world—not only with descriptive information about daily events, which is the goal of journalism.

Existential Sociologists are Different from Everyday Members. Existential sociologists become members of various groups in order to gain an existential awareness of the lives of the members. They try to grasp the everyday realities of the members, but then they try to go beyond those of the members to experience and analyze the situation from a variety of perspectives. They try not to have "an ax to grind" as most members do. Most important, the concern of existential sociologists is not only with the social scene but with the derivation of generally valid sociological statements—theories about human beings.

Existential sociology finds its most extensive and systematic expression in the recent work of Jack Douglas, John Johnson, and their many co-workers.[65] The topic of inquiry of Douglas and Johnson's work is human beings and their book examines how various groups navigate the uncertainties of everyday life. We learn that chronic pain patients often choose to present a front that does not betray their pain, letting only their doctor and their spouse behind their stoic front of normalcy. We learn how problematic a day becomes when a simple walk to the coffee machine may cause agonizing pain and how a chronic patient manages his reality by avoiding a variety of tasks that would entail painful movements. We also learn that behind the facade of normally operating members of society one does not find persons who rationally calculate the cold scientific options opened to them in their future life. Rather, we find concrete individuals who tremble with terror at the tragic possibility of what the future has in store for them:

> The thing that bothers me the most about my accident is that I gotta sit home all the time. Christ, I'm about going crazy! Don't forget, I've been working most of my life, so I ain't used to sitting around like an old man.[66]

In another essay we view the confusion of gay people vis-à-vis their public identity:

> We were drinking and dancing and after the men left I said to her "Are you a lesbian?" and she got very embarrassed . . . and I said if you ask me about myself the first thing I will tell you is that I am a lesbian.[67]

Revealing one's identity as a gay person can be an anguishing experience, regardless of one's rational beliefs. "Coming out" in the open can be very problematic in itself:

Out of the closet, well that means different things to different people, it could mean you tell your mother you are gay, or it could mean—um—you march on city hall . . . There are degrees you know, of being out of the closet. I think essentially it just means to be more open and up front about your gayness. You know.[68]

The field researchers also reflexively turn a mirror upon themselves, thus providing a view of what exists beneath the cold rhetoric of scientific discourse. For example, John Johnson, who usually appears to be a composed researcher, literally breaks down when confronted with a harsh decision by Juvenile Court on a case he had been studying closely:

> . . . I also began to cry. As we say in the trade, I presented the appearance of one who had lost all self-control. And then, when alone on the grounds of the juvenile facility several minutes later, I presented the appearance of a formally-rational (expletive deleted) social scientist beating his (deleted) fist against a tree. Shortly after that, I doubled over and puked my guts out.[69]

Other existential sociological works are beginning to appear. Among these is the recent monograph that examines the explosive topic of sexuality on nude beaches.[70] The heated public controversy over the legality, morality, and desirability of such nude beaches provides a sociological gold mine. The differences between the nude bathers' rational public accounts, which depict the beaches as safe places for "nature lovers," and the actual events, which are heavily charged sexually, provide an excellent insight into the ways in which social performers construct daily reality and hide themselves from threatening strangers. In this setting, members' rational accounts, the stuff of conventional sociological fieldwork, pale before the power of uncontrollable feelings that drive individuals. The nude bathers find themselves in an extremely problematic situation when confronted by the recalcitrance of their own body to support their social front. Thus we are able to see the situatedness of their actions, actions that are but a remedial attempt to cover the embarrassment caused by their bodies:

> A case in point was a threesome of college students . . . two males and one voluptuous female. They started desuiting right away . . . one of the males promptly proceeded to get an extension that threatened momentarily to turn into a full scale erection . . . The girl, no doubt recognizing the situation, dashed for the water. The boys, probably realizing the impropriety of chasing after the female in this situation, were forced to put off satisfying their need for the cold water and immediately began a vigorous game of frisbee.[71]

Another work in the same vein is *The Last Frontier*,[72] which explores the meaning of growing old in the United States. The rational meaning of growing old wanes into insignificant gibberish when confronted with highly charged emotional issues such as the death of a loved one, the prospect of facing a musty, squalid hotel room for the rest of one's life, or the loneliness of being old:

> It sneaks up on you, you're going down the street, and you're a young man feeling good, working at something . . . and all of a sudden, you quit your job . . . it hits you between the nose all of a sudden . . . I'm old . . . and then it begins to scare you . . . and . . . it gives deep . . . deep sentiments of things that's coming . . . and then . . . you kind of wish that you'd kept some friends . . .[73]

The poor old people stagger onward a day at a time in the emotional confusion of what they once were, of what they are now, and the uncertainty of what they will be.

Other existential works are emerging. They explore different situational aspects of life, from the problematic shifting of momentum [74] in sports that renders the games highly situational, to the examination of the daily uncertainties and the hedonistic feelings that dominate a drug-dealing subculture.[75] All of these new existential sociological studies are beginning to provide us with a better understanding of human processes, and with a fuller picture of humanity.

Other Sociologies and Existential Sociology

To present existing critiques of existential sociology is a hard task because it is such a new approach. Earlier in this chapter we emphasized the differences between existential sociology and other disciplines, such as existential philosophy, phenomenological sociology, naturalism, and journalism. We also pointed out the difference between existential sociologists and everyday members of society. In spite of this clarification it is probable that many of the critiques of existential sociology will confuse it with some of the above-mentioned disciplines.

Basically, there are two camps from which criticism is likely to be levelled at existential sociology. The first, positivistic sociology, would probably deny that existential sociology is in fact a sociology since it is "subjective," "un-scientific" and "high-level journalism." This group of critics would say that, given the relativistic approach of existential sociology, no solid truths are possible and we are left with a solipsistic world. This claim would probably be made by relying on the absolutist notions that sociology is a science, as are the physical sciences. These traditionalists would claim that its aim is to produce absolute objectivity, and that a hypothetic-deductive (or inductive) model is necessary to produce scientific results. In other words this group of critics would hold fast to traditional, positivistic sociology.

The second group of critics would be composed of phenomenologically oriented sociologists. They would readily acknowledge the shortcomings of positivistic sociology. However they would very likely deny that existential sociology is the answer to current sociological problems. This group of critics would equate existential sociology with earlier ethnographic approaches. They would say that existential sociology lacks tangible data (such as videotapes or conversational transcripts). They would claim that to uncover people's feelings is an immoral enterprise. They would say that existential sociologists are "snoops." And they too would conclude that existential sociology is "unscientific."

Both groups of critics view sociology as a rigorous discipline seeking absolute knowledge about human beings, although they claim different ways to gain it. They both are still floating in a maze of abstractions and refuse to see the bridge to the concreteness of the everyday world that existential sociology offers, just as Galileo's detractors refused to look through his telescope when confronted with a new universe.

Existential sociology provides a heightened awareness of our problematic situatedness as beings-in-the-world. We act not out of certainty but out of doubt, which in the end remains our only certainty. Existential sociology understands the futility of oversimplifying the world and challenges us to study it in its complex nuances, in its intricate weavings, as well as in its abysmal cruelty.

Notes

1. Walter Kaufmann (ed.), *Existentialism from Dostoyevsky to Sartre* (New York: World Publishing Co., 1972), p. 11.

2. For an excellent analysis of various forms of existentialism, see William Barrett, *Irrational Man* (New York: Anchor Books, 1962).

3. For a misunderstanding of the relation between existential sociology and the phenomenology of Husserl, see James L. Heap and Phillip A. Roth, "On Phenomenological Sociology," *American Sociological Review* 38, 1973.

4. John Johnson, *Doing Field Research* (New York: Free Press, 1976); and Jack Douglas, *Investigative Social Research: Individual and Team Field Research* (Beverley Hills, Calif.: Sage Publications, 1976).

5. See the work of Robert Park, especially *The City* (Chicago: University of Chicago Press, 1925).

6. See David Matza, *Becoming Deviant* (Englewood Cliffs, N.J.: Prentice-Hall, 1969).

7. See the works of Alfred Schutz, listed in the Notes for chapter 5 of this book.

8. Jack D. Douglas, *Creative Deviance and Social Changes,* forthcoming.

9. For an interesting, although unorthodox account of the separation of the two realms, see Robert M. Pirsig, *Zen and the Art of Motorcycle Maintenance* (New York: Bantam Books, 1974).

10. Brown, in Douglas and Johnson, *Existential Sociology.*

11. Frederich Nietzsche, "La nascita della tragedia dallo spirito della musica," in *Il Meglio di Nietzsche.* Milano: Longanesi, 1956.

12. See Plato, *Republic,* and Ralph Dahrendorf, "In Praise of Thrasymachus," in *Essays on the Theory of Society* (Stanford, Calif.: Stanford University Press, 1968).

13. Niccolò Machiavelli, *The Prince* (New York: Washington Square Press, 1970).

14. For an analysis of Machiavelli as a humanist, see Maurice Merleau-Ponty, *Humanism et Terreur,* 8th ed. Paris: Gallimard, 1947. Also see S. Lyman and M. Scott, *A Sociology of the Absurd* (New York: Meredith Publishing Co., 1970).

15. A. Koyré, *From the Closed to the Infinite Universe* (Baltimore: Johns Hopkins University Press, 1958).

16. See Bertolt Brecht, *Galileo* (New York: Grove Press, 1966).

17. Physiological Epistles, 1847, in John Passmore, *A Hundred Years of Philosophy* (London: Gerald Duckworth & Co., 1966).

18. See Passmore, *A Hundred Years of Philosophy.*

19. Fyodor Dostoyevsky, *Notes From the Underground* (New York: Thomas Y. Crowell, 1970).

20. Leo Tolstoi, *The Death of Ivan Ilyich and Other Stories* (New York: Signet Books, New American Library, 1960).

21. Ibsen, Henrik. *Brand,* in *The Works of Henrik Ibsen* (New York: W. J. Black, 1928).

22. See Barrett, *Irrational Man.*

23. The discussion of Dilthey's hermeneutics draws heavily from Richard E. Palmer, *Hermeneutics* (Evanston, Ill.: Northwestern University Press, 1969).

24. Ibid., pp. 108–109.

25. Ibid., p. 13.

26. Martin Heidegger, in W. Dilthey, *Patterns and Meaning in History* (New York: Harper & Row, 1961), pp. 18–19.

27. See Palmer, *Hermeneutics.*

28. See A. Fontana, "The Existential Thought of Jean Paul Sartre and Maurice Merleau-Ponty," in J. Douglas and J. Johnson (eds.), *Existential Sociology* (New York: Cambridge University Press, 1978).

29. Jean Paul Sartre, *Nausea* (New York: New Directions, 1949), p. 15.

30. Jean Paul Sartre, *Troubled Sleep* (New York: A. Knopf, 1951), p. 193.

31. Jean Paul Sartre, *Nausea* (New York: New Directions, 1949), p. 112.

32. Jean Paul Sartre, *Roads to Freedom* (New York: A. Knopf, 1947).

33. See Fontana, "The Existential Thought of Jean-Paul Sartre and Maurice Merleau-Ponty."

34. See Spiegelberg, Herbert, *The Phenomenological Movement,* vol. II (The Hague: Martinus Nijhoff, 1971).

35. Maurice Merleau-Ponty, *Phenomenology of Perception* (London: Routledge and Kegan Paul, 1970), p. xiv.

36. Ibid., p. 158.

37. H. Spiegelberg, "Husserl's Phenomenology and Sartre's Existentialism," in Joseph Kockelmans (ed.), *Phenomenology* (New York: Anchor Books, 1967).

38. For a misunderstanding of this point, see Heap and Roth, "On Phenomenological Sociology."

39. See Aaron Cicourel, *Method and Measurement in Sociology* (New York: The Free Press, 1964).

40. See Jack D. Douglas, *American Social Order* (New York: The Free Press, 1971).

41. James D. Watson, *The Double Helix* (New York: Signet Books, 1968).

42. Ibid., pp. 125–126.

43. See, for instance, P. D. Ouspensky, *In Search of the Miraculous* (New York: Harcourt, Brace and World, 1949).

44. Robert Morrison, *Primitive Existentialism* (New York: Philosophical Library, 1967).

45. Ibid., p. 1.

46. Ibid., pp. 26–27.

47. Ibid., p. 27.

48. Alan Blum, "Theorizing," in Jack D. Douglas (ed.), *Understanding Everyday Life* (Chicago: Aldine Publishing Co., 1970), p. 304.

49. Ibid., p. 308.

50. Ibid., p. 312.

51. "Logos . . . is that which is conveyed in speaking . . ." "Phainomenon [is] . . . that which shows itself." See Palmer, *Hermeneutics,* pp. 127–128.

52. Peter McHugh, Stanley Raffel, Daniel C. Foss, and Alan Blum, *On the Beginning of Social Inquiry* (London: Routledge and Kegan Paul, 1974).

53. In Hugh Mehan, and Houston Wood, *The Reality of Ethnomethodology* (New York: John Wiley & Sons, 1975), p. 168.

54. Edward Tiryakian, *"Existential Phenomenology and the Sociological Tradition,"* in *American Sociological Review* 30, 1965, pp. 674–688.

55. Ibid., p. 686.

56. Peter Manning, "Existential Sociology." *The Sociological Quarterly,* No. 14, Spring 1973, 200–225.

57. Ibid., p. 204.

58. Ibid., p. 209.

59. Lyman and Scott, *Sociology of the Absurd.*

60. Ibid., p. 2.

61. George Orwell, "Shooting an Elephant," in *The Orwell Reader* (New York: Harcourt, Brace & World, 1956), p. 6.

62. Joseph A. Kotarba, "Masking Official Violence: Corporal Punishment in the Public Schools," in J. Johnson and J. Douglas (eds.), *Crime at the Top* (New York: J. B. Lippincott, 1978).

63. Ibid., p. 262.

64. David Matza, *Becoming Deviant* (Englewood Cliffs, N. J.: Prentice-Hall, 1969).

65. Jack D. Douglas, and John Johnson (eds.), *Existential Sociology* (New York: Cambridge University Press, 1976).

66. Joseph Kotarba, "The Chronic Pain Patient," in Douglas and Johnson, *Existential Sociology*, pp. 270–271.

67. Carol Warren, and Barbara Ponse, "The Existential Self and the Gay Community," in Douglas and Johnson, *Existential Sociology*, p. 283.

68. Ibid., p. 285.

69. John Johnson, "Behind the Rational Appearances," in Douglas and Johnson, *Existential Sociology*, p. 215.

70. Jack D. Douglas, and Paul K. Rasmussen, with Carol Ann Flanagan, *Nude Beaches* (Beverly Hills, Calif.: Sage Publications, 1977), p. 83.

71. Ibid., pp. 130–131.

72. Andrea Fontana, *The Last Frontier* (Beverly Hills, Calif.: Sage Publications, 1977).

73. Ibid., pp. 130–131.

74. Peter Adler and Patricia A. Adler. "The Role of Momentum in Sport," *Urban Life*, Vol. 7, No. 2, July 1978, 153–176.

75. Patricia A. Adler, Peter Adler, Jack Douglas, with Paul Rasmussen, "Organized Crime: Drug Dealing for Pleasure and Profit," in *Observations of Deviance*, 2nd ed. (New York: Random House, 1980).

APPENDIX

A Brief History of the
Sociologies of Everyday Life

JACK D. DOUGLAS

All human beings are at certain times in their lives, especially in those quiet moments of contemplation that come with leisure and the full experience of mature years that spur fears of death, concerned with their own nature and the sources of their actions. Who am I? How am I and all of us alike or different from other animals? Why do I act the way I do? Are my actions caused by my genes, by my socially learned values, by my immediate situation? Or am I *free to choose* how I will act in each situation I face?

Most of the philosophies and religions of the world, including the so-called primitive philosophies, which we today are more apt to call common-sense philosophies, are based on answers to such basic questions about human life. This is true of all the great philosophies of the Western world and of all the social sciences. Herodotus and Aristotle were just as concerned with the basic questions of human life and their answers as scholars in behavioral biology, psychology, sociology, anthropology, history, economics, and political science are today. The questions are stilled during certain eras when pat answers are assumed by presumptuous professionals. Social scientists went through such an era from the 1930s to the 1960s. The complacency of one era is always ended by a new era of urgent questioning and searching when the accepted answers are challenged and changed to take into account new findings and ideas about human beings. This is what the sociologists of everyday life are doing today.

The Emergence of the Classical Paradigm of Positivist-Structuralism

Just as they are today, the classical ideas of the social sciences were dominated by one major issue: individualism versus collectivism; or the individual versus society; or the great-person theory versus the theory of collective behavior; or the nominalist versus the realist (as the Greeks had first put it); or the concrete versus the abstract; or the concrete versus the ideal; or empiricism versus idealism. Although there were many specific differences between these many different terms, they all revolved around two basic, interrelated questions. First, can human actions be explained in terms of concrete individual factors (such as individual will, choice, or the concrete situations individuals face) or in terms of something outside of the individual (such as culture or social structure) that determines or causes what they will do? Second, are we to determine the answer to our first question by observing individuals in concrete situations of everyday life, or by observing something (such as a social structure), supposedly outside of the individuals, by experimentally controlled methods? In a very general way, we can say that psychology chose to explain life from the individual's perspective and the social sciences (with some important exceptions, especially in economics) chose the collectivist approach. Both psychology and the social sciences chose to study human beings abstracted from their natural, concrete situations and subjected to experimental controls.

In trying to understand better exactly what these early social scientists were arguing about, it will help, as it does in all other matters, to first consider how we deal with these basic questions about human life in common-sense experience. In our everyday world all of us deal with other people, animals, tools, or other things that have concrete existence as concrete, individual things that *exist*. When I encounter Sue in the hall I do not hail her as a member of an abstract category of the human species—"Oh, hello there, you human being." Quite to the contrary, I greet her as a concrete person—"Hello, Sue." Unless I am so withdrawn from the situation as to be seen by Sue and most other people as insane, I in part deal with her in terms of exactly what I perceive her as doing in that exact situation. Indeed, the unwritten law of common-sense, everyday reality is that her concrete existence in that concrete situation takes precedence over *almost* any other things I might have thought about her. (Sartre long ago insisted that "Existence comes before essence," by which he meant that concrete realities of life come before our symbolizations of them; you must live before you can think symbolically. Sociologists of everyday life have increasingly insisted that existence also normally dominates essence, but not always, as we shall see.)

There are certain abstract, symbolic and trans-situational ideas I have about Sue that have some effect on my thinking and acting toward Sue in this concrete situation. Because of the shape of her body, her smell, the feel of her hand, the shape or length of her hair, the form of her clothes, her voice, and possibly many other things about her, I immediately respond to her in part as a member of the general category of *female.* (This is, of course, part of our animal nature. All animals do the same thing in many situations. But the human animal is a rare kind of animal, one which has an almost continual readiness for sexual response. Thus, humans have an almost continual concern with their sexual identities, although the degree varies greatly.) The more I respond to Sue in terms of that or other abstract categories, the less I respond to her concrete, individual existence. If I carry that to an extreme (such as "Hello, female," or "Hello, human being"), almost everyone would see my behavior as bizarre, or worse. On the other hand, if I deal with her only as a concrete, individual existence (what Hegel referred to as a "here-now-this" experience), I would be seen as equally bizarre or worse. (If you consider my asking her things like, "What kind of a being are you?" you will see the point.) In some very complicated way that we do not yet understand very well, human beings put together a vast number of these abstract categories of meaning and concrete details about a concrete person and situation to deal "effectively" with them in concrete situations. In oversimplified terms, we can say that the entire history of human thought, and especially of social science thinking, has revolved around this complex and problematic duality of concreteness and abstractness in our everyday realities. The tendency of most people in thinking abstractly about human beings is to seize upon one of the two poles of this duality (generally the abstract pole) as the only one of ultimate importance. This has been the source of endless human difficulties.

The difficulties appeared in the very beginning of Western social theory. Herodotus was the first important recorded social thinker in the Western (note the abstract distinction) tradition of thought. Herodotus, who lived in the 5th century BC, was concerned with explaining how the vastly outnumbered Greeks had defeated the Persians. Unlike so many of his contemporaries, he did not simply attribute it to the will of the Gods, or to the "great men" who led the Athenians, Spartans, and other Greeks, or to the Fates, or to historical accident. Instead, he thought there was something that differentiated the Greeks in general, as "Greeks," from the Persians in general, as "Persians." After much snooping around the Middle East asking endless questions and reading all available literature on the subject, Herodotus concluded that there was something very important about Greece in general and about Persia in general that explained the victories of Greece.

As Aubrey de Selincourt has summed it up, "He was able to keep before his reader the sense that Greece, the centre of his interest, was still only one country in an immense and diverse world which it was yet to dominate by virtue of certain qualities which that world lacked, above all by that passion for independence and self-determination which was both her glory and her bane" (1962: 23). The intense desire to be free was the motive that drove the Greeks to heroic feats. Their individual initiative continually allowed them to outwit and outmaneuver the immense hoardes of dictatorially ruled Persians. Herodotus, then, believed there were some general characteristics shared in some way by most Greeks (obviously not all), which allowed them to defeat most Persians most of the time. These general characteristics eventually became known as Greek civilization and, later, Greek culture.

Not long after Herodotus' great work, Thucydides wrote another great work in Western historical thought, the *History of the Peloponessian War*. In this he described and tried to explain the great war between Sparta and Athens that led eventually to the defeat and conquest of Athens. Although relatively few years separated Herodotus from Thucydides, their works are very different. Having been an Athenian general in the war, he had an insider's view, but also a remarkable ability to search out, question, analyze, and present all of the conflicting facts he thought relevant.

Where Herodotus tended to be naive about what people told him, Thucydides continually discounted and rejected self-expressed motives. Where Herodotus found cultural differences, Thucydides was more apt to find individual differences or human nature responding to different concrete situations. (Thucydides also was dealing with the defeat of the most free and individualistic of the Greeks (the Athenians) by the least free and individualistic (the Spartans), which clearly could not be explained in the general terms Herodotus used.) More important, Thucydides, while sometimes concerned with possible cultural differences between Athenians and Spartans, was much more concerned with the effects of individual differences within each city state on the outcome of the battles and eventually the war and with the ways in which each commander fought his battles. Sometimes the strategy of the commander was seen as overriding other differences. (For example, in the beginning of the book Thucydides argued that the Hellenes took ten years to defeat the Trojans because their leader Agamemnon had few supplies when they landed, chose to disperse his forces to gather food, and did not for ten years bring his force to bear on the Trojans.) Thucydides looked at the battles and the war in the way a military strategist does, as something won or lost in terms of what is done in the concrete situation by concrete individuals. Herodotus, on the other hand, looked at such events in terms of abstractions he believed characterized the social groups involved. One was more of an individualist and (concrete) situationalist; the other more of a culturologist and believer in symbolic (abstract) determinism.

These differences in thought were soon embodied in the thought of Plato and Aristotle and thence transmitted to all highly educated members of Western societies down to our own day. Plato argued that one can know the truth about individual things only in terms of the symbolic abstractions (ideas or types) about them. His view of society is always very abstract, going from what he believed in general (in the abstract) about human society to any concrete society. Aristotle took a much more complex view, but one that is basically the opposite. He preferred to amass huge amounts of information about the concrete realities first and then abstract from them their common characteristics. When he wanted to analyze flora and fauna, Aristotle sent out research teams with Alexander to bring back specimens from all over the Middle East. When he wanted to analyze politics in Greece, he studied the specific, concrete forms of political life in the city states of Greece. (See Plato's *The Republic* and *The Laws* and Aristotle's *Politics*.) The Platonists were known as the "realists." *Symbol realists*, however, would have been a better name because the Platonists believed reality consisted always in abstract ideas. (This view became known in the nineteenth century as "idealism." "Idea-ism" would be a better name.) The Aristotelians first were known as the "nominalists," but by the nineteenth century were more commonly known as "empiricists." The Platonists argued that the nominalists could study individual things only in terms of the symbolic categories or forms they already had. The nominalists argued that a true category, one that really represented the concrete things, could only be formed by first looking at the concrete realities.

Sociologists of everyday life would argue that the issue is much more complex. Human beings do form or create new symbolic categories, such as "lasers" or "corporations," to fit new concrete realities. But they create new categories in part out of previously learned categories. And once a category is created, its meaning is learned and transmitted independently of the concrete realities used to first form it, sometimes with no reference to the concrete realities at all. As an extreme example, modern words like "conservative" and "liberal" have almost the opposite meanings in terms of their concrete referents today from what they had in the nineteenth century. This is common with political symbols because people use them to manipulate political sympathies.

Plato won the argument, not by his logic or practice, but by the strength of his supporters. The Christian church more or less adopted his view and argued that the abstract truths were those of God and his Word. St. Augustine's *The City of God* was similar in approach to that of Herodotus's and Thucydides's earlier works. In trying to explain the conquest of Rome by the barbarians, St. Augustine explained it in terms of the words of God as revealed in the Bible—not in terms of different cultures or historical individual decisions and situations. In Biblical terms, the Romans deserved it.

This kind of argument did little to advance the fledgling Greek social sciences. Instead, such arguments eliminated science from the Western world. Only in the eleventh century were these ancient ideas of science reintroduced from the Islamic World where they had continued to develop. By the thirteenth century, the Christian paradigm of knowledge and human life had been synthesized with the Greek ideas into medieval scholasticism. This paradigm allowed for possible observations of concrete realities, as is easily seen in the intense interest shown by Albertus Magnus and Roger Bacon in natural observations. But scholasticism did not in any way encourage such concrete observations and in fact subordinated them to the preconceived, abstract ideas of Christianity, logic, mathematics, and related areas of thought. The scholastic paradigm has never really disappeared. It is still found in many philosophical ideas about humans, in almost any of the rationalist theories of human thought and action, in ideas such as "use value" in Marxism and "distributive justice" in welfare economics. Scholasticism contributed greatly, although indirectly, to the theories of Descartes, Spinoza, Rousseau, and Durkheim. Almost all of the modern ideas that assume in some way that abstract and preconceived values or other ideas are the basic determinants of human actions can be traced in a very general way back to scholasticism and beyond that to Platonism.

The Abortive Revolution in Social Thought: The Scottish Moral Philosophers

By the seventeenth century the partly empirical forms of thought used by natural scientists were increasingly being applied to human actions, especially in Britain where the natural sciences were so strong. By the eighteenth century the British had developed a highly empirical form of philosophy and a highly empirical form of "moral philosophy" (see Schneider, 1967), which we would now call social science. These social scientists relied primarily on their own direct observations of concrete realities in their everyday lives. They often called their work "the philosophy of common sense," what we would call "the sociology of everyday life." They were interested in national differences or racial differences, but not much. Like Thucydides, the Scottish moral philosophers were quite concerned with human nature as the background for human motives. Also like him, they were concerned with how and why concrete individuals act the way they do in concrete situations. They analyzed British society in terms of these complex variables, not in terms of Britishness or some other abstract idea about the British. For example, they saw smuggling and all other forms of black market activity as a simple result of human beings acting to fulfill their material desires in a situation in which an inefficient government bureaucracy tried to advance its human material interests at their expense. They did not see it as a result of culture or any other abstraction about the British. This form of thought, known primarily as "liberalism" (the opposite of its present meaning), became dominant in British economic thought. It was always the major stream of British sociological thought and the dominant form of American sociological thought, often called social psychology because of its individual orientation, until the advent of Durkheim's "structural-functionalism" (see below) in the 1930s.

On the continent there were always some thinkers who held similar views. (The famous "Viennese School" of liberal economics is most obvious.) Jacob Burckhardt, whose life experiences in a society (Switzerland) even more pluralistic * than Britain's may have encouraged his historical orientation, always looked at history as very complex, made up of many different realms and of concrete individuals. In his great works, especially *The Civilization of the Renaissance in Italy,* Burckhardt was very concerned with the relative independence of major institutions and styles and individuals of any given society. He also recognized that there were interdependencies among institutions and that individuals of many societies tend to have some characteristics that are different from individuals in other societies. In the highly pluralistic societies of Switzerland, Britain, and the United States, one would be hard put to specify much that individuals have in common. What do the German, French, Italian, and Romansh Swiss have in common? Swissness? But what would Swissness look like? In a nation with four languages and where differences and heterogeneity are so obvious, the question of similarities has always been hotly debated. In a very similar vein, when de Tocqueville visited America in the nineteenth century, he concluded that there was very little (not even language) that most Americans held in common.

The Positivistic-Structural Reaction

The ideas of the Scottish moral philosophers remained of minor significance on the continent and by the end of the nineteenth century were losing influence in Britain, especially in anthropology where they were rooted. By the 1930s, they were on the retreat in America as well, even in sociology and economics. At the risk of encouraging the same homogenization of thought that we have suffered so much from in this

---

* A pluralistic society is one made up of more than one group with more than one set of shared meanings. Switzerland, for example, has four different cultural and linguistics groups (German, French, Italian, and Romansh).

century, we will discuss three overriding sub-cultures of thought in the past century and before that were combined by intellectual entrepreneurs in ways that progressively excluded the more individualistic and situated views of human life from consideration (see Merz, 1965).

First, there was, of course, scientific thought. The drawback of the social sciences is that they were created after the basic natural sciences had become highly successful. Most of the early social scientists had been exposed to the natural sciences in their educations and professions, and so were led to build the social sciences on the same foundations as the natural scientists. Although they are now almost entirely forgotten because their theories proved so useless, almost all the social scientists from the seventeenth to the twentieth centuries were "social mechanists." That is, they literally applied the basic laws of the natural sciences to the social life of humankind (see Sorokin, 1928). For example, they tried to show that human society followed precisely the law of gravity, such that the further away one is from a given body, the less one is affected by it. Indeed, the "social effect" supposedly decreased as the inverse square òf distance. This seems ridiculous today, especially in an age when Americans are deeply concerned about what happens in nuclear-armed Russia and, for better or worse, care little about what happens in Mexico. But to scientists convinced by the success of Newton's universal principle, the idea seemed true.

Imitation is often a great force in human life, probably because that is one basic way we learn in infancy and childhood. But, just as a baby cannot properly learn to drive a car by merely watching his or her father do it successfully, or a poor nation cannot become rich by adopting vastly expensive and complex technology that no one in the nation knows how to operate efficiently, so a science cannot be successful by merely imitating the earlier successes. Each realm of nature has its own special properties that its science must develop methods to deal with. And the more different the realms of nature, the more different the methods used to study it must be in order to produce the valid and reliable findings of a science.

While the natural sciences of the nineteenth century were dominated by empirical, heterogeneous ("looking for differences") thinkers, there were certain major forms of nineteenth-century science that emphasized the homogeneous, closed, system-like nature of some natural processes. These forms were highly successful and well publicized in the nineteenth century. The most important of these forms of science were statistics, statistical mechanics, thermodynamics and, most important, parts of the theory of evolution. Statistics, statistical mechanics, and thermodynamics had profound effects on the school of social thought in France known as "moral statistics" that led directly to Durkheim's (1952) structural-functional theory of society (see Douglas, 1967). (The effects are most obvious in a work like Quetelet's *Social Physics* published in the last century.) Structural-functionalism involved looking at a mass of interacting parts as a closed, single whole, a "system," which produced statistically measured effects or outputs (such as temperature or, in society, suicide rates).

In the early twentieth century this orientation changed dramatically in the natural sciences with the successive revolutions of relativity, quantum physics, uncertainty effects, Gödel theorems, non-Euclidian geometries, and the vast complexities and uncertainties of elementary particle theory. By then, the social sciences were already set on their course by nineteenth-century scientific thinking. They have never to this day reconsidered their historical foundations in the light of the new natural sciences.

Evolutionary thought had a somewhat similar effect on the social sciences. The idea of evolution actually started in social thought, in the works of Spencer, and then was reinforced by the biologists, especially Darwin. All evolutionary ideas dealt with two major aspects: homogeneity (similarity of the individuals of a species) and heterogeneity (differences of some individuals within one species and between species). Heterogeneity was seen as more important than homogeneity because it was the difference in individuals (mutations) that led to evolutionary adaptations (called "progress" by social thinkers). The works of Spencer, which emphasized heterogeneity and "progressive" complexity, were all but forgotten.

In the early twentieth century, most evolutionary social thought became race theory and was put in the service of the great wave of nationalism. It argued for homogeneity within one race ("purity of the blood"), resulting in the exclusion and stigmatization of many races and cultures.

The second great wave of social "thought," a far more virulent and fateful one in its political ramifications, was nationalism. Earlier forms of absolutism of the monarchs in the sixteenth and seventeenth centuries had tried to convince the masses that the state or nation was absolute and the monarchs, being the mystical embodiment of the state, were also absolute. Some intellectuals were sincerely convinced of this idea, and many more were convinced for political reasons. But Louis XIV's supposed claim that "the state is me" was too egoistic to encourage much identification with the state by the masses. The new nationalism of the French Revolution changed the absolutism of monarchies. Now the people, the masses, were seen as the embodiment of all virtue, merely by the fact of being the people. All men were equal and the great mass of the people were partakers in the sublimity of the nation, whether or not they did anything to achieve this exalted status. Bonapartism and all succeeding forms of modern tyranny and democracy also presented the mass of people as sublime, virtuous, unerringly right, the fount of wisdom, sovereignty, rights, etc. The "great leader" or "great party" was always presented as merely the *only* sincere spokesman of the masses, either of one nation (as in the "National Socialism" of Germany) or of all nations ("international socialism"). The emphasis of this new political and social thought was always on the total equality (homogenization) of all the members of the mass and the mystical identification of all the members with the nation-state and with its leader. This idea worked in most of the major nation states in one way or another and to varying degrees. The masses and their intellectual spokesmen swept the competing forms of individualistic thought aside.

The third great wave of social thought was romanticism. Romanticism actually was a predecessor and partial creator of nationalism. Rousseau was the first famous romantic and his thought was a precursor, especially in its most violent form of Jacobinism, of the forms of thought that helped prepare the way for the French revolution. Romanticism was a highly varied, deeply emotional movement that influenced the forms of thought involved in nationalism. Although there is much controversy over the properties of romanticism, it was clearly a form of revolutionary feeling and thinking *against* traditional forms of more rationalistic thought and living. It was a kind of modern mystical religion, inspired by a deeply emotional conviction that people could sweep away all existing forms of life and thought and by the mere sublimity of their natural goodness, which all human beings possess, could achieve heaven on earth.

In some ways it was a Second Reformation in France, because it struck out against the Church's corruption and rationalism, which had not been swept away by the First Reformation in Northern Europe. Voltaire, who helped to prepare the way for Rousseau, put it simply and emotionally: "Erase the infamy."

The mystical anti-rationalism of romanticism did even more to prepare the way for both nationalism and the culturological forms of thinking in the social sciences. Romanticism was a revolt against the earlier forms of rational thought, but not in the way scientific empiricism was. Scientific empiricism was fundamentally aimed at opening the mind to the external, natural world. Romanticism was fundamentally aimed at opening the mind or reason to the internal realm of mythical thought and emotion (and thus has direct historical links to the ideas of the unconscious mind of Freud). Poetry was the great realm of romanticism. As one might expect, the academic and intellectual thinkers did not take very well to its anti-rational extremes. The intellectuals produced a synthesis, but one which made rational ideas co-equal with the emotional thoughts or else dominant over them. The co-equal view of feelings and thought led to the idea that "science is superstition and superstition is science," which formed the basis of vital new forms of modern Platonist social thought.

The clearest form of modern Platonism was found in German idealism, first developed by Schelling. Ernst Cassirer's description in *The Myth of the State* (1955) of Schelling's ideas show how they helped to form the foundation of both nationalism and the culturological view of human society:

> The consequences of this romantic philosophy were drawn by Schelling in his *System of Transcendental Idealism*. . . . There can be no sharper contrast than that between the views expressed in these lectures and the judgment of the philosophers of the Enlightenment. What we find here is a complete change of all former values. Myth that had occupied the lowest rank was suddenly elevated to the highest dignity. Schelling's system was a "system of identity." In such a system no clear-cut distinction could be made between the "subjective" and the "objective" world. The universe is a spiritual universe—and this spiritual universe forms a continuous unbroken organic whole (1955, pg. 4–5).

This form of mythical thought was important in supporting both (1) the overgeneralization that depicted all the members of a nation-state and all their social activities as an organic whole and one homogeneous mass; and (2) the subordination of the vastly varied world of concrete, practical activities to the realm of the abstract, "super-organic" ideas that supposedly constitute culture or society independently of individuals.

The best-known descendant of this romantic super-organicism, and one of the foremost proponents of the nationalism that flows naturally from it, was Hegel. Hegel thought that the "universal spirit" is totally independent of the mundane world of everyday conflicts and complexities. Eventually the universal spirit overcomes and determines what happens in the world through the progressive evolution of ever higher forms of the state. This thinking is the direct and indirect progenitor of numerous forms of the philosophies of history, philosophies of nature, and the so-called social sciences. Marxism was one of its most successful embodiments for the simple reason that Marx wedded the Hegelian historical ideas to the powerful rhetoric of nineteenth-century science. Hegel sounded like a theologian. Marx sounded like a scientist.

There were many other forms of "super-organic," nationalistic thinking in Germany that had more direct links with the theories of the modern social sciences. Leopold von Ranke looked at each nation-state as an organic whole that should determine what individuals do. He dominated German and, indirectly, much of Western history, not Jacob Burckhardt. In German anthropology this "super-organic" whole was called "Kultur," a word which in English had meant only higher class manners and sentiments. (In English, the closest term used by intellec-

tuals was "civilization," but it did not connote the meanings of a super-
organic and homogeneous whole.) The term *culture* was introduced in
its German sense into England by anthropologists such as James Frazer
in *The Golden Bough*. This work agreed with Schelling's romantic ideas
that science and magic were basically the same and, even more importantly, with Edward Tylor's *Primitive Culture* (first published in 1871).
The idea of the super-organic, shorn of some of the magical romanticism,
was later imported directly from Germany into American anthropology
in the works of Franz Boas and Alfred Kroeber, who had profound
effects on American anthropology. While most anthropologists have
moved away from these earlier ideas, some have even reintroduced the
idea of super-organic evolution.

The contemporary view of culture is summed up in the definition
of the term proposed by Clyde Kluckhohn and Alfred Kroeber in 1952
after an exhaustive study of what anthropologists meant by it:

> Culture consists of patterns, explicit and implicit, of and for
> behavior acquired and transmitted by symbols, constituting the dis-
> tinctive achievement of human groups, including their embodi-
> ments in artifacts; the essential core of culture consists of traditional
> (i.e., historically derived and selected) ideas and especially their
> attached values; culture systems may, on the one hand, be con-
> sidered products of action, on the other as conditioning elements
> of further action (Kluckhohn and Kroeber, 1952: 181).

This is certainly a much more complex and naturalized version of the
"universal spirit," but it is only a modification of the more idealistic,
Platonic ideas of Hegel and others. Anthropologists, especially in Britain
and the United States, came to look at cultures as highly relativistic.
That is, each culture was seen as very different from most others. (This
is called "cultural relativism.") With some important exceptions, anthropologists looked at each particular culture as a homogeneous whole for
all important aspects of their analyses. They saw human cultures as extremely different and attacked any arguments about cultural similarities that resulted from human nature or the human condition. These
anthropologists (the cultural relativists) saw culture as internally homogeneous and symbolic in a somewhat Platonic sense; it was a neo-
Platonism.

In France the social sciences followed a similar but more mixed
path. The two major streams of thought affecting the development of
sociology were introduced by Auguste Comte and the moral statisticians
(Douglas, 1967). Like Durkheim after him, Comte saw society as a moral
phenomenon, as a homogeneous moral whole, made possible by a "universal consensus" that transcends and determines individual thought
and action. Comte believed morality was different in different societies,

but was a whole system within any one society. Within each society there is, he believed, a "universal consensus" of morality. He looked at morality in secular terms, but, as T. H. Huxley said, his positivistic view of society was essentially "Catholicism without Christianity." The universal consensus of Comte was a moralistic spirit that permeated and united all social relations in a great organic whole. In time, Comte even came to talk of humankind as "The Great Being," and his "science" became more a religion of science and humankind in which human beings were to worship themselves through the means of science.

Although there are the inevitable differences in details and style, Comte's notion of society was the same as the romantic and nationalistic neo-Platonist "culture"; and his "sociologist" was the same as the German (and, later, English) "anthropologist." One cannot escape the suspicion that Comte was merely using his own brand of names as part of professional entrepreneurship—making himself the founder and great man of the new Church of Scientific Secularism. To Comte the most mischievous, even evil, social analysts were the English liberal (individualistic) social thinkers; and Adam Smith was almost the Devil incarnate.

The moral statisticians were far more traditional in their natural scientific approach to society. Statistics, statistical mechanics, and thermodynamics constituted their scientific proclivity. This meant they were predisposed to look at society as a closed system of interacting parts that could not be directly observed and that produced statistical out-puts (such as suicide rates), which constituted measures of the overall action of the parts of the closed system.

Influenced by Rousseau, Comte, and the moral statisticians, Durkheim (1952) looked at society as a moral phenomenon. He believed society existed as a level of reality separate from the individuals that made it up. Durkheim believed society acts to constrain and determine individuals' actions independently of their own wills or intentions; that society exists outside of its individual members. Morality also existed as a whole outside of individuals, rather than in the feelings or thoughts of particular individuals within the society. With this conception of society, Durkheim thought it should be analyzed in terms of its statistical outputs (such as suicide rates), which represent the state of the whole society.

Durkheim steadfastly opposed the liberal and utilitarian ideas of the English. He believed all parts of society are functionally interdependent so that the whole operates as a system, with morals being the basic determinant of the functioning. Because the Western societies Durkheim studied, especially France, were much more complex and conflictful than most of the societies studied by anthropologists, Durkheim's works have more divergent and complex strains of thought than those of the anthropologists. Still, when all the dust of controversy has settled, Durkheim's "society" is Comte's "society" and the Germans' "Kultur." It is also the same system of ideas as Talcott Parson's "social system" (see, for example, Parsons, 1937).

Social Structure and
Patterns of Social Action

Regardless of this history of conceptual baggage that modern social thinkers inherited, they remained partly empirical and, with few exceptions such as Comte, their empiricism was not a mere pose. The inherited conceptual baggage may have obscured some of their empirical observations, but most modern social thinkers remained sincerely curious about the world and partially open to new insights and eventually to new generalizations about the world. After only a hundred years of nineteenth-century abstractions, more and more social scientists became aware that there were problems involved in explaining the vastly complex and conflictful kaleidoscope of everyday life in Western societies. Especially in societies such as the United States, where there is no majority group, and where even small, tightly knit groups of social scientists cannot agree about many features of that society, social scientists found explanations in terms of homogeneous culture or social structure tenuous.

The first crucial insight was that it was very common to observe widespread patterns of social action that obviously were in conflict with (or had nothing to do with) the supposedly shared culture or society. This insight came especially from studies of deviant behavior. If it was true, for example, that all Polish peasants shared values opposing extramarital sex, how could one explain the widespread existence of such sexual behavior in Chicago among Polish-Americans (Thomas and Znaniecki, 1958)? If everyone shared values against stealing, how could one explain widespread juvenile delinquency among the poor and supposedly lower rates among the better off (Merton, 1957)?

Anthropologists and sociologists slowly came to distinguish between "culture" or "society," "social structure," and "social actions." The general nature of the distinction is seen in the classic work by Robert K. Merton (1957) on anomie, social structure and deviance. Merton distinguished between culture as a set of universally shared and transmitted symbols (such as values and beliefs) and culture as a set of external variables such as "opportunities for success," which were seen as the "social structure of opportunities." Merton argued that all Americans are taught the cultural value of achieving success. The structure of opportunities generated by the class structure, however, was such that opportunities decreased as one went down the class structure. There was thus a difference between what one was culturally trained to want (success, for example) and what one could expect to get from the structure of opportunities. This difference caused a strain, called "anomie" by Merton, within the individuals, which led some to deviant behavior in order to achieve the success. In a similar vein, the Chicago sociologists explained such things as sexual deviance by Polish-American girls in terms of "social disorganization."

The same distinctions were increasingly being made in anthropology. Values were distinguished from patterns of behavior, and it was recognized that normatively prescribed patterns of kinship behavior might happen or might not. The so-called social structure was increasingly being used to explain the variation between cultural patterns and patterns of action.

But there was a crucial problem involved in this whole structural argument. Where did the class system originate, the system that supposedly constituted the social structure, which in turn supposedly produced the differences in opportunities for success? Was the class system produced by something in the human animal (pecking orders, territoriality)? Or was it merely to be taken as part of the human condition? Some structural-functional sociologists in fact argued that the class system was a result of the natural selection over time of those societies with class differentiations, That is, only societies that rewarded achievers more than non-achievers would win in the struggle of societies. Such an argument made social action ultimately dependent on non-social, non-cultural factors such as human nature and the human condition. It was rejected by most social scientists. Instead, they tried to show that the class system was itself derived from the shared values of society. But this argument meant that social structure (the class system in this case) was a result of culture, in the same way that the value on success was. That would mean that culture was in conflict with itself, which violated the basic assumption by the structuralists of homogeneity and functional interdependency. Most of the structural-functional sociologists shied away from recognizing the contradiction and went on their conceptual ways. But this kind of contradiction led more and more social scientists to see the need to break out of the many neo-Platonic conceptual traps of the nineteenth-century concepts of "culture" and "society."

Cultural and Social Heterogeneity, Pluralism and Conflict

In economics and political science there remained into the twentieth century important strains of theory that interpreted social competition, conflict, pluralism, etc., as fundamentally important in Western societies in determining what people did. Everyone might profess to be Judeo-Christian and this might involve a universal commitment to brotherly love, but the *fact* was that almost everyone acted very greedily in the great struggle of the marketplace. Competition and conflict were endemic, vital parts of what made the world go around, whether or not Comte or other devotees of the universal consensus or great spirit liked it.

In addition, there was always an important stream of political science that is best called English (or Burkian) conservatism to distinguish it from continental conservatism. (The continental-type conservatives were apt to be called outright monarchists in England.) Continental conservatism shared with the social scientists the idea that there was one great, over-arching, universal set of morals (or other spiritual things) that were necessary to hold society together. The difference was that the conservatives found their great spirit in God, the Church, or sometimes the *ancien régime,* which was a hierarchy dominated by the king. Edmund Burke's conservatism in England, combined with the liberalism that dominated the thoughts of the American political thinkers and leaders, was very different. Burke was the fiery opponent of both romantic idealism (embodied in Rousseau and the Jacobins) on the continent and of monarchical power in England. He believed that social order is necessarily an organic growth because no human minds are capable of constructing such a vast complexity, but that the growth comes from the bottom up, *not* from the top (culture, king, etc.) down. Britain was a pluralistic society. That is, there was a high degree of sharedness in morality, beliefs, and practices within the many different parts of the society, but not much that was universal. In America, the same was more true, and it was possible to form a central government only by designing it in such a way that the founders from all the regions believed it would always be weak compared to their local governments.

English and American conservative thought was, then, what we now call a *pluralistic or sub-cultural theory of culture or society.* It argued that these societies and probably all Western nations could only be understood by understanding the many different parts that were in conflict with each other, but which commonly had considerable agreement within themselves. (This theory actually complemented liberal English thought insofar as the liberal thought emphasized each individual as the ultimate level of analysis. It disagreed insofar as the conservatives believed that social consensus of some degree was essential at the local level.) The conservative theory believed that social order in general and at the national level could only exist if it grew "naturally" out of the more local order and, consequently, remained in harmony with those local orders. (This form of social theory is probably best represented today by the works of Robert Nisbet and Friederick Hayek.)

Much of anthropology and sociology in the past several decades has been involved in rediscovering, usually quite independently, these basic ideas. (Indeed, the same is more or less true of economics because for decades the macro-structural theories of economics eclipsed the earlier liberal theories, until the macro theories simply proved incapable of dealing with current problems.) Even anthropologists came to distinguish between different levels of cultural integration or consensus in different groups and to see that some cultural patterns could be almost universal in a given group, while others were restricted to one small part of the group. In sociology the Chicago sociologists and, far more, their critics became aware in the 1930s that the myriad ethnic, racial, economic, and regional groups in America are very different from each other, even when they form very homogeneous groups. A long series of works from the 1930s to 1950s increasingly emphasized the importance of sub-cultural differences as the basic causes of deviance from some of the laws by some groups. As William Foote Whyte put it, the sex code of an Italian-American slum is not the same as the sex code of the New England Yankees who made the laws that apply to both Yankees and Italian-Americans in Boston slums. Sociologists increasingly came to see that some sub-cultures can become *contra-cultures,* or sub-cultures that oppose either other sub-cultures or supra-cultures (which cross-cut all the sub-cultures, as the police do). Now called "counter-cultures," these cultures are very common in highly pluralistic, conflictful societies like American society.

Some social analysts (such as Suttles, 1968; and Douglas, 1971) have argued that complex, pluralistic, and conflictful societies like the United States can only be understood by considering the many different levels and realms of social life. They argue that there are some few almost universally shared values and ideas (such as the values on democratic government) and a generally shared system of communication, language. These constitute the "public realm" of life and are a *least-common-denominator set of meanings* that are widely enforced in *public settings.* In highly public settings, such as national political communications in the mass media, there are widely shared ideas about what is proper and improper. These ideas are very different from our ideas about private communications. For example, in the presidential race of 1976 Jimmy Carter was widely considered, at least in the media, to have improperly discussed his personal sexual views in terms that would be very bland in private conversation but which are almost never heard in the mass news media. There are even a few rules of public life, such as the rule against public nudity, that are almost universally upheld (but see below). The social analysts argue that this kind of *public culture* is very useful in avoiding conflicts in a conflictful, pluralistic society. Some analysts have made the same point by pointing out that conflict becomes widespread in a society when the "rules of civility," the rules of public discourse and behavior, break down.

At the same time, social analysts argue that most of the lives of individuals in such societies are not affected by an over-arching public culture. Instead, our lives are far more affected by the more local, more private realms of life and by sub-cultures we live in.

Social analysts argue strongly that all of these shared aspects of our lives are essential if we are to be able to construct social order in pluralistic societies. They agree with the culturological and structural theorists that *some* basic shared meanings (cultural) are necessary to have social order, but they disagree greatly over how much is necessary and, above all, over how much cultural sharing of meaning exists in societies such as the United States and most of the other major nations of Europe today. They tend strongly to agree with those social analysts (such as

Rosenberg, Gerver, and Howton, 1971) who argue that there is a process of *massification* going on in our societies. That is, most forms of sharedness of life meanings are being progressively eroded by many different social developments. More important, they argue that this *de-culturation* of our society, often called "fragmentation," makes the culturological and structural types of social theories more and more irrelevant for explaining our social world. In a world of "do your own thing," cultural or social meanings are less and less shared, and social determinism gives way increasingly to individual determinism, unless social disorder becomes so great that a government tyranny imposes order from outside. Individuals increasingly must construct their own meanings for the situation they face and must choose their own situations and responses to them. Almost all the readers of this chapter know about these problematic searches for individual meanings and actions.

Social Action

Let us return to the simple situation of my encountering Sue in the hall. In some very simple societies with long histories of stable life patterns, it *may* be possible to argue that the culturally learned and transmitted meanings of the persons involved allow the individual to predetermine most of the possible responses to Sue's presence. In fact, however, even anthropologists studying very small and stable societies have come increasingly to recognize that even something as unvarying as kinship relations does not allow great predetermination of symbolic response. The kinship terminology may be highly stable, so in such a society Sue's classification by me might be highly predictable. But the behavior, while far more predictable in such a society, is still much more unpredictable than the language. In a society like ours the things I say to Sue are much more unpredictable, regardless of how much we know about the cultural roles (such as neighbor, older girl, or Italian-American boy). Certainly one can say things such as, "an American man is likely to say something like 'Hi, Sue' and an English man to say 'Hello, Sue'." But even such a simple thing is *not very* predictable. We all know that I may say nothing to Sue, because I may be mad at her for something, or I may wink at her for other reasons. We must know the *situation* in which the encounter takes place.

There are some very complex, culturally shared definitions of such situations that will give us some more predictability, but they still do not carry us very far. With the exception of some few very taboos, we all know what I say to Sue will depend very much on past personal relations which no one else can predict on the basis of cultural knowledge. My approach will be determined by what I intend or want in the situation. (I may want to escape her or seduce her or marry her or. . . .) It also depends on what she intends or wants in the situation, and on the precise developments of the concrete situation. Our culture provides me and Sue with a vast baggage of learned ideas and rules. But we construct just what will happen in that concrete situation. (There are also situations that are externally determined, such as a car coming along and running us over, as well as those which result from our behavior.)

Although he never conceptualized it that way, that is just the sort of thing Thucydides was saying about the Peloponessian war: sub-cultural differences between Athenians and Spartans, which were vast, may have some importance. The concrete persons, strategies, actions and outcomes, some of which are beyond human control, are what make the big difference, however. In anthropology this sort of thinking led to great emphasis on *cultural process* and many works on "structure versus process" (or structure *and* process). In economics it led to elaborate ideas about economic policy. But the implications were carried furthest by sociologists in a great number of different kinds of theory, beginning with symbolic interactionism and stretching through dramaturgy, labeling theory, phenomenology, ethnomethodology, and existential sociology.

In general, these sociologies constitute the *sociologies of everyday life*. Although they have many important differences, we have seen that they all look at the observation of the concrete, natural (or un-controlled) events of everyday life as the starting point of their scientific studies, rather than abstract speculations about culture or social structure. As the eighteenth-century English liberal thinkers and the American pragmatists (*see* chapter 2) did, they see concrete individuals constructing their lives in concrete situations as the beginning of all society, and the foundation of all social science. On the other hand, most of them would partially agree with the conservative thinkers and the structural sociologists that individuals have to have some culturally shared meanings if they are ever to construct any order out of their lives and get along together. And they would argue that any social science theory about what is or is not shared in society must begin with concrete everyday events and from that point infer abstractions. Social scientists of many kinds seem to be launched on a very creative path of studying the vastly complex relations among culturally shared meanings, structural pluralism and conflicts, and concretely situated individual constructions of meanings and actions. Scholars have commented that the culturologists, structuralists, and other neo-Platonists of the nineteenth century turned eighteenth-century social science upside down and wound up studying concrete realities through preconceived ideas about whole cultures. The sociologists of everyday life believe they are turning the social sciences right-side-up again, going from the concrete realities to the abstractions (or theories) these realities support.

References

CASSIRER, ERNST. *The Myth of the State.* New Haven: Yale University Press, 1946.

DOUGLAS, JACK D. *The Social Meanings of Suicide.* Princeton, N.J., Princeton University Press, 1967.

DURKHEIM, EMILE. *Suicide.* New York: The Free Press, 1952.

KLUCKHOHN, CLYDE and ALFRED L. KROEBER. *Culture.* Cambridge, Mass.: Harvard University, Peabody Museum of American Archaeology and Ethnology Papers, vol. 47, no. 1, 1952.

MERTON, ROBERT K. *Social Theory and Social Structure,* Glencoe, Ill.: The Free Press, 1957.

MERZ, JOHN THEODORE. *A History of European Thought in the Nineteenth Century,* vol. I. New York: Dover, 1965.

PARSONS, TALCOTT. *The Structure of Social Action.* Glencoe, Ill.: The Free Press, 1937.

ROSENBERG, BERNARD, ISRAEL GERVER, and F. WILLIAM HOWTON. *Mass Society in Crisis,* New York: the Macmillan Company, 1971.

SCHNEIDER, LOUIS. *The Scottish Moral Philosophers.* Chicago: University of Chicago Press, 1967.

DE SÉLINCOURT, AUBREY. *The World of Herodotus.* Boston: Little, Brown and Co., 1962.

SOROKIN, P. A. *Contemporary Sociological Theories.* New York: Harper & Row, 1928.

THOMAS, W.I. and FLORIAN ZNANIECKI. *The Polish Peasant in Europe and America,* New York: Dover, 1958.